Praise for My Friend Anna

"*My Friend Anna* is sensational."

—Alice Broster, *Bustle*

"Unbelievable, unforgettable, and unputdownable: that's *My Friend Anna*."
—*Book Riot*

"*My Friend Anna* is the dishy story you've been craving ever since Anna Delvey first made headlines . . . a harrowing account of what it's like to be conned."

—*Refinery29*

"If you gobbled up every last detail of the Anna Sorokin 'Fake Socialite' trial this spring (and really, who didn't?), your addictive summer beach read has arrived."

—*New York Post*

". . . a behind-the-scenes look at the [Anna Delvey] scam and how she got away with it . . . until she didn't. This one's nonfiction but feels too wild to be true."

—*The Skimm*, July 30, 2019

"It started out as an article in *Vanity Fair* and ended up a national obsession. Read for an inside look at NYC's elite—and a lesson in how people aren't always what they seem."

—*The Skimm*, May 28, 2020

"Beach reads should be light, fun, and serve a lot dish. That's why number one on my summer reading list is *My Friend Anna: The True Story of a Fake Heiress* by Rachel DeLoache Williams."

—*Town & Country*

"... the Sorokin scam [has] everything: glamour, greed, lust for power, great clothes (or at least expensive ones), rich people being ripped off, cameos by fellow millennial con artists like 'Pharma Bro' and the Fyre Festival organizers, and lots of satisfying clichés about the rotten core of the Big Apple."

—*The New York Times*

"... the gritty, glittery story of the woman who defined the Summer of Scam."

—Cristina Arreola, *Bustle*

"... a thrilling tell-all that I have no doubt will be one of the most talked-about releases this summer!"

—*Audible.com*

"*My Friend Anna* is a powerful account of Anna Delvey's life and crimes, but also a searching portrait of confidence artists and hustlers at large, and the kinds of communities that seem especially vulnerable to them."

—*CrimeReads.com*

"William's book is a detailed retelling of her experience, building far beyond the initial account she published in *Vanity Fair* in April 2018."

—*Insider*

"I'm embarrassed to say how much I enjoyed it."

—*Entertainment Weekly*

My Friend
Anna

THE TRUE STORY OF A FAKE HEIRESS

Rachel DeLoache Williams

GALLERY BOOKS

New York   London   Toronto   Sydney   New Delhi

Gallery Books
An Imprint of Simon & Schuster, Inc.
1230 Avenue of the Americas
New York, NY 10020

First Gallery Books trade paperback edition February 2022

GALLERY BOOKS and colophon are registered
trademarks of Simon & Schuster, Inc.

For information about special discounts for bulk purchases, please
contact Simon & Schuster Special Sales at 1-866-506-1949
or business@simonandschuster.com.

The Simon & Schuster Speakers Bureau can bring authors to your
live event. For more information or to book an event, contact the
Simon & Schuster Speakers Bureau at 1-866-248-3049 or
visit our website at www.simonspeakers.com.

Interior designed by Laura Levatino

Manufactured in the United States of America

10   9   8   7   6   5   4   3   2   1

Library of Congress Cataloging-in-Publication Data
has been applied for.

ISBN 978-1-9821-1409-1
ISBN 978-1-9821-1410-7 (pbk)
ISBN 978-1-9821-1411-4 (ebook)

For my parents

and

in loving memory of my grandparents
Ruth DeLoache Thompson and Fletcher D. Thompson

Contents

Contents

Part III

Preface

You are here to read about Anna Delvey, and I don't blame you. I, too, found her charming—while we were friends. The best villains are the ones you can't help liking despite their malevolence. That was Anna's power. I liked her so much that it took me six months to realize my dear friend was a con artist. The truth was right under my nose.

From the outside looking in, people may think they comprehend the story of my friendship with Anna. It may seem easy to presume my motivations or assign blame based on stories in the news. But nothing about what I went through with Anna was simple. By telling my story here in all of its detail, I hope people will come to better understand what it was really like to live through this experience.

Ultimately, I believe that it's natural to want to trust people. I'm not sorry about that. Having this impulse doesn't make a person stupid or naive; it makes her human. In my opinion it's a mark of good fortune not to have developed the type of cynicism that comes with so-called street smarts. If you'd asked me before I met Anna, I wouldn't have thought I lacked this type of common sense. I was skeptical of strangers, suspicious of new people. But I didn't see Anna coming. She slipped through my filters. You read about those characters in books, you see them in movies, but you don't expect to meet one in real life. You don't think it's going to happen to you.

If you haven't yet had the experience, I can tell you: it is deeply unsettling to learn that someone you care about, a person you think you know well, is an illusion. It messes with your head. You replay the scenes, the words, the implied understandings. You pick them apart. You hold each bit up to the light and ask what, if any, truth it contains.

Regret is an unproductive emotion. What's done is done. All any of us can do is choose how to react in each moment—informed by the past, we decide how to move forward. I don't have regrets, but I can see how this happened. And there is *something* to be learned from that. I say *something*, which is vague, because what I learned seems to evolve and expand with time. I've processed this ordeal in waves, privately and publicly. Looking back on different parts, I feel a long way from myself—from the way I used to be.

This is my story.

Part I

Chapter 1

Mayday

The three of us—Kacy, the fitness trainer; Jesse, the videographer; and me, the friend—had come to Marrakech at Anna's invitation. She had offered to pay for our flights, a luxurious private *riad* at La Mamounia, complete with three bedrooms, a butler, and a pool, and all of our expenses. It sounded like a dream. But my last full day in Morocco—Thursday, May 18, 2017—got off to a rocky start.

I had woken up to three new messages on my phone. The first was from Kacy, who had succumbed to a stomach bug and wanted to go home: *Morning Rachel, I think I need to leave today,* it read. The other two were from Jesse. He had gone to the tennis courts to film Anna during her private lesson, but when he arrived, she wasn't there. She was asleep beside me, in the room we were sharing.

"Anna," I whispered. "Don't you have tennis?"

"Humph—no, I postponed it," she said groggily, then turned away and fell back asleep.

Anna said she postponed tennis, I texted Jesse. Evidently that was news to him, and he sounded annoyed: *K. Yeah, I went to tennis and the trainer was there without Anna,* he wrote back—and a hotel manager had come by looking for her, he added.

Wanna go to breakfast with me? I asked.

Yea, he replied. *Give me 5. I'll meet you in the living room.*

3

In the meantime, my focus returned to Kacy. She hadn't had the energy to make any travel arrangements, she'd told me. I did a search on my cell phone and sent her a screenshot of a 12:40 p.m. flight that looked like it might work, although it was already a little past ten.

If u could help me pack I can make it, Kacy wrote back.

Before I could respond, I got a text from Jesse. *Ready,* he said.

Start packing, I told Kacy. *I'll call the concierge [for a car]—have you booked [the flight]? I think you need to leave within about 15 minutes to make it! Calling the concierge to see if they think it's possible.*

I used the landline next to my bed. Awakened by my voice, Anna sat up to reach for her cell phone. She blinked rapidly before using a fingernail to separate the long lashes on the outer corner of her right eye.

"Kacy's leaving," I said, hanging up the phone. "I need to help her pack."

"Why?" asked Anna. "You're not her maid. She shouldn't be asking you to do that."

"Yeah, but she's sick," I reminded her.

Anxious about Jesse, who was waiting for me, and Kacy, who needed to hurry, I swiftly changed out of my pajamas into a cotton dress. When I grabbed my cell phone from the bedside table, I saw that Anna had fallen back asleep.

I met Jesse in the living room. "Hey, you should go ahead without me," I said. "I'll meet you there." The breakfast buffet was next to the pool, about a five-minute walk from our *riad.* Jesse seemed aggravated by the morning's disjointedness—first at the tennis courts, waiting for Anna, and now here, waiting for me. I was in too much of a hurry to pay him any mind.

"Okay," he said brusquely before leaving.

When I entered Kacy's bedroom, on the opposite side of the *riad* from mine, the air felt stale and smelled faintly of coconut. She was lying on the bed, where she had spent most of the last two days. I stood beside her and pulled up a travel website on my phone. Kacy got up slowly. After finding her wallet, she gave me her credit card and I used it to purchase her ticket. Noting that her car hadn't arrived, I called the concierge for an update. "She really needs to leave," I implored. I frantically helped her pack.

Kacy was out of sorts, and her movements were labored as she ambled around her bedroom, picking up clothing and shoes. After helping for about ten minutes, I paused to see if her car was out front. But one step into the living room, I saw two men standing across from me. Their patterned silk jackets with mandarin collars told me they were hotel management.

"Where is Miss Delvey?" the taller one asked, his tone stern. The men's faces were familiar—they'd spoken with Anna the night before, too—but they didn't look friendly.

There had been an issue with the debit card Anna had given the hotel to pay for our stay, and after two days of polite but firm pressure from the management, she still hadn't fixed the problem. Anna resented institutional authority and seemed to shirk rules and regulations as a matter of principle. The hotel made it very clear that they needed to have a functioning card on file, but Anna answered their entreaties with flares of condescension and flashes of anger. How dare they interrupt her vacation with such unpleasant badgering! Anna had always expected special treatment because of her wealth, but this time she had gone too far. I had seen touches of this before Morocco, and liked her despite it, but never before had it involved me so directly or to such a degree. Now that we were in Marrakech, an ocean away from Manhattan, where our friendship was born and based, I saw Anna's aloofness in a new way—and it unnerved me.

"She's asleep," I answered curtly. Our decadent vacation had taken a dark turn. I was frustrated but unsure whether to direct my anger toward Anna or the hotel's staff. The men's unannounced presence in our private lodging felt invasive, so for the moment I aimed it at them—not that they'd have noticed. I quickly shelved my emotions and snapped into action mode, the same thing I'd been doing all morning. Thanks to my job putting together complex photo shoots at *Vanity Fair* magazine, defusing stressful situations had become second nature—and, as exhausting as it was, I was good at it. I strode across the room and down the long hallway, determined to wake up our host.

"Anna," I prodded. "Anna, those guys from the hotel are here. Can you see what they need?"

"Ugh," she grunted.

"They're in the living room."

I skipped off to rejoin Kacy, assuring the managers that Anna was on her way. At this point, I realized that my panicked phone calls asking the concierge for an urgent car to the airport had set off alarm bells. They thought we were fleeing. My heart raced. Kacy's illness, Anna's nonpayment, our general disorganization—the troublesome winds that had gained force through the week were now whirling into a perfect storm.

I picked up the telephone next to Kacy's bedroom. "Hi, I'm checking on that car." There was a pause. My next words came out in one breath: "Okay, he needs to please hurry! We're not all leaving—the managers are here—we have one sick traveler who needs to get to the airport."

Now that Kacy was finally up and moving, she was ready to go, her attention focused only on going home. Wheeling her suitcase, I walked beside her past the managers. In her haste and malaise, I'm not sure Kacy even noticed them. But they eyed us watchfully. Anna had not yet appeared, but Kacy's car finally had. I passed her suitcase to the driver, and while he loaded it into the trunk, Kacy and I exchanged a modest farewell.

"You'll tell Anna I said bye?" she asked.

"For sure," I answered. Kacy got into the back seat and closed the door. I was relieved that she was on her way to the airport and would make her flight, but when my thoughts returned to Anna, I felt a growing sense of dread. I went back inside.

"I'll go check on her," I said to the men before they could ask.

Why was she taking so long? I jogged along the dark corridor that led to the master bedroom and found Anna speaking on her phone in German, pacing around in her bathrobe and wearing a serious expression. Her gaze was cast downward, eyes shifting from side to side, as if she were processing information or waiting for an answer. She listened more than she spoke.

"Anna," I interrupted, "you gotta go." She nodded without looking up and, after a moment, left the room. I stayed behind. I understood why Anna might have had trouble reaching her bankers the night before—it had been late when the manager had flagged her down in the lobby. Now that it was morning, I trusted she could contact whomever she needed to and that she would soon have the situation under control.

6

My Friend Anna

Glad to have a moment to myself, I went online to find my travel itinerary. Unlike the rest of the group, I had booked my flight out of Morocco before we left New York. I would fly to France directly from Marrakech and spend a few days traveling alone before meeting colleagues in Arles for the opening of an Annie Leibovitz exhibition. My flight to Nice (with a connection in Casablanca) was at 10:05 a.m. the next day, less than twenty-four hours away, so I checked in online. Wanting to avoid an experience like Kacy's, I called the concierge to schedule a 7:30 a.m. car to the airport. Once that was done, I considered our agenda for the day.

We planned to visit Villa Oasis, the private home of Pierre Bergé and Yves Saint Laurent, which bordered the couple's beloved Jardin Majorelle, tourist-filled gardens that we'd seen on Tuesday. The villa itself was closed to the public and could be seen only by special request, with an obligatory $1,600 donation to the Jardin Majorelle Foundation. Ordinarily, that wasn't something I'd have ever considered realistic, but because Anna was paying, she called the shots. We were scheduled to leave the hotel at 11:00 a.m., and since it was already a quarter till, I was worried. I rushed to gather what I'd bring with me for the day: my Fujifilm X-Pro1 camera and the beige leather pouch that contained my passport, credit card, and receipts.

I'd have to skip breakfast, I assumed, but without caffeine I'd likely get a headache. So I sent a text to Jesse: *Can you order me a coffee to go?*

Before he responded, I entered the living room through its dining area and saw Anna, still wearing only a bathrobe, sitting on a plush gold sofa across the room. Her arms were crossed at the wrists, resting lightly on her thighs. The two managers stood on the tile floor between us, in the same spot they'd been for almost an hour. No one was talking.

Anna's cell phone sat blankly on the coffee table in front of her. It struck me as odd, with the men still there, that she was done making calls—even odder that she'd stopped using her phone altogether. Desperate to understand, I looked to her face for a clue. She appeared neither worried nor particularly calm—if anything, she seemed strangely detached. This was the frightening part. It was clear that the men were waiting for her to do something. What was she waiting for?

"What's going on?" I asked her. "Were you able to sort things out?"

She made a lazy gesture toward her phone. "I left messages," she said. "They should be calling me back."

"How long will that take?"

"I don't know—I've been promised to have this resolved already."

"Is there no one else you can call? Your banks should be open, right?"

"I called them already. They shall be taking care of this."

Anna's detachment was startling, and it made me angry. The tension in the room was unbearable—did she think this could wait? I considered briefly that she might be dragging her feet out of spite. I'd known her to be contemptuous toward hotel managers before. Back at the 11 Howard hotel, where Anna lived, for instance, she had been enraged when they insisted that she begin paying for her reservations in advance. But here and now, Anna didn't seem mad at all.

Another thought occurred to me: if Anna received monthly trust fund disbursements (as I had every reason to believe), maybe she'd already exceeded her allowance for May. The weekend before our trip to Morocco, at the start of the month, Anna had chartered a private jet to travel from New York to Omaha and back in order to attend the Berkshire Hathaway Annual Shareholders Meeting. I'd booked charter flights for photo shoots before—not many, but enough to be familiar with their expense. If Anna hadn't made prior arrangements to access more funds for her travels, it might explain why she now seemed to be mired in red tape.

Back in New York, occasional mishaps like this hadn't seemed like a problem. Anna could afford to make mistakes—financial or otherwise. I remembered one night in late March when she and I had gone to a nautical-themed cocktail lounge in Manhattan called The Ship. It was less than a block away from 11 Howard. We'd never been to The Ship before, and we went with a few hotel employees after their shift.

"I'd love to buy everyone a drink!" Anna proclaimed. The 11 Howard crew gleefully accepted her offer, cheering "Drinks on Anna D!" She reveled in other people's delight, and it showed: her cheeks grew rosy, her eyes danced, and the corners of her mouth twisted up into dimples. The bartender took our orders and passed out the round before requesting a card for the $130 tab. As it turned out, Anna had her hotel key and nothing else. "Will you get it and I'll pay you back?" she asked me discreetly. I did. And because she was always so generous, I never bothered to remind her.

———————————

The La Mamounia managers listened to our conversation with their patience visibly ebbing. Not only had they been in our *riad* all morning, they'd gone through the same ordeal with Anna the night before. They had stopped her as we passed through the lobby after dinner and followed her to the *riad* to wait as she made calls. Thinking it best to give her privacy, I had excused myself and gone to bed. When I left the room, the men were standing just where they stood now: at the edge of the living room by the steps to the foyer, effectively blocking our path to the main door.

"So, you're gonna sit there and wait?" I asked Anna.

"There's nothing else I can be doing. I told them, but they don't want to leave, so . . ."

I glanced at the managers. *No shit, Anna,* I thought. The men were firmly planted with their hands clasped: one man's behind his back, and the other's in front. They weren't going anywhere.

The taller one turned to me, exasperated. I saw the train coming before it hit me, but I couldn't see a way off the tracks.

"Do *you* have a credit card?" he asked.

I looked at Anna and suppressed an urge to vomit. *Jump,* she seemed to say. *I'll catch you.* In an instant, her bearing went from obstinate to conciliatory, and her expression softened, particularly around her eyes. "Can we use it for now?" she coaxed.

Adrenaline surged through my body. Irresolute, I looked at the managers, hoping for latitude. "It's just for a temporary hold," the tall one said. "The final bill will be settled later."

"And I shall be hearing back," Anna added, picking up her phone.

Seeing no alternative, I buckled under the pressure, unzipping my beige travel pouch and removing my personal credit card. A manager stepped forward to take it. "The block will only be temporary," he again assured me.

The episode couldn't have lasted more than fifteen minutes, but it felt like eons. When the men were gone (along with my credit card), I turned to Anna in disbelief.

"Did you tell your parents you were going to Morocco?" I asked.

She shook her head no.

"But you'll fix this, right?"

It was a statement more than a question. I didn't need to tell Anna what she already knew—that she had boxed me into an extremely unpleasant position.

"Yes, I'm taking care of it. Thanks so much for stepping in," Anna said cheerily.

My attempts to rationalize the situation did not make me fine with it, but once the standoff had ended and the air had cleared, I convinced myself that it would all be okay. The managers had said that the hold on my account would only be temporary, and Anna would settle the final bill upon checkout. I was glad to be departing before her.

But a short while later, while Anna was getting dressed, the taller manager returned to the living room just as I was leaving to meet Jesse. He was the same man who had taken my credit card, so I assumed he was there to return it. It was either a clipboard or a tray that he passed me—I can't recall—but it held a slip of paper that looked like a receipt, which he asked me to sign. My stomach dropped. The slip of paper displayed a block of numbers—date, time, some unintelligible coding—and farther down, in a slightly larger font, "30000.00 MAD."

I froze. *Receipts came after charges, not before them,* I thought. *What was this?*

"I thought my card wasn't going to be charged," I said.

He pointed to a word on the ticket printed in all uppercase letters: "PREAUTORISATION." It was French, a language I had studied, but in this context the word's meaning eluded me.

"Your signature for the block," the man said.

My Friend Anna

God, I wish I had said no, had walked away, had flat-out refused.

It was over in a heartbeat. It wasn't even my full name that I scribbled: if you didn't know any better, you'd think it was signed "Rah." That was enough.

It was past our scheduled departure time for Villa Oasis, but Anna had only just begun to get ready. I left her in the *riad* and walked toward the hotel's main building along the wide central allée that cut through La Mamounia's sprawling gardens. My head was spinning. Had Jesse ordered my coffee? I glanced at my phone for his reply.

His first message said: *I'll ask.*

His second: *Why don't you ask [the butler]?*

I let out a sigh. *I'm not in the villa,* I replied. *Don't worry.*

On my way to meet him, I decided to stop by the front desk to tell the concierge that we were running late. But then, considering how hesitant the staff had been to send a car for Kacy, I began to wonder whether the outing had been scheduled at all.

The concierge listened to my question, shifting his weight forward to the balls of his feet and back again to his heels. Then he nodded and picked up the telephone. After a brief call, he turned to me and said, "Your car will be here shortly."

As the restaurant's name suggested, Le Pavillon de la Piscine ("The Pool Pavilion") was adjacent to the hotel's lake-size swimming pool. Le Pavillon featured a lavish buffet breakfast with a bounty of fresh fruit, yogurts, and pastries, in addition to meats, cheeses, and eggs cooked to order. The dining tables were outside, which is where I found Jesse.

We sat shaded from the harsh sun by a white umbrella. I was preoccupied with an internal call-and-response: a dull aching in my stomach that yanked downward in tugs, which my chest would answer with flutters of vague warning. I buried my apprehension beneath a willfully cheery exterior.

Anna appeared just as my coffee was cool enough to sip, floating across the tile patio to join us. She was wearing one of my dresses. It was the short, cotton, white one with blue stripes that I had recently purchased at a sample sale and hadn't yet worn. The tag was still attached when I last saw it hanging on my side of the closet. Anna hadn't bothered to ask if she could borrow it.

I felt a jolt of anger. If my sister had done something like that when we were kids, it would have provoked a temper tantrum. But I was an adult now, I reminded myself, and Anna wasn't my sister. It was only a dress. Besides, just one more day and I'd be gone.

"That suits you," I conceded, worrying about whether her frame would permanently alter its shape.

Anna smiled and struck a cutesy pose. "Yes, I thought it would look good in pictures," she explained.

After a morning fraught with tension, I was relieved to be leaving the hotel for our excursion to the Yves Saint Laurent villa. It would be good to get out. We'd spent most of the week lounging around the resort, and it felt silly to have come all the way to Morocco to spend so much and see so little.

We set off with our driver and arrived at the Jardin Majorelle entrance fifteen minutes later. Our guide, a handsome man with gray hair, emerged to greet us. He wore thick-rimmed glasses and a denim shirt. His round belly rested atop a camel-toned belt and green khakis. We followed him through the garden's entrance, past the tourists, and over to a discreet second gateway, where a dusty path lined with tall palm trees and hardy flowers led to the private grounds of Villa Oasis.

The gardens around us were filled with citrus plants and whimsical cacti, wild shapes from the pages of a Dr. Seuss book. The walls of the villa itself were peach-hued with turquoise and ultramarine accents, nestled behind spiky green foliage. We paused regularly along the way to take photographs.

My Friend Anna

Anna always made sure she featured in the pictures. She knew how to pose. Unlike her, I was camera-shy and self-conscious. There's a rare photo of us together that was taken in front of a fountain, an eight-point star made of multicolored tiles, centered in front of the villa's main entrance. Anna has her legs artfully crossed in a way that emphasizes her femininity. She has one hand on her hip, which flatters her figure. Large sunglasses shield her face, except for a composed, thin smile. In contrast, I am tucked a tad behind her, facing the camera straight on in my loose-fitting dress, cheeks round and eyes squinting as I grin widely in the bright sun.

Before we entered, our guide announced that filming and photography were forbidden inside the villa. This was disappointing news, especially to Jesse. Anna didn't appear particularly upset, even though she had said she wanted to use the trip to Morocco as an opportunity to make a film, partially to justify its large expense. In New York, she had been working on the Anna Delvey Foundation, a visual-arts center she was developing that would house gallery space, restaurants, members-only lounges, and more. She was considering making a documentary about its creation, and she wanted to see what it felt like to have someone around with a camera. It seemed to me that Anna cared more about the idea of having Jesse there than she did about what he shot—his presence was more about the feeling it gave her: of being interesting enough to film. By coming to Morocco, he'd agreed to do a job, and he took it seriously. He maintained that for the film to work, it would need to be more than just a montage of Anna gallivanting around La Mamounia. Trying his best to capture an adequate variety of footage, he decided to record audio of our conversations during the Villa Oasis tour, given the photography ban. His handheld microphone was on as we entered through the patterned cedar front doors.

The contrast between the bright exterior and the dimly lit entrance hall was staggering. A feast of texture and color surrounded us, the most intricate ornamentation I'd ever seen: mosaic tile-work, hand-carved plaster, elaborate paintings. We paused for a moment to let our eyes adjust before circling the space as one would in a museum, each moving at our own pace and direction under our guide's watchful eye. I was struck by the entrance

13

hall's vastness, its high ceiling and marble floor, which, in combination with a tile fountain in the room's center, made it feel more like a place of worship than a home.

The other rooms were cozier, smaller but still grand, with textured handwoven fabrics on overstuffed pillows, inviting furniture, and plenty of nooks. There wasn't a single object that appeared to have come from a store, at least none that I had ever been to. It all looked handcrafted, hand-painted, and handpicked. The place and its contents were clearly the result of loving attention over the course of many years.

I was overcome with reverence for the mystery and splendor of the villa, but something about Anna's presence made me suppress the impulse to lean into my interest too profoundly. Letting her see that I cared too much about anything made me feel vulnerable. I moved through the villa taking notes with my eyes, as though I was scouting a location that I might come back to later in life, someday when I could appreciate it properly, on my own time and with different company.

We took photographs on the roof terrace and patios, wherever we were permitted, as we made our way through the tour. We finished in a sunny blue drawing room, taking a moment to admire a square table with a chessboard set into its center. Anna was especially interested in chess. She once told me that her younger brother played at a competitive level, in tournaments and such. Talk of her brother seemed to reveal a soft spot in Anna, an access point to something warmer, more human, a familial affection to which I could relate. As a result, anytime I was with her and saw anything relating to chess, I went out of my way to point it out. She seemed as taken with the game as her brother must have been.

After our tour, the four of us sat on low stools around an etched silver table in the property's outdoor pavilion. We drank glasses of fresh orange juice and ate crescent-shaped cookies called *kaab el ghazal*, or "gazelle horns," from a scallop-edged blue dish.

Then we followed our guide toward the exit, back out through the door-way into the public gardens. He led us down a path and around the side of a bright-blue building, the Berber Museum, a place we hadn't seen. Wooden shutters with metal rivets framed the front door of the museum's bookshop, pale against the vibrant cobalt of the building's exterior. The guide led us inside, to the shop's cash register, and came to a stop. Was this the end of the tour? An exit-through-the-gift-shop farewell?

"How would you like to take care of the donation?" he asked.

We turned to Anna. "Oh, I thought the hotel took care of that," she replied. "I'd understood it could be billed through our reservation at Mamounia."

But it was clear that payment was required there, in person, at the bookshop. Anna and Jesse turned to me, which caused the tour guide and the cashier, a trim man in a dark uniform, to follow suit. My face warmed. I unzipped my leather pouch and riffled through receipts looking for my credit card. It wasn't there. I felt a surge of panic as I flipped through again. The manager had returned it to me when I signed the preauthorization slip, right? I frantically thought through my steps. Did I drop it in the *riad*? Leave it on the concierge counter? Did I carry it with me to breakfast and accidentally leave it there?

Flicking through the pouch's contents a third time, I was forced to accept that I definitely did *not* have my credit card—only my debit card, which was tucked away carefully next to my passport. I felt stuck. I handed it to the cashier with a heavy heart, knowing that my account, which contained only $410.03, would go into overdraft.

The cashier attempted to run my card once, twice, again, and again— but the transaction was repeatedly denied. Since I hadn't used my debit card in Morocco, nor informed my bank that I would be traveling there, the irregular charges had been declined.

None of us had a way to pay. I was mortified. What now?

The guide insisted we return to our hotel to collect a card for payment. To ensure that we didn't just disappear, he would accompany us.

Over the year or so I'd known Anna, I had noticed how determined she was to be taken seriously. Following the guide away from the cash register, I felt a shift as we transitioned from guests to potential criminals, and suddenly I understood how it hurt to have your validity questioned. I felt

15

misunderstood, as if we'd finished dinner in a restaurant and forgotten our wallets (an honest mistake), and the staff didn't believe that we had intended to pay.

We filed out from the garden's main entrance to the street, where our driver sat waiting in the van. The four of us climbed into the back seat. The guide was quiet and increasingly withdrawn. During our tour, I had learned that he was actually the director of the Jardin Majorelle Foundation and had been a lifelong friend of Bergé and Saint Laurent's. His incongruous presence in the crowded back seat of our vehicle, bouncing along the road to our hotel, felt humiliating and wrong. I apologized repeatedly for taking up his time. Certainly he was busy with more important matters than ours, especially since the foundation was working on the Musée Yves Saint Laurent, which was set to open later that year.

Our van pulled into the drive nearest our villa, at the side of La Mamounia's walled grounds. My friends stayed in the vehicle while I sprang out and set off at a jog. In the moment, faced with problem after problem, my growing anger and frustration toward Anna was overshadowed by my frenzied struggle to keep our ship afloat. I was simply too busy plugging holes to waste time being angry about why they kept appearing.

Our butler, Adid, spotted me coming and opened the front doors. I searched our villa: my credit card was nowhere to be found. I looked again and again in the living room, on my bedside table and the desk, scanning the floors in case I had dropped it. Could I have put it in my suitcase? I opened the compartment where I had hidden other cards for safekeeping. Nothing. In desperation, I grabbed my American Express corporate card, the one given to me by Condé Nast (*Vanity Fair*'s parent company) for work expenses, slipped it into my travel pouch, and ran back down the soft gravel path to the hotel's main building. My heart was racing and the air-conditioned lobby felt cool against my skin.

I signaled to a manager behind the front desk.

"Do you still have my credit card?"

He answered with a slow nod. He did! It was there. I felt a pang of relief and thought of everyone waiting in the van. "I need it back," I choked.

But to my dismay, he refused. The billing for our accommodations was unresolved, he told me. My card was being held hostage because Anna was responsible for payment, which hadn't yet materialized.

I pleaded, explaining that I needed the card to pay the gardens, that it was our only functioning method of payment, and that the man from the foundation was there with us in the car. My desperate words fell on apathetic ears.

Thinking fast, I unzipped my travel pouch and removed the corporate American Express card.

"Here," I said placatingly. "Give back my personal card and you can hold this while I'm gone."

He reached for the corporate card, but before he took it, I said firmly, "You may *physically* hold it; you may not charge it." He nodded.

"Where is Miss Delvey?" he asked.

"She's waiting in the van."

"We need to speak with her."

His tone was chilling. I knew the situation was getting serious. I walked fast across the grounds back toward the driveway.

I passed Jesse on my way. He looked peevish. "I'll be in the villa," he said. "This is ridiculous."

Anna and the guide were still in the van. Its rear sliding door was open. "Anna, they're asking for you at the front desk," I said.

Her audible scoff made me feel like the tired mom of a petulant teenager. Without further discussion, she climbed out of the van and walked away, leaving me alone with the director.

It wasn't like in some places, where they can take down a card's details or use a device to scan a credit card remotely. We had to return to the bookshop. Sitting on bench seats in the rear of the van, the director and I awkwardly faced each other on the journey back to the Jardin Majorelle. I tried to make conversation but could tell he wasn't interested.

"I'm so sorry again about taking up your time like this," I said. In the silence that followed, I couldn't bring myself to look him in the eye.

———

Once at the cash register, the director stood beside me as a shop employee ran my Amex card.

It was declined.

He tried again.

It was declined.

I had nothing else. The employee behind the counter tried dialing the number on the back of the card. The call did not go through. Were they going to let me leave? Could we pay them later?

With the wave of a hand, I was ushered from the register, led by the shop employee and director away from the beauty of the bookshop, with its carved wooden shelves and vaulted tile ceiling, a space where nothing bad could happen. They took me into a narrow back corridor, filled with banal office supplies and a low counter that ran along one side.

I stood alone between the two men. My hands became sweaty and started to shake. I struggled to maintain my composure.

"How do you propose we resolve the situation?" one asked.

I stared at the wall in front of me. It was covered with instructional papers and employee announcements, rules and diagrams written in French. The visual details are blurry but I remember thinking how far away my normal life seemed. I was on the edge of nowhere.

"I need to make an international phone call," I said.

The shop employee picked up the receiver on a landline phone and again tried the number on the back of my American Express card. When it didn't work, he turned to me and said that the number was wrong. I asked to try for myself and after several attempts—experimenting with the country code—I heard a clicking sound, then a tone, and at last a singsong robot voice: "American Express. Please tell me in a few words how I can help—"

"Representative," I interrupted. The robot went on. "Representative," I cut in again. I repeated the word until I reached a human. His voice was deep and Southern. He sounded like home.

With the men standing on either side of me, I explained the situation, doing my best to stay calm while also conveying my distress. Why had the card not worked? He told me that "Responsible Lending" had flagged my account for irregular spending activity when La Mamounia put through a charge for $30,865.79.

My vital organs shut down, caught fire, and floated to the top of my chest.

No, no, I assured him, that was only a block—it would not stay on my account.

The duress in my voice must have registered. Instead of belaboring the fine points, he asked how much money I'd need to get safely out of Morocco. If it had been possible, I'd have hugged him through the phone. He raised my spending limit, and I hung up.

I fought back tears as we left the back room, swallowing hard to contain my emotions. I was furious to be there alone, to be put in that position, to be cleaning up Anna's mess.

Re-entering the bookshop, I was surprised to see Anna and Jesse walking toward the cash register. Another car from the hotel must have dropped them off. They looked relieved to have found me, but they didn't seem overly concerned or even apologetic. Regardless, it was too late. The damage had already been done: the museum employee had run my card again, and this time the transaction went through.

The three of us walked back to the van in silence. It's a wonder I didn't explode.

———————

All of this happened before we'd even had lunch. I don't remember the conversation that followed, how it was decided we'd go to the medina, who suggested the restaurant or knew how to find it. Our driver stopped on the edge of the labyrinth, let us out, and agreed to wait.

It was the first time we'd ventured into the souk without a guide. I was irritable and impatient. We wound our way through narrow alleys, dodging speeding motorbikes and the aggressive heckling of pushy vendors, on a search for the Places des Épices.

By the time we reached Nomad, a rooftop restaurant overlooking the Rahba Lakdima spice square, it was late afternoon. The lunch crowd had already come and gone, and the place was nearly empty. We sat alone in the open air, quieter than usual. I was too shaken up to talk about what had happened. On the verge of sobbing, I ordered vegetables on a bed of couscous even though I wasn't hungry. All I wanted to do was return to the hotel and add up the charges on my credit card.

On our way back to the van, we got lost. We walked in circles, passing the same scenes again and again. Anna and Jesse took turns choosing which way to go. I trailed behind them, barely holding it together, ready to collapse into a heap of self-pity and despair.

Just before panic set in, the knot untangled. Anna managed to call our driver. He found us on the edge of a busy street, and we set off for the hotel one last time.

At La Mamounia's front gates, as usual, security guards used mirrors on long rods to check our vehicle's undercarriage for signs of anything sinister. That afternoon, they appeared to move in slow motion. As soon as we were out of the van, I strode to the front desk, where I collected my corporate card and asked why, according to Amex, the block on my personal card had gone through as an actual charge, rather than as a temporary hold. Hadn't the hotel said that my card wouldn't be charged? What was the definition of a "block" anyway? Was it just a euphemism for a temporary charge?

The front-desk clerk explained that a credit for the same amount would appear in my account; it was just a preauthorization, a formality, only temporary. I couldn't understand his logic or why he was speaking in such vague code. After a few minutes of talking in circles, I was physically and emotionally spent, and returned to our villa with both of my credit cards.

Anna had ordered a bottle of rosé and was pacing around our private pool, modeling one of her new bespoke dresses. Its white linen was sheer, revealing her black thong underneath. A glass of wine occupied one hand, a cigarette the other. I walked right past her and went straight to our room.

I sat cross-legged on the bed and focused on my laptop. I made an Excel sheet tabulating the expenses I'd incurred relating to our trip, beginning

20

with four one-way flights. On the morning we were scheduled to leave from New York, Anna had been stuck in meetings and our flights still hadn't been booked. Pledging to wire reimbursement within a week's time, she'd asked for my help. So I'd purchased the tickets. (One-way only, rather than round-trip, in order to maximize flexibility, she had said.) Then there were the restaurant charges, clothing from the souk, and our visit to Villa Oasis. I didn't factor in the hotel, since that block was, apparently, only temporary.

I took a screenshot of the itemization and sent an email to Anna, as she'd requested, including my bank account information so that she could wire reimbursement:

> Hi Anna,
> The total amount is $9,424.52
> Let me know if you need anything else.

I hesitated before signing off:

> —Thank you so much.

I took a deep breath. Sending the email provided some relief: the ball was no longer in my court. Anna now had the information necessary to get repayment underway, and I was almost done with the whole experience. I felt a burst of energy, the slaphappy mania you get when you've not slept or you've come through a stressful event. I joined Anna and Jesse by the pool. I told Anna I'd sent her an email outlining the grand total of what she owed me. She smiled without batting an eye.

"I'll wire $10,000 on Monday," she promised, "to make sure all expenses are covered."

My mood lifted further. When Anna handed me a glass of rosé, I took it from her gratefully. We finished the bottle, I changed into a dress—one like Anna had on, but in black—and we went to Le Marocain, the hotel's Moroccan restaurant, for our last dinner in Marrakech.

The *riad*-style restaurant was situated in the gardens near the hotel's main building. We sat on the terrace, next to a lily pond, surrounded by candlelit lanterns, at the same table where we'd eaten on the first night of our trip. It felt like an appropriate ending. While we waited for our food, Anna pecked at her phone. She looked pleased, almost giddy, glowing with self-satisfaction. Andalusian music floated through the air as a trio of musicians waltzed from table to table, offering each of their songs like an intoxicating dram. The trip had been tumultuous, to say the least, but as the three of us sat there on our final night, the mood was pleasant and calm. We talked about Anna and Jesse's plan to depart the next day for Kasbah Tamadot, Sir Richard Branson's hotel in the High Atlas Mountains where we'd all had lunch the day before.

After dinner, I gathered my belongings while Anna finished a cigarette in the courtyard and Jesse went to his room. Packing was soothing: finding, folding, and stacking. It allowed me to re-establish a feeling of control.

"You should have all of these," piped Anna, back inside and holding an armful of clothing. "I don't think I'll really be wearing them again." She handed me the garments she'd picked out in the medina, including a red jumpsuit and gauzy black frocks, all but the two dresses she'd had custom-made. I crumpled them into my suitcase. I didn't like or want the dresses, but there was something in Anna's eyes that I couldn't refuse. I thanked her for the gift. She beamed.

My departure was early the next morning, but in my mind I had already left. Bag: packed. Alarm: set. Car: booked. I clung to my mental checklist, thumbing each of its tasks like beads on a rosary. The more organized I felt, the better I would sleep. Anna's presence threatened my efficiency. Finally, I changed into my pajamas, washed my face, and brushed my teeth. Anna's back was to me as I turned down the covers on my side. Gently, I lifted a long pillow and placed it between us on the king-size bed as a barrier. I hoped to leave before she awoke.

Chapter 2

New York, New York

M arrakech was a long way from Knoxville, Tennessee, where I was raised, the eldest of three children. Neither of my parents was from the state, but they attended graduate school in Knoxville and returned to raise a family, attracted by the city's livability and its proximity to my mom's parents, who lived just over the mountains, in Spartanburg, South Carolina.

My siblings and I were taught the importance of good manners from an early age—that they were an essential way of demonstrating consideration and respect for others. It didn't matter if it was a relative or the lady making milkshakes at Long's Drug Store: through politeness we acknowledged another person's dignity.

Our parents wanted us to work hard and follow our passions, and they gave us the tools to do it. They energetically supported us in our pursuits but also gave us the space to find our own way. They didn't seem terribly focused on the mistakes we made because they wanted us to meet tough challenges with excitement rather than a fear of failure. I know now that I was quite fortunate. I had been given the strength and confidence to follow my dreams and I believed there was at least a kernel of goodness in every person.

New York entered my mind's eye through stories my dad told. Being from Brooklyn defined him. I pictured the city like the grainy, black-and-white photographs he'd taken when he lived there, street scenes of panhandlers and vagabonds, friends and strangers. In some ways, it was the thing that made my dad feel *other*—that and his Jewishness, which in our house didn't mean much except that we got presents on both Hanukkah and Christmas. But to the society around us, it seemed a distinction worth noting. When I said a word with too much of an East Tennessee twang, he'd jokingly fine me a quarter. (Movie "thee-AY-ter" got me every time.) He was irreverent and loud and loved a good laugh, and I identified his way of being as symptomatic of his Brooklyn-ness.

My Grandma Marilyn lived in New York, and we'd visit her once a year or so. We came at Hanukkah, when the northern cold was bitter and numbing. I dressed for the weather, in an excessively colorful poofy jacket, earmuffs, and mittens. I wanted people on the street to understand that I belonged. I snuck a shy glance at each passing stranger, smiling when our eyes met, the way we did in the South. It would be a long time before I learned that New Yorkers played it much cooler than that.

The summer after my freshman year at Kenyon College, I got an internship in New York at the Planned Parenthood Federation of America. I moved into the spare bedroom in Grandma Marilyn's apartment, unpacked my new "work clothes" into the closet and drawers she'd cleared out for me, and began my professional life in the city.

Planned Parenthood was a bold choice for my first summer away from Knoxville. In my East Tennessee high school, there was a vocational track with a course in teen parenting. There was even a child-care center, where teenage parents could leave their babies for the school day. Young parents were not an anomaly—the abstinence-based sex "education" taught in our lifetime-wellness class made that clear.

"Raise your hand if you're a virgin," said the educator in one of the classes I attended. She came from an outside Christian-based organization and was brought in by the school to teach this portion of the health curriculum. "Okay, now raise your hand if you're a second-time virgin." This meant that you had already lost your virginity, but having seen the error of your ways, you had repented and declared your virginity anew, presumably until marriage. We looked around and shifted uncomfortably in our seats. Some girls exchanged knowing glances. Others raised their eyebrows and sat up straighter in their chairs, perhaps thinking good posture was evidence of purity. A two-day program consisting of a graphic PowerPoint presentation and several interactive exercises taught us that sex before marriage inevitably led to heartbreak, irreversible physical damage, and diminished human worth. The abstinence pitch centered on saving the prize of your "diamond zone" (an invisible area that starts at your neck, goes out to include your breasts and mid-region, and concludes at your crotch) for your future husband. You saved your diamond until you got a diamond (wedding ring).

Accepting an internship at Planned Parenthood was an act of rebellion in my mind against ineffective parochial constraints like abstinence-based sex education. And coming to New York offered a glimpse of how life could be in a city so much bigger—in size and worldview—than where I was from.

That summer proved revelatory. By the end of it, I had an intensified respect for people who worked tirelessly for organizations whose means were insufficient and whose successes were always measured against how much remained to be done. Public health wasn't the profession in which I wanted to build my career, but New York was the place for me.

For the summer after my sophomore year, I landed an internship at a creative agency called Art + Commerce, which the entertainment management company IMG had recently acquired.

My college boyfriend, Jeremy, wanted to pursue work in the New York restaurant industry, so he and I moved into an apartment together along with two of his best friends from home, Matt and Corey. We lived in a studio just north of Union Square that had been converted into a two-bedroom apartment. After a week or so in the kitchen of a busy restaurant, my boyfriend changed his mind, left the city to join his family on vacation in Croatia, and then returned home to Los Angeles. I was left to live with Matt and Corey.

Matt and Corey were magnetic, attractive, and relentlessly social. By day, Matt interned for *Late Night with Conan O'Brien* and Corey worked as one of the shirtless models that used to greet customers inside Abercrombie & Fitch stores. By night—and I mean late at night—they promoted for clubs. I spent those months tagging along like a little sister, during what I came to call my summer of "models and bottles."

Out with the boys, I thought everyone seemed taller and more mature than I was. I didn't have fancy "going out" clothes. I attended college in Ohio, where we wore mismatched clothes from American Apparel, oversize tank tops, boots, and flannel. That summer, I wore mostly vintage and thrift-store finds, and a short dress I'd sewn myself from a brown paisley fabric. I tried not to let it shake my confidence, but I knew that my baby face and off-brand shoes were to blame if we ever got turned away from a door.

Even though I wanted to be included, going out every night could sometimes be tedious. On occasion, I'd do an experiment to entertain myself. I'd speak to strangers with an exaggerated Southern drawl and gauge their reactions. When I used a slower cadence, people would hang on my every word. Jokes were funnier. Stories were sharper. The only trouble was the inevitable disappointment—or, worse, disinterest—when I returned to my usual way of speaking. I suppose, to varying degrees, we all try on different identities in college, on the path to finding our own.

My internship with Art + Commerce was eye-opening. In addition to supporting photography agents who represented industry legends like Annie Leibovitz and Steven Meisel, I helped orchestrate photo shoots with the agency's in-house production team. My responsibilities on the shoots were mostly menial—organizing contact lists, sourcing supplies, picking up coffee—but I was working behind the scenes to create pictures like those I'd admired in magazines for as long as I could remember. In the process, I discovered my passion for production, and fell in love with the fast-paced and glamorous world of photography.

My Friend Anna

I studied in Paris during the spring semester of my junior year and turned twenty-one the month I arrived. It was the first time I had traveled abroad on my own. My friends had all chosen to study in other places, like Amsterdam, Buenos Aires, Cape Town, and Jaipur, so I had to find a roommate. Through the grapevine, I arranged to live with a friend of a friend, a girl who'd gone to high school at Harvard-Westlake, in Los Angeles, with my Kenyon roommate Kate. We lived on the Left Bank of the Seine, in the Latin Quarter, a stone's throw from Notre-Dame. In our little apartment, the living room doubled as my bedroom and the pullout couch was my bed. I got to know Paris as it turned from winter to spring, all while studying photography, the history of haute couture, drawing, and French. It was magical.

Toward the end of my time abroad, I considered my plans for the summer. I had my heart set on interning within the photo department of a magazine. *Vanity Fair* was the dream.

From my Paris apartment, I scanned the magazine's masthead and found the name of a woman listed as the senior photography producer. Then I looked online to see how Condé Nast formatted their email addresses: firstname_lastname@condenast.com. It was worth a shot.

"Dear Ms. MacLeod," my note began. I described my experience at Art + Commerce, expressed my fangirl enthusiasm for *Vanity Fair*, and ended by saying that "I would give my left hand to work in the photo department, but [would] also [be] willing to try something totally new!"

Kathryn MacLeod emailed her response a couple of hours later. "Hi, thank you for your email," she said. "I quite like your letter, let me check on this for you . . . I'm not so involved with the internship process at *V.F.* I will see who is and recommend you—I promise your left hand can remain intact."

At the time, this felt like the most miraculous thing that had ever happened to me. I was giddy to have received a response. A few days later, I was granted a phone interview. The call from Kathryn's assistant, Leslie, came as I was walking past the Pompidou Center on my way home from an early class. Caught off guard, I stopped on the edge of a plaza in the shadow of the hulking modern art museum and sat on the ground.

Unfortunately, the full-time internships were already filled, Leslie explained. I was disappointed, but I had always known an internship was a long shot. I was pleased to have made it as far as I did, and managed to secure an internship in the photo department at *Harper's Bazaar* instead.

During my final semester of college, I went to a dinner in the dean's house at Kenyon. The chairman of the school's board of trustees was seated to my right. He had seen my senior art exhibition in the college's gallery space earlier in the day, which led him to ask about my plans postgraduation. I described my past internships in New York and told him I'd like to find something along the same lines.

"If you could work for any publication, which would it be?" he asked.

"*Vanity Fair,*" I answered, without hesitation.

"Oh, Graydon is a friend of mine," he said. "I'd be glad to put you in touch." Graydon Carter was the magazine's editor in chief. This offer felt too good to be true. "Send me an email a week before you move to the city," he went on, "and I'll connect you to set up a meeting."

To my astonishment, it happened. I moved into the spare room in Grandma Marilyn's apartment and a meeting was set, but on the day before my appointment, I had an unpleasant epiphany: *I have absolutely nothing to say to Graydon Carter.* I was suddenly afraid of that muted train wreck that occurs in an interview when you're asked, "Do you have any questions?," and your brain goes blank. *Questions,* I reasoned. I needed some questions, so I prepared an exhaustive list.

That evening I received an email from Mr. Carter's assistant:

Dear Ms. Williams,

Regretfully, Graydon's calendar has just been overrun with unavoidable appointments at the magazine—tomorrow and through the rest of this week. So he has asked if you might please meet with Vanity Fair's managing editor, Ms. Chris Garrett, tomorrow in his stead. Ms. Garrett's

assistant, Mark Guiducci, is copied on this email. And he is looking
forward to welcoming you here at the magazine tomorrow, before
your 4:00pm meeting. If anything opens up in Graydon's calendar at
or around that time, I will of course reach out to you so that you might
have a brief meeting with Graydon.

. . . I hope that you understand. Please let me know if you have any
questions.

Many thanks,
David

The next day, as promised, Mark stood waiting on the twenty-second
floor. He was exactly as I imagined a *Vanity Fair* assistant would be, polished and charismatic. From the lobby, I followed him through a set of glass
doors into a carpeted hallway. Vintage magazine photos floated in frames
along the walls.

"Chris, Rachel's here to see you," Mark said, leaning into an office. An
elegant, birdlike woman stood to greet me.

"So, tell me why you're here," she began as we sat down. Her request
came wrapped in a beautiful cadence, the intonation of a 1950s English
movie star. I let slip a small laugh before noting her sincerity, and then
I broke into an earnest explanation: because *Vanity Fair*, above all other
magazines, perfectly synthesized my passions for writing and photography,
and because my mother always said to "acquire taste not things," which is
what I aspired to do. Her face softened as she listened, before breaking into
a faint smile.

"I'd love for you to consider an internship with the magazine," I heard
her say. At this, my heart sank.

"Thank you, but I've already done so many internships," I told her. "I'm
really looking for a job."

"People don't tend to leave *Vanity Fair*," she explained; there were no
job openings at the time.

Over the next two weeks, I sent Ms. Garrett a handwritten thank-you note and followed up with human resources. I had nearly given up hope when, one afternoon, two emails arrived in my in-box. The first was from Kathryn MacLeod, the same Ms. MacLeod that I'd picked off the masthead and emailed the previous year. The second was from Chris Garrett. A position had suddenly opened to be Kathryn's assistant. Unaware that I had ever contacted Kathryn before, Chris Garrett thought of me for the job and sent Kathryn my résumé. Kathryn received the recommendation and remembered our correspondence. The next day, I went in for an interview. I received a job offer that same afternoon.

"Williams! I'm glad to see you back, my dear. Does this mean you got the job?" Adam asked from behind the security desk. We'd met when he checked me in for my interview. I nodded and smiled. "Congratulations," he said, offering a high five and then a temporary ID, to use until my official badge was ready.

The elevator opened on the twenty-second floor to a long foyer, blocked on each end by sets of closed glass doors. The voice in my head made a suggestion: "Act like you've been here before." It was a line my soccer coach used to say when my team scored a goal or won a game. I was overflowing with excitement, but it was better to stay calm, to take note of how I got there, and to focus on what would come next.

Over the following months, I learned more than I could have imagined, much of it the hard way. Indeed, I strongly believe now that you should approach your first real job with some very specific guidelines, especially if you're a recent liberal arts graduate. I propose the following:

1. Don't be defensive.
2. Expect minimal feedback if you're doing okay or better. No news is good news.
3. Check your ego at the door.

4. Don't assume. Check. And check again.

5. Long-windedness has no place in email correspondence; get to the point.

6. Understand why you're doing something.

7. Think ahead.

8. Hell hath no fury like a boss who receives an email containing bad news that ends with a frowning-face emoticon.

9. In fact, scratch emoticons from all professional correspondence.

10. For birthdays, holidays, or special occasions, just a card will do.

I moved out of my grandmother's spare bedroom after a year and moved with a friend into a tiny, overpriced two-bedroom rental on Christopher Street in the West Village.

My bed was positioned in the corner of my room, beneath the room's window, the lower half of which bit down on an AC unit. There was a strange period of time where mysterious spider bites appeared on my arms and upper legs, one at a time. Red circles started as sore spots and grew into swollen mounds. I went to walk-in clinics, took courses of antibiotics, and cleaned my bedding, my clothing, and the room, but to no avail. I lasted a full year with the spider bites before cracking, and decided at long last that I needed a fresh start. I moved into a nearby studio apartment, where I paid less rent, had more space, and lived alone.

So, there I was: I had a great job, I was living on my own, and I had a new boyfriend named Nick and a feral cat called Boo, whom I'd scooped up from the streets of the West Village as a scared three-month-old kitten hiding under a car. My New York dreams had finally come true, and for four more years they hummed along.

In that time, I got promoted from assistant to associate and, finally, to photography editor. Kathryn was no longer my direct boss (by then, several assistants had come and gone in my wake), but she still sat right next to me and we were very much a team. My days were filled with all the details necessary for organizing *Vanity Fair*'s elaborate photo shoots—everything from securing locations and ordering catering for the top photographers and movie stars to cleaning up garbage on set and dealing with logistics. The work was challenging and rarely glamorous, but it was extraordinary just to be there, to have a minor role in the big leagues, contributing to the creation of iconic images featuring the most notable cultural influencers of our time. I traveled from the office to photo-shoot destinations around New York City, as well as in Los Angeles, Paris, Belfast, and Havana. Schedules would often not be confirmed until the very last minute, so I learned to be nimble. I was motivated, happy, busy, and fulfilled.

And that's when I met Anna.

Chapter 3

Foundation Work

I was six years into my job at *Vanity Fair* when she appeared. From the get-go, there was something about her that demanded attention, an enigmatic otherness that was captivating. I met her one night when I was out with friends. It's funny in hindsight to consider the impact of such an otherwise unremarkable evening. Although Anna struck me as a bit odd, meeting her would have been forgettable had it not set into motion a chain of events that would alter both of our lives forever.

It was a Wednesday in February 2016, a few weeks after my twenty-eighth birthday. I had just recovered from a nasty cold, which had kept me cooped up for several days watching *The Great British Bake Off*, a television series I had recently discovered and had become obsessed with. *Vanity Fair*'s annual Hollywood issue was on newsstands, its cover featuring thirteen women, including Jennifer Lawrence, Cate Blanchett, Jane Fonda, and Viola Davis.

As usual, I went to work at *Vanity Fair*'s headquarters, now located on the forty-first floor of One World Trade Center, the tallest building in the United States, into which Condé Nast had moved two years prior. I spent the morning catching up on my expenses: tracking down receipts for charges that had been made on my credit card before and during photo shoots. I taped down each receipt, carefully entered its details into an online portal, and then typed in the assignment code that tied each charge to its corresponding project. I finished the report after lunch, scanned in the receipts, and clicked *Submit*. Within a few weeks, Condé Nast would approve the line items and disburse payment directly to American Express. The rest of the workday was slower, mostly emails back and forth pertaining to upcoming shoot dates. By 5:30 p.m., I was antsy from a day of paperwork and in the mood to socialize. I sent an email to my colleague Cate, to ask if perhaps she wanted to have dinner together. She had plans already but suggested we grab a quick glass of wine. We went to P. J. Clarke's in Brookfield Place, close to our office. She had to leave after forty-five minutes, but I settled in to order food.

Maybe it was that glass of wine or the slowness of the workweek. Maybe I was on a high after my sickness or especially liked the outfit I had on. Whatever the reason, on that particular evening I was full of energy and eager for some fun. As Cate left, I scrolled through my phone to plan my next move.

I sent a text to my friend Ashley, an upbeat blonde with good lipstick sense and a kind heart, whom I'd known since the first summer after I moved to the city. Back then, she was working at *Interview* magazine with one of my best friends from college. Ashley had since found her way through the fashion editorial scene to become a freelance writer. She would travel to parties, events, and fashion shows and then write about them for publications such as *Vogue*, *AnOther Magazine*, *W*, and *V*. She was always fun to be around, and it was Fashion Week, so there was a chance she would already be out and game for an adventure.

Hi!! I just finished my last show! she quickly replied. *Want to grab a drink maybe?*

That was exactly what I wanted. We made a plan: I would finish my dinner, she would wrap up some of her Fashion Week coverage, and then, at eight p.m., we would meet at Black Market, a cocktail bar in Alphabet City.

She arrived on schedule and got us a table. Because of a pit stop in my apartment (to drop off my workbag and change into boots with more of a heel), I walked in fifteen minutes late, full of apologies. The two of us were

34

cheerful as we caught up over cocktails. In a few days' time, Ashley would travel to London Fashion Week and then to Havana before another week of fashion shows in Paris.

Once our drinks were finished and we had caught up on each other's news, we decided to join forces with some of Ashley's fashion friends who were also out that night. We walked twenty minutes to meet them at a place called Happy Ending, a trendy spot on the Lower East Side with a restaurant on the ground floor and a popular nightclub past the bouncer one flight down.

We found our group finishing dinner, tucked into a booth in the back. Mariella was there, an Australian with short brown hair and a natural sassiness that was endearingly exaggerated by her accent. I'd met her recently through Ashley. She worked in PR for luxury brands. There were a couple of other girls there, too, whom I didn't know that well: a fashion associate from a Hearst magazine and a publicist who worked in-house for a fashion label.

Tagging along with this crowd made me feel like I was on the inside of something special. Their knowledge of fashion and a certain slice of who's-who trivia exceeded my own, but I knew the language and got the jokes. They were friends with publicists, models, musicians, and designers. Wherever we went, they knew the guy at the door—the one who decides if you're tall enough, rich enough, or attractive enough to enter; who might, if he's in the right mood and you know the right person, say the right thing, or wear the right shoes, let you pass. Select patrons only—it's a funny idea. Why is exclusivity appealing? We all want to be included. We crave validation, from friends and from strangers. If you'd said that to me then, I'd have been defensive. I might have said, "Oh, sure, the door is silly, but inside you'll have more fun than you would in some other random bar," and I'd have been right. On this night in particular, I wish the door policy had been even more discerning.

Tommy came by the table as the dinner plates were cleared. "Tommy" was a name I'd heard mentioned many times. In his early to mid-forties, from Germany by way of Paris, he worked with businesses on the creative direction of their branding, marketing, and events. I knew him as someone who threw exclusive parties for Fashion Week types—in an assortment of popular venues (from hot-spot hotels like the Surf Lodge, in Montauk, to buzzy nightclubs like the once fun, now defunct Le Baron in Chinatown). If you were looking for him in a crowd, you could ask any stranger. "Oh, Tommy? He was just here a minute ago" would be a likely response. He always—and I mean *always*—wore a hat.

It was thanks to him that we had a reservation in the more exclusive lounge downstairs. We walked in as the space was kicking into gear, not empty but not crowded. Young men and women made laps through machine-pumped fog, scouting for action and a place to settle in, as they sipped their vodka soda through black plastic straws. We made our way to the right and back, where the fog and people were denser and the music was louder. We spilled onto the banquette and small stools flanking a low, round, red-topped table.

I can't remember what arrived first: the expected bucket of ice with a bottle of Grey Goose and stack of glasses or "Anna Delvey." She was a stranger, and yet not entirely unknown to me. I'd noticed her for the first time one month earlier, tagged in Instagram photos with Ashley and other girls whom I had recognized. Curious about the unfamiliar face, I'd clicked the tag over her image and discovered that @annadelvey (since changed to @theannadelvey) had more than 40,000 followers. After scrolling through her posts—pictures of travel, art, and a few doe-eyed selfies—I assumed that she was a socialite. She smiled and made herself at home in our company, a relaxed, new member of the crew. I was looking forward to meeting her.

Anna, in a clingy black dress and flat black Gucci t-strap sandals with gold bamboo-inspired accents around the ankle, slid into the banquette on the other side of Mariella, who was sitting to my left. She methodically smoothed her long auburn hair, arranging it over her shoulders, as Mariella introduced us. Anna had a cherubic face with oversize blue eyes and pouty lips. She greeted me in an ambiguously accented voice that was unexpectedly high-pitched.

Pleasantries led to a discussion of how Anna first came into our group of friends. She had interned for *Purple* magazine in Paris and become friends with Tommy back when he was living there, too. It was the quintessential nice-to-meet-you-in-New-York conversation: hellos, exchange of niceties, how do you know X, what do you do for work?

"I work at *Vanity Fair*," I told her. The usual dialogue ensued: "In the photo department," "Yes, I love it," "I've been there for six years." Anna was attentive, engaged, and generous, ordering another bottle of Grey Goose and picking up the tab. I could tell that she liked me, and I was happy to have found a new friend.

Not long after that evening, I was invited by Mariella to join her and Anna for an evening at Harry's, a downtown steak house not far from my office. It was the first time Mariella had reached out to me directly, and I was pleased. Until then, we'd only seen each other when I was out with Ashley, whom I knew best out of the group.

The vibe at Harry's was masculine and upscale, with leather seating and wood-paneled walls. Anna was there when I arrived, and Mariella came a few minutes later, impeccably dressed, having rushed from a work event. We were shown to our table and we settled in, removing our jackets and setting our bags to the side. *These girls are pretty cool,* I thought to myself, slightly nervous and aching for a cocktail. Anna was testing out an app for a friend, she told us. She had used it to make our dinner reservation and would also use it to pay. I wasn't hungry—we'd had pizza that afternoon in the office—but Anna ordered appetizers, entrées, several side dishes, and a round of espresso martinis for the table.

Conversation rolled along just fine, as did the cocktails. The evening had a distinct New York glamour to it—martinis in a steak house, chatting about our workday.

Mariella went first, filling us in on the successful PR event she'd finished just before dinner. Then I told her and Anna about my day, which was unexceptional by comparison. Last up, our focus turned to Anna. She had spent the day in meetings with lawyers, she said.

"For what?" I asked.

Anna's face lit up. She was hard at work on her foundation—a visual-arts center dedicated to contemporary art, she explained, referring vaguely to a family trust. She planned to lease the historic Church Missions House, a building at Park Avenue South and Twenty-Second Street, to house a lounge, bar, art galleries, studio space, restaurants, and a members-only club. She was meeting every day with lawyers and bankers in an effort to finalize the lease.

I was impressed. Anna and Mariella embodied a level of professional empowerment that I respected and wanted to emulate. Anna's ambitions, in particular, were remarkable—her plans were grand in scale and promising in theory—but what was just as fascinating, if not more so, was her hypnotizing manner. She was endearingly kooky, not polished or prim. Her hair was wispy, her face was naked, and she was constantly fidgeting with her hands. She was a zillion miles away from the cotillion-trained debutantes I'd known in my youth, and I liked her more because of it.

The evening went on, more food arrived, and finally it came time for the bill. Anna offered her phone to the waiter, who obligingly studied its screen.

"I don't think it's working," he said.

"Are you sure?" Anna asked. "Can you try it again?"

The waiter took the phone to a computer across the room and typed in the numbers manually before coming back to us a minute later.

"I'm sorry, there's still an error," he said, returning Anna's cell phone. Mariella and I assuaged Anna's obvious frustration with the offer of our credit cards. It had been a nice evening with new friends, and even though I hadn't eaten more than a few oysters, I was happy to take on a third of the check, less for the food and more for the pleasure of the company. I thought nothing more of it.

I got together with Ashley, Anna, and Mariella every few weekends. Our friendship was filled with late nights in SoHo and occasional after-work events. We once went to one of Mariella's functions—a book launch at the Oscar de la Renta flagship store on the Upper East Side—where we crossed paths with real estate developer Aby Rosen, whose company, RFR Realty, owned the building Anna was working to lease. When Anna spotted him, she walked over excitedly to say hello. I watched from across the room, marveling to see an assertive young woman holding her own in conversation with such a prominent businessman.

Nights would start with Ashley and me making plans to meet for drinks. By the end of our hang time, a group would have joined us. One at a time they would arrive: Mariella, Anna, and sometimes others. We had a more-the-merrier mentality, and those New York nights had a flow: we'd start at a restaurant, stop by a bar, and end with a dance floor or two. Most of the places we frequented have since closed and their names have been forgotten. Whatever their particular theme, they were iterations of the same core concept, designed to draw the fashionable crowd of the moment.

As the months went on, Anna was in touch with me independently from the rest of the group. I was flattered she had singled me out, and we started getting together on occasion, just the two of us. That's when our friendship began to solidify. Nick and I were still together, but as a photo assistant for Annie Leibovitz, he traveled nonstop for work. My college friends mainly lived elsewhere and the ones in New York were Brooklyn-based and preoccupied with all-consuming jobs. So when I wasn't out with Ashley and the rest of the gang, I was often by myself.

As far as I could tell, Anna was single, but romance and relationships were never her chief concern. In passing, she would mention old flings but nothing much else. This made it difficult to get a read on her taste in men, which I was curious about. Her apathy toward dating added to her mysteriousness. It seemed like she chose to be alone on purpose, and that independence was one of her hallmarks.

One afternoon in a cab on my way downtown, I received a text from Anna asking me to swing by. At the time, she was living in the Standard, High Line, not far from my apartment. The Standard was a hotel I associated with three things: partying, thanks to the two nightclubs on the top floors of the hotel; exhibitionism, since one wall in each of the guest rooms featured a large window that revealed the uncensored activities of its inhabitants to the Meatpacking District below; and André Balazs, the hotel's owner. Little did I know then that only one of these factors was of interest to Anna: the millionaire hospitality mogul whom she would later meet.

I arrived as the sun was setting, the lounge area out front saturated in a soft crimson glow. I found Anna there, on a mod, curved bench with red cushions atop its white base. She was with someone I hadn't seen before, a Korean-American guy, dressed in all black, who looked to be in his early thirties. I can't remember if she told me he'd be there or if I thought I was meeting her alone. Either way, as I approached, she stood to greet me and then introduced a person I'd heard her mention before: Hunter.

Hunter Lee Soik was a tech entrepreneur. I've since heard him called a "futurist"—whatever that might be. I couldn't tell if they were "together" or not at the time. She would later refer to him as her ex-boyfriend, but their relationship status was ambiguous. They were not overly affectionate, but since Anna told me they were sharing a hotel room, I assumed they were sleeping together. Hunter was visiting from Dubai, where he'd moved after living in New York. He was a little cold at first, inscrutable, as he reclined to watch Anna and me chitchat. He engaged me slowly, asking the usual questions about who I was and where I worked. When he described his background, we realized that we had Art + Commerce in common. He'd worked for them as a consultant, he said.

Hunter became more talkative as the evening went on. Once he'd warmed to me, I found him interesting and eloquent. He seemed to know at least a little about a lot.

After a bit, we decided to relocate to the Boom Boom Room, the hotel's swanky lounge upstairs. It was quieter than I'd seen it before, since I'd only been for parties and on weekends. We sat at a table in the back, next to a glass wall that looked out over Manhattan.

Hunter told me about his job at the Dubai Future Foundation, explaining that he worked to curate the country's cultural and artistic offerings. His responsibilities sounded formidable, if a little overstated. He went on to say that he had created an app called Shadow, back when he was living in the US, which was designed to foster a "community of dreamers." The tool functioned like an alarm clock, but its wake-up call was gentle so that you could better remember and then transcribe your dreams as you came out of them. The app would then use an algorithm to extract keywords from users' recordings. Those keywords would anonymously upload to a global dream database, so that users could track the content of dreamers around the world. Hunter had launched a crowdsourcing campaign on Kickstarter to raise capital for the project. I admired his initiative.

So, not only was Hunter helping to shape the cultural future of an entire country, he'd also come up with an app. I'd google him later and discover that his concept for Shadow had been covered by *The New Yorker*, *Wired*, *The Atlantic*, *Forbes*, *Fast Company*, *Business Insider*, and *Vice*—he'd even given a TED Talk.

As far as I could tell, whether they were together or not, Anna and Hunter had all of the makings of an international power couple. Watching the two of them, I could see the marks of time spent together. Much of their communication was nonverbal: secret messages exchanged through casual glances, nods, and smirks. They shared a history on which their mysterious dynamic relied—a history about which I knew very little.

I soon learned that Anna had been introduced to many of her acquaintances through Hunter, including a fashion designer, one of the founders of the video-hosting platform Vine, and Mariella. Evidently, Hunter was well connected in certain circles. He went back to Dubai shortly after our visit, but Anna stayed in touch with their shared contacts.

One such connection was a philanthropist named Meera, a divorced woman in her fifties who had been married to the former vice-chairman of a leading financial services company. On a Saturday in June, Anna and I took a Metro-North train up from the city to visit Meera at her estate in Hyde Park on the Hudson River. She was hosting a lunch, and Anna had been invited. Anna, in turn, had asked me to come.

That morning, I arrived to Grand Central Terminal early. Anna was running late, so for the sake of expediency I waited in line and bought round-trip tickets for us both.

Five minutes before departure, I stood anxiously on the platform next to our train. Anna claimed to be in the station, but she had yet to appear.

Finally, with only seconds to spare, I spotted her. She was jogging toward me, in a black fitted dress, with her sunglasses on, carrying a black leather jacket, a Balenciaga tote, and a shopping bag full of gossip magazines to read on the journey. On board, we managed to find two empty seats side by side.

Nearly two hours later, we arrived at the Poughkeepsie train station. We taxied to the Hyde Park address and arrived to a tasteful, old-looking mansion. Meera answered the front door and welcomed us warmly, air-kissing each side of our cheeks.

"Thanks so much for having us," Anna said cheerfully, stepping inside. We followed our host into the kitchen, where a household staff was busy preparing for lunch. Meera gave a few instructions and then pointed Anna and me toward the adjacent living room. "Come meet the others," she said, leading the way. The living room was a rustic open space with beams stretched across its vaulted wood ceiling. Off the living room was an outdoor deck with sweeping views of the estate's grounds, its tennis court, the distant Catskills, and the Hudson River.

A circle of casually dressed young adults, roughly the same age as Anna and me, were sitting on the plush sofas chatting. They paused in their conversation and turned to look as we entered. I noticed they studied Anna more than me, which wasn't unusual—she had that effect on a room.

Meera introduced us. "This is Anna Delvey," she announced, "a talented young woman who is working on her own art foundation." Some people raised their eyebrows, while others nodded approvingly. I was described as Anna's good friend, and then as a photo editor for *Vanity Fair*. I felt like a sidekick, and in essence, I suppose I was.

Through snippets of conversation, I deduced the gathering was a reunion associated with United World Colleges, and surmised that Anna had been invited by Meera even though she wasn't an alumna of the schools. I was intimidated as I surveyed the room, aware that everyone already seemed to know each other well. I remember thinking that, despite my nerves, I should make an effort to talk with new people. It would be the polite thing to do (which I knew because of my upbringing), and it might even be interesting.

The food was laid out buffet-style, which encouraged people to mingle. I helped myself to pasta salad and roasted vegetables, and waited for Anna so we could join a group of other guests. But it was soon clear to me that Anna had other plans. She had no interest in engaging with anyone aside from the host and me. She led me to a corner of the dining room table, and we put our plates down before returning to the kitchen for drinks.

"Do you have any rosé?" Anna asked a server. "I'll just take a glass of that." Impulsively, I followed suit. We returned to our plates. I felt uncomfortable about our standoffishness, I was nervous that we were being rude, but I stuck with Anna, since I was her guest and she didn't know anyone else. It was a relief when the host came to sit beside us.

Meera chatted with Anna and asked about her art foundation. As usual, the topic made Anna particularly animated. By then, I'd gotten used to hearing her repeat the keynotes of her progress: from the historic building on Park Avenue South ("the perfect location") to the nonstop meetings with bankers and lawyers in her effort to finalize the lease. I was essentially invisible while the two of them spoke, but the role of quiet observer suited me nicely.

After we finished our food, we briefly joined the others in the living room before Anna suggested the two of us split off to check out the swimming pool. She refilled her wineglass, and we made our way outside, down a footpath that led to a gate in a rectangular white fence. There was another woman in the pool area, watching her young daughter swim. She supervised, with care and amusement, as the girl turned flips and emerged from the water feet first, in a handstand, toes pruned and pointed as her legs wavered. I felt a contrast in energies as I watched, aware of myself as some sort of buffer between their domestic innocence and Anna's wildness and spontaneity.

Next to the pool, Anna drank and played with Snapchat, admiring herself in different filters as she held her phone up with one arm, selfie-cam engaged. I joined in, smiling by her side as we looked at ourselves on her iPhone's screen, with pink noses and cutesy puppy ears. Then the rest of the group entered the pool area, led by the host on a tour of the property.

At my suggestion, we abandoned our photo session to join in. Only Anna still had a wineglass. Her drinking seemed conspicuous, but maybe just to me. Was I overly sensitive? I cared what people thought of me—of us. I saw this in myself, and faced with Anna's willingness to do whatever she wanted whenever she wanted, I felt that I should be more free-spirited, like her, or at least try not to worry so much.

Once the tour finished, people got ready to leave. A group that had driven up from the city in a rental car politely offered to give Anna and me a ride back. We accepted, agreeing to scrap our return train tickets. Three of us squeezed into the back seat, Anna in the middle.

Not long into our drive, Anna asked if there was an auxiliary audio cable, so that she could plug in her iPhone to play music. I marveled at her audacity (or was it confidence?) in making such a request, Anna having said little else up to that moment. She put on an album that felt incongruous to the passing scenery and the carful of mellow strangers, but it was Beyoncé, so no one objected. Conversation lulled and we wound our way back to the city, mostly silent save for Anna's soundtrack.

That was one of the last days I spent with Anna in 2016. Over the summer, I was busy traveling. I went to weddings in Georgia, Maryland, Pennsylvania, and New Hampshire. I went to South Carolina with my family, to Montauk with Nick, and on weekend trips to visit my best friends from college. For work, I went to Paris for a photo shoot of Bruce Springsteen, to Los Angeles for more photo shoots, and to Toronto to help with a portrait studio at the Toronto Film Festival.

By the time fall began, my schedule had calmed down, but Anna was already gone. She had been in New York on an ESTA visa, she said, which lasted only three months at a time. When it lapsed, she went back to Cologne, Germany, where, she explained, she was from.

That October, *Vanity Fair* hosted its annual New Establishment Summit in San Francisco, a conference which Anna had planned to attend. I'd even put her in touch with the magazine's deputy director of special events to purchase a ticket, which would have cost her $6,000. She was aware of the price and didn't seem to have a problem with it. But a few days before the event, Anna texted to say that a family friend had passed away and, at her mom's request, she would stay in Germany for the services. I was focused on work, so her cancellation had little impact on my mood or plans.

During the months that followed, I hung out with my college friends more than I did with Ashley and Mariella. I gave almost no thought to Anna. She was out of sight and out of mind. Until she returned one day, nearly half a year later, and jumped back into my life.

Chapter 4
Fast Friends

In February of 2017, a year after I first met her, Anna returned to New York. I had heard from her only a couple of times while she was away, occasional messages from an international number in which she said she was eager to get back and excited to catch up. It was a Sunday when she arrived. She checked into 11 Howard, not far from my apartment, and she invited me to lunch that same day.

She wanted to try Le Coucou, a fancy French restaurant that had recently opened to rave reviews, in the same building as her hotel. It was a place to be seen, as Anna was aware. "I've been dying to go," I told her, knowing full well that reservations were impossible to come by, tables booked months in advance. As a guest of 11 Howard, she assumed the concierge could make a last-minute booking, but I wasn't surprised when that didn't pan out.

We decided to meet at Mamo instead, an Italian restaurant on West Broadway. As much as I was looking forward to seeing Anna, I wasn't really sure what to expect. I didn't actually know her very well, and it had been such a long while since I'd seen or even talked to her, it felt like we were meeting for the first time. I was also a bit confused as to why she'd picked me out as someone she wanted to see so soon after landing. Nonetheless, I took her invitation as a compliment and felt optimistic as I left my apartment. Working at *V.F.*, I'd become good at cold calls and meeting strangers, but new friends had an incubation period, and it took time for me to feel comfortable. I had butterflies in my stomach as I pulled open the restaurant's front door.

The décor had a Provence-does-Meatpacking feel, even though we were technically in SoHo. The dining room had bistro chairs, white tablecloths, and a rosé-colored banquette running along its left-hand side. A band of mirrors stretched across the rectangular room's long walls, below vintage Italian movie posters in dark frames.

Anna had settled into the L-shaped booth closest to the door. Above her hung a poster of Lino Ventura and Jean-Paul Belmondo, both holding guns, floating above a dark cityscape. "ASFALTO CHE SCOTTA," it read, in caps-locked Italian—"Hot Asphalt," the Italian title of a film called *Classe Tous Risque* ("The Big Risk").

Anna was smiling, her cheeks flushed, as she stood up for a hug. She wore fitted black casual attire, with a feathery fur coat draped over her shoulders, soft to the touch. Her round face was bare—surprisingly free of makeup, not even mascara—and her hair was down, freshly blown out, auburn, and still long. She rearranged her belongings on the banquette to her left, steadying a large shopping bag as she sat down.

"How long have you been here?" I asked, taking a seat across from her. She'd only just arrived, having come directly from the Apple Store, where she'd purchased a laptop and two iPhones—one for her international number and one for a new local one, she explained.

Anna ordered a Bellini when the waiter came by—a young Italian with puppy-dog eyes—and I followed suit. She was ready to have a drink. She told me her parents weren't big drinkers, and if she drank alone, "they'd think I had a problem or something." According to Anna, her visit home had been a good time to get organized and to detox.

While she was away, she told me, she had enjoyed going for long hikes. I responded with enthusiasm: having grown up near the Smoky Mountains, I liked to hike, too. It would be a month or so before I realized that where I interpreted "hikes" to mean arduous treks up hilly trails, Anna used the words "hike" and "walk" interchangeably. No matter, she also seemed glad that we had an affinity for the same activity—we both liked to walk. It was a connection.

On her hikes at home, Anna said, she would put on headphones, listen to music, and explore the countryside, allowing her to clear her head.

"That sounds so nice," I remarked. Nature and open spaces were luxuries I craved most while living in New York, with its endless cement and inescapable crowds. This comment did not land as I expected.

"It was totally *boring*," she said dismissively.

I was surprised and disappointed, but I made an effort to justify Anna's boredom, dismissing her blasé attitude as a symptom of her youth and privilege. After all, in some crowds one must appear bored to be "cool," and enthusiasm is often the mark of a rube.

The young server returned. I hadn't even glanced at the menu, but he clearly wanted to take our order. I was overwhelmed with menu indecision.

"Capelli d'angelo alla carbonara for the princess?" he suggested.

"Sounds great," I replied.

"Oh, we should have a bottle of wine," said Anna, still scanning the menu.

"I told myself I'd clean my apartment today, and I should really do some work," I said, mostly to acknowledge these facts aloud to myself. "But that does sound good . . ."

"It's only, like, *two* glasses each. We don't have to finish it."

"Oh, whatever—let's go for it," I agreed.

I liked having someone push me in this way. Anna made it feel as though choosing to indulge wasn't a yes-or-no, all-or-nothing decision. It happened one step at a time. She even made it sound reasonable. Her sense of logic was at times so different than mine—like her choice to live in a hotel rather than an apartment—but it made her worldview all the more transfixing.

New York attracts such a wild range of people: artists and bankers, immigrants and transients, old money and new money, people waiting to be discovered and others who never want to be found. Everyone here has a story to tell—some more elaborate than others. But without exception the people have texture, and texture is character, and character is fascinating.

Anna was a character—I knew this already but had forgotten just what it was that made her so distinct: the exotic way she spoke in that pan-European accent and how casually she chose to have, say, and do whatever she wanted. In the mood for the carbiest, creamiest, most truffle-covered pasta on the menu, she had ordered it without offering a single excuse, and with zero discernible trace of guilt. I, on the other hand, was the complete opposite.

It would be a long lunch. Emboldened by my tipsiness, I decided to broach the subject of Anna's family, which she hardly ever discussed. When I asked her whether she was close to her parents, she said that their relationship felt rooted more in business than in love. This was hard for me to fathom, on so many levels. *Business?* What did she mean? Were they disinterested in her as a person, doling out money with no affection? Or did they use their money as leverage and demand that she meet their expectations? She didn't strike me as someone who'd been to boarding school (her interpersonal skills were too . . . *brash*), so I pictured her at home, emotionally neglected in a country manor outside of Cologne, some drafty old house with so many rooms that days could pass before Anna might see another soul. That would explain her autonomy, I reasoned, and it made me feel sorry for her.

Her father worked in solar energy, Anna said, but their family's money came from her grandfather, who had died when Anna's mother was young. Her parents didn't understand her world and ambitions, she went on, but they trusted her to make her own decisions. Business aside, it appeared there wasn't much else on which they could build a relationship: "I mean, like, what are we supposed to talk about? They don't really get what I am doing." Anna didn't see the point. When she hinted that her mother had expressed some sadness at their distance, I sensed a fleeting wistfulness in Anna's tone.

"Well, what about siblings?" I asked, hoping for something more cheerful. She said that her brother was twelve years younger, so, in essence, she was raised as an only child. Her mother had been careful to keep them totally separate, she explained, to prevent Anna from becoming inconvenienced or jealous.

Anna said this as though it was normal, as if her mom had done a particularly good job of governing sibling relations, and perhaps she had. Maybe Anna's temperament didn't mix well with others. However, it gave me the sense that Anna was troubled.

She reminded me of a girl I'd known in elementary school. We'll call her "Sarah Jean." Sarah Jean had it rough. Her mom was the leader of my girls' choir—at least, she was until the other parents noticed her difficulty with anger management. It was a performance at Christmastime that finally sealed the deal, when, in front of an audience, she screamed at us, "*Put a smile on your faces! This is joyful!*"

Sarah Jean had a hard time fitting in with the other girls. She was slovenly and obtrusive. She craved attention and her behavior made the other girls uneasy. To make matters worse, she was the first one of us to hit puberty, so her awkwardness was a step ahead.

I had witnessed my mom take an active interest in Sarah Jean's well-being. She made a special effort to pay attention to her, to listen to her opinions, and to treat her with extra kindness and warmth. She had encouraged me to do the same. Years later, when I asked my mom why she had done this, she said that she "could see the damage unfolding in that little girl."

"It takes a village?" I suggested.

"It takes individuals who are willing to look," she said. "Girls need special care."

There were glimmers of Sarah Jean in Anna. The parallel made me step closer where I otherwise might have stepped back. I thought I could be there for her in a way that others were not. Anna's self-assurance could be excessive, but I came to see it as a testament to her resilience. I didn't have a trust fund, or even any savings, but my family had given me all of the love and encouragement in the world—and still, chasing dreams was an unending and treacherous business. It blew my mind to think that Anna, who I now knew to be three years my junior, had conceived of a dream as big as her art foundation and was working to make it happen, all by herself.

A warm plate of angel-hair pasta appeared in front of me, steaming through a lattice of grated Parmesan. I took one bite and put down my fork.

It was my fault for not being more assertive: I was lactose intolerant and my dish was covered in cheese. It would have been rational to wave down our server and simply explain the misunderstanding, but that's not what I did. Not wanting to cause a fuss, I decided to make a quick run to the nearest pharmacy for a box of Lactaid pills: voilà, easy solution. Anna rolled her eyes and smiled when I told her my plan. I excused myself and slipped out the door.

After fifteen minutes (and fruitless searches of two different stores), I found myself in a quaint local pharmacy on Centre Street. Nestled between the Gas-X and Tums, I found my target: Lactaid Fast Act—bingo! One box left. I paid in a hurry and hustled back to Mamo, wondering what Anna and the waiter must think.

Anna was in the process of de-boxing her new phones when I walked back into the restaurant. As I sat down, she excused herself to the restroom and the waiter approached holding a dish. In my absence, Anna had taken the liberty of explaining my predicament, and the kitchen had prepared a fresh plate of pasta without dairy. Clearly, it hadn't been the most sensible solution to run around town while my food grew cold. I appreciated that Anna had taken the initiative to speak up on my behalf.

After we finished eating, the waiter brought over a dessert bowl of cut strawberries dusted with confectioners' sugar, along with his phone number on a small slip of paper. "He wanted to know if you were single," Anna said, "and I told him to ask you for himself." Although I wasn't interested, it was true that Nick and I were going through a rough patch. We'd gotten into a fight around the time of my birthday, and shortly thereafter—having recently left his job working for Annie Leibovitz—he took off for a month-long sojourn in Costa Rica and had since been bad at keeping in touch. It was an in-between period where we were neither fully together nor fully split up. So, no, I was not available to date the server, but I *was* especially glad to have Anna back in town, just when I needed a diversion.

When the check arrived, Anna put down her card and pushed mine away. Because she had invited me, she insisted on being the one to pay. I argued, relented, and thanked her in earnest.

My Friend Anna

By the time we left the restaurant, it was almost five o'clock. We walked toward Anna's hotel, and she invited me in for a drink. We passed through the hotel's modern lobby, heading straight for the steel spiral staircase to the left, which swooped twice around a thick column, rising to the floor above. On the second level, we entered the Library, a stylish lounge that was like an outpost of the Soho House (a private members' club for creative types)— only better, because it felt undiscovered and we had the place to ourselves.

The room's design had distinctly Scandinavian overtones. Every element of its décor, from furniture to lighting, was a work of art. There was a concierge desk to the left as you entered, staffed by two employees sitting at laptops and answering the phone. The rest of the space was divided into pockets of seating areas: a sculptural sofa and lounge chairs surrounded a Nordic-looking coffee table; minimal two-tops punctuated the right side of the room, nestled between chairs with wide seats; in the middle of the space, next to the windows, was a round six-top table, overwhelmed by a tall branch-filled floral arrangement; and beyond that, in the back, was a long wooden dining table beneath a chandelier that looked like a toy jack.

My eyes scanned the setup and stopped on a photograph that hung in a frame across from the concierge desk, a black-and-white image of an empty theater—part of a series by Japanese photographer Hiroshi Sugimoto. Light emanated from a seemingly blank, rectangular movie screen, casting its glow out from the center of the composition onto the empty stage, seats, and theater. Sugimoto used a large-format camera to capture a movie's thousands of still frames within a single image. The result was otherworldly. Looking at his work always reminded me of Shakespeare, a play within a play. It captured kinetic energy, portentous and alive with emotion and light. The viewing experience was meta and inverted: I was the audience, looking into an empty theater, beneath a blank screen.

Anything was possible, or maybe it had already happened. Maybe it was all already there.

Freshly resettled in New York, Anna had an agenda: she wanted to establish a personal fitness routine. I'd recently canceled my gym membership in order to save money (I barely ever went anyway) and was feeling out of shape. Anna had heard about an app that allowed you to book personal training sessions on demand, so we decided to try it together. We scheduled our first workout for Wednesday of that week.

On Wednesday morning, I woke up earlier than usual. I pulled on a sweatshirt and skipped down my building's four flights of stairs feeling energized and enthusiastic. After a ten-minute jog, I reached Anna's hotel, and I sent her a text to let her know I'd arrived. While I waited for her response, I studied the lobby of 11 Howard. In the early-morning light, it struck me as cold, full of hard surfaces, minimal, and modern—much less inviting than it had seemed on Sunday evening. There was no word from Anna, so I pinged her again and finally got a response: she told me to come to her room.

The ninth-floor hallway was dimly lit and its carpet muffled all sound. When I knocked on the door of Room 916, Anna answered. Her face looked puffy. She was wearing some sort of high-performance, ridged scuba suit fresh from Net-a-Porter that was nicer than my work clothes. Standing there in my old soccer shorts and oversize T-shirt, I realized that I'd misunderstood the dress code.

"Come in," she said.

Once inside, I noticed a bathroom to my immediate left. I saw that every inch of its marble-topped sink was covered with high-end beauty supplies. Her bedroom itself was small, and also cluttered with stuff. Hard-shell suitcases were pushed into the near-left corner, behind an oval table, which was buried beneath papers and a cluster of shopping bags from Supreme and Acne Studios. On the far side of the room, in a small gap between the bed and the window, Anna had wedged a metal rolling rack, on which hung the feathery jacket she'd worn on Sunday and other garments in shades of black. *So this is what it looks like to live long-term in a hotel,* I thought. On the console beneath her television, I noticed empty boxes from Net-a-Porter and Amazon, along with workout equipment in clear plastic bags—a jump rope embedded with LED lights and an agility ladder like the one I'd used for soccer footwork drills—that she'd clearly purchased online. It was obvious to me that Anna ordered room service, designer clothing, fancy-pants workout gear, and anything else she might want with only the push of a button.

Anna grabbed her water bottle. Its contents were cloudy—a beauty elixir, I assumed. Then she picked up her key card and we left, the heavy door clicking shut behind us. That morning's workout session with Anna would be the first of many. Inside an empty room that the hotel used as a multifunctional space, a trainer guided us through sets of pushups, lunges, squats, and crunches. Anna was semi-serious as we went through the exercises. She followed instructions, up to a point, but focused on speed more than form. She also focused on her cell phone, which she used to play music. That was when I discovered Anna's passion for Eminem, an affinity I hadn't seen coming. Its randomness made me laugh. "Lose Yourself," that song from the 2002 movie *8 Mile*, played at full volume.

To me, it was a throwback; to Anna, it was an anthem.

At Anna's invitation, the trainer and I joined her for breakfast in Le Coucou after the workout. She was clearly dead set on trying the restaurant—and luckily, at this hour, we had no trouble getting a table. It was a decadent place to start the day—stunning natural light poured in through tall windows onto our white tablecloth as we sipped coffee from china cups. I did feel slightly self-conscious to be sitting in sweaty clothing on such a gorgeous, velvet-upholstered Thonet chair. Nervous about getting to work on time, I excused myself before Anna left the table. I texted her afterward to ask if I could split the $85 cost of our workout session. *No!* she wrote back, as I'd assumed she would, though I'd have been equally happy to pay. I was thankful for her generosity.

It was quiet in the *Vanity Fair* office that day. We were wrapping up our April issue and a sizable portion of the staff had already flown out to Los Angeles for the magazine's annual Oscar party, which would take place on Sunday. My flight wasn't until later in the week. I wanted to get a pedicure before my travels and wondered if Anna might like to join me. It was nice to have a friend who didn't keep normal office hours and lived downtown. I sent a text message to see if she was free.

I'm about to see apartments in SoHo, she responded. *Want to join? Yes, I need [a] pedicure,* she added. *[We] can do that after.*

The front door of 22 Mercer Street made a buzzing sound as it opened. I passed a doorman and took the elevator up one floor. Apartment 2D was easy to find. Its gatekeeper was a suave Realtor in an immaculate suit. Everything about him was symmetrical: mouth, ears, eyes, hair—like a factory-made appliance. I eyed him distrustfully as he led me down a long entry hall lined with white shelving and colorful objects. We passed the open door of the master bedroom—the softness of its curtains and a button-tufted headboard gave it a feminine feel—and then, farther down the hallway, there was a large window, through which a tiny courtyard was visible, more ornamental than functional, with a giant red apple sculpture in its center. For photo shoots, dinner parties, and trips with friends to visit their families, I'd been in apartments this extravagant before—even ones far nicer—but never with a friend my age who was looking to buy one for herself. I felt honored that Anna wanted my company, maybe even counsel, to help make such an important and personal decision.

The Realtor and I entered the loft's open kitchen, and I saw Anna, on the opposite side of a long counter, next to a wall of lacquered white cabinets, looking focused and right at home as she took in her surroundings. She was wearing all black, as usual. A leather tote bag hung from the crook of her left arm. That's when I noticed another couple in the adjacent sunken living room, talking to a different broker.

"That's Fredrik Eklund," whispered the Realtor. I didn't know who that was, but I nodded in feigned understanding.

Anna greeted me while opening a kitchen cabinet. Together we peered inside and discovered ceramic jars, uniformly spaced, each labeled according to its contents.

"Is this apartment staged?" I asked the Realtor.

"No, a famous actress lives here," he replied.

It felt like a movie set. Where was the dust? Where was the mess? Everything looked brand-new and kind of sterile. I kept my opinions to myself, not knowing Anna's taste. After all, if she was used to living in hotels, maybe she cared more about amenities than character. (I would later learn that the apartment belonged to Bethenny Frankel from *The Real Housewives of New York City*, and that the apple sculpture in the courtyard was a nod to the TV show's logo. I also learned that Eklund was a reality TV personality who costarred with Frankel in a show on Bravo.)

We continued on our tour, not speaking, while Anna's Realtor diligently opened doors and pointed to important, marketable details with catchphrase narration: arched windows, imported marble, built-in storage, walk-in closet. Anna wore a poker face while taking stock of every detail.

After ten minutes, I could see that Anna was bored and her attention was rapidly expiring. Seeming to sense this as well, the Realtor gave us a quick peek at the building's basement gym before we returned to street level. Anna summoned an Uber. When it pulled up, we piled in—all three of us—and set off for the next location.

"Do you have an aux cord?" Anna asked the driver. He passed back the cable that would allow her to plug in her phone to play music. The song was "Tunnel Vision," by Kodak Black, and Anna cranked the volume to a level inhospitable to conversation.

Anna was interested in one more listing, an apartment at 1 Great Jones Alley, a building that hadn't actually been built yet. Instead, we saw an architectural model, renderings, and a mockup suite in an adjacent property housing a sales office.

At the end of the tour, back on the sidewalk, the Realtor handed Anna a plastic bag of glossy pamphlets for various multimillion-dollar properties. She accepted it reluctantly and promised to keep in touch. The moment he was out of earshot, she complained about the bag of garbage she now had to lug around. It was a nuisance, I agreed, thinking that would end the conversation. But Anna went on: "Ugh, like *why* would I need this? It's so annoying!" She hated unnecessary stuff, she explained. It was an attitude related to her lifestyle. Living in a hotel, she had space only for the essentials.

I pictured her room, chockablock with stuff, and puzzled over this apparent contradiction.

Anna continued. When she was younger she had cared so much about getting new things and keeping them obsessively organized, but at some point she'd made a decision. Why should possessions control her? "None of it matters anyway," she had realized. "Things, like money, could all be lost in an instant."

I was glad to hear Anna say this. It made me think that she wasn't precious about the trappings of her wealth. "You can't take it with you," I said in agreement.

———————

So, on this particular Wednesday, I had already joined Anna to exercise, eat breakfast, and hunt for apartments. In three and a half days, I had spent more time with her than I did with most of my best friends over the course of a month. Still, our marathon day together wasn't over. Garbage pamphlets in tow, we grabbed a bite to eat before going to the nail salon. In Blue Ribbon Sushi, on Sullivan Street, we sat at the bar. At eye level, just in front of us, colorful cuts of seafood were displayed in a curved window. I stared at a lone octopus tentacle on a plate, admiring its spectacular array of tiny suction cups. Simultaneously repulsed and delighted, I took an iPhone photo to document it.

"I like sushi, but it's kind of new to me," I confessed. "My mom doesn't like fish, so we never ate it growing up." To me, that octopus tentacle looked like a severed monster's tongue—it did nothing to pique my appetite.

Anna had eaten sushi often with Hunter, she said, so I left the ordering up to her. Ordinarily, I'd have chosen something on the "safe side"—like a California roll or rock-shrimp tempura—but I was happy for an excuse to try something new (so long as it was tentacle-free). She rattled off the names of unfamiliar-sounding dishes like an expert: hamachi, spicy scallop hand rolls, *uni*, *ikura*, and two glasses of white wine.

Anna was frequently giving me an education in popular culture references. At this meal, for instance, she was surprised to learn that I knew nothing about Danielle Bregoli, a young teenager who'd recently become famous for coining the phrase "Cash me outside, how 'bout dat" on an episode of *Dr. Phil*. Anna played me the segment, entitled "I Want to Give Up My Car-Stealing, Knife-Wielding, Twerking 13-Year-Old Daughter Who Tried to Frame Me for a Crime." While we waited for our food, she showed me the YouTube clip, in which Bregoli, a baby-faced teenager with flat-ironed hair and huge hoop earrings, described her bad behavior without an ounce of remorse. When she noticed members of the talk show audience laughing at her, Bregoli smugly called them "hoes" and dared them to catch her outside. When Dr. Phil asked what she meant by that, Bregoli's mother chimed in to clarify: it "means she'll go outside and do what she has to do."

I guess Bregoli's bravado, and her self-proclaimed "street" talk, made the scene funny. I watched as Anna laughed. I wanted to see the humor in the same way that she did, but Bregoli reminded me of people from my middle school, kids who came from tough neighborhoods, from tough families, who acted out in class because they craved attention so badly that they got it however they could. It made me sad. Noting my mixed reaction, Anna quickly pointed out Bregoli's resulting fame, citing her Instagram account as evidence. But this bit of information only made me feel worse. The show's ostensible purpose had been to teach this girl that her delinquent behavior had negative consequences. Instead, it had made her "Internet famous."

I was aware of my own disapproval and was afraid it made me prudish, so I actively worked to dismiss it. Why did I have to take everything so seriously? Did it matter? Couldn't I just go along with the joke?

The dynamic of my friendship with Anna was beginning to fall into place. She challenged me to be less uptight and less judgmental, to cut loose and have fun. At the same time, she invited me into her world of hotels, restaurants, and offbeat activities. I became both her audience and companion. I guess part of me aspired to be more like her.

———————

I paid the bill for lunch, and on our way to get pedicures, we perfunctorily evaluated our fingernails in the back seat of an Uber. Anna's looked like pumpkin seeds, painted a sandy nude tone and filed to a dull central point. "I figured it out," she said, referring to their shape. "I keep them this way and they don't break." Anna had a signature fidget—she did it when her mind seemed to wander—as she demonstrated just then in the car. She would use the fingers of one hand to pinch the nails on her other, like making two shadow puppets kiss.

"It drives my father crazy," she said, aware that I was looking. He thought her habit gave the impression that something was wrong with her, she said. Her face broke into a grin as she wondered aloud if he was right.

On the inside of Anna's right wrist was a tattoo, in black ink, a cartoon outline of a ribbon tied into a bow. I'd seen it before but never asked about its significance. "How long have you had that tattoo?" I said.

Anna had gotten it when she was young, she told me, as an ode to Marie Antoinette. She had written an essay about the ill-fated queen for school, and developed a subsequent fascination. I couldn't imagine why she'd have looked up to a woman rumored to have said, "Let them eat cake," when she heard people were starving, so I thought of Anna instead as a fifteen-year-old, watching Sofia Coppola's *Marie Antoinette* and idealizing Kirsten Dunst. Surely, *that* was the Marie Antoinette she idolized.

"I've had it for so long, I barely notice it anymore," she told me. Her tone was suddenly dismissive, implying that her admiration for such a person had faded.

We arrived at Golden Tree Nails & Spa, which I had chosen because the staff was always so nice and attentive. We entered to a wave of hellos and proceeded to the shelves of multicolored polish. Bordeaux red was my pick. I can't recall Anna's. We sat next to each other in massage chairs, looking down at our phones while our technicians filled the water basins at our feet, testing the temperature and readying their tools. Anna, who had a way of making routine activities into an adventure, announced she wanted some wine.

"Go for it," I said, agreeing to join her for a glass. I was already a little light-headed from the glass of wine at lunchtime, but I went along with her plan, as usual. Anna ordered a bottle of white wine through an app on her phone to be delivered directly to the nail salon. We sat quietly as our feet were groomed and the automated chairs massaged our backs.

Anna broke the silence. "We should do the infrared sauna," she suggested. She'd mentioned this before. From what I understood, it was like a microwave, using infrared light to heat bodies from within. I had no idea what that meant.

"Let's do it," I said, up for anything.

Anna held her phone with her left hand while the nails of her right clicked against the screen. "They have an opening for tonight," she reported. She made the booking at an infrared spa called HigherDOSE.

"Great," I replied.

As Anna and I sat at drying stations, a woman entered the nail salon holding a black plastic bag. Anna waved to catch her attention. "Postmates?" the woman asked.

"Yeah," said Anna. At this point, we were rushed to make our infrared appointment, so without opening the wine, I paid for our pedicures and we left in a hurry. On our way out, Anna grabbed two plastic cups from a stack beside the water dispenser, and in the back seat of our Uber—aux cable plugged in, rap music playing—she twisted off the cap of the wine bottle and poured each of us a cup. Drinking in a car made me uncomfortable, but I kept it to myself.

We finished our cups as we arrived at East First Street. The infrared spa was located within a shop called the Alchemist's Kitchen, which looked closed. But we found the front door unlocked and entered past an unmanned tonic bar. Farther inside, there were shelves displaying a hodgepodge of herbal cure-alls: tinctures, ointments, palo santo, and sage. Anna and I were the only ones there. We proceeded directly to a staircase in the back of the room and located a HigherDOSE check-in desk downstairs.

There was a Shailene Woodley lookalike stationed at the counter. "Is this your first time?" she asked. Her voice was raspy and mellow.

"Has anyone ever told you that you look like Shailene Woodley?" I blurted out. I was a little bit tipsy.

"Yes," she laughed; it happened all the time. "My name's Becca, though."

She started to describe what we could expect in the sauna. "Don't worry if you notice black marks on your towel," she said. "The heat is great for de-toxing, and you might release heavy metals as you sweat." She pulled towels down from a closet shelf as she spoke and then led us into a private room.

The square interior was dark and quiet with a wooden booth at its cen-ter. There was a faux candle, water dispenser, and drinking glasses on a table in the corner of the room, along with a small bowl from which Becca lifted a remote. "This is how you adjust the booth's colors," she said, push-ing a button. She then picked up a laminated guide to chromotherapy and outlined the vibrational energy created by each color. Blue, for example, is said to promote relaxation and alleviate pain; whereas red increases the pulse and supports circulatory functions. I was skeptical but intrigued and egged her on by asking questions. Anna couldn't have cared less. Next, Becca lifted a little cord from the bowl and told us how it could be used to play music. Anna listened to this part.

Finally, she left us alone to begin our treatment. I stepped to the far side of the sauna booth to undress privately and then wrapped myself in a white towel. Anna stood on the opposite side of the booth and did the same. Then she removed the wine from her Balenciaga tote bag and poured it into the two glasses on the table. I monkeyed around with a spray bottle and stepped through a mist of rose water to accept my cup as it was offered.

Opening the booth's glass door made a sound like the opening of a shower, as the magnetic closures popped apart. Inside, the two of us sat on a wooden bench with our shoulders just a hand's distance apart. "Do you wanna deejay?" I asked Anna. And, as usual, she did. This time, she chose a more varied playlist than her usual Eminem-centric rotation.

Ten minutes into the forty-five-minute session, we were drenched. If someone had entered the room at that moment, they'd have seen two red-faced girls in white towels sweating profusely with their hair in topknots, taking sips of wine between giggles as they listened to music inside of a light box that changed color every few minutes. It sounds like a lot, I know, but it really was a blast.

Occasionally, Anna would sing along to a song under her breath, songs that I hadn't expected she would like, such as Bob Dylan's "It's All Over Now, Baby Blue." These songs reminded Anna of Olivier Zahm, she said, the editor in chief from *Purple* magazine, where she'd interned. She told me that he'd played music like that when they rode in the car together. It didn't occur to me to ask where they'd been driving—maybe I assumed it was around Paris or to *Purple*'s printer, which Anna had said was not far from her hometown in Germany.

Anna told me much more about her life than I told her about mine, which was fine by me. I've been a private person since I was a little kid and was happy to be the listener.

Drinking wine in a sauna is a bad idea. Anna and I had joked about it, telling ourselves that the combination would make us break even—that we'd sweat out the toxins as we took them on board—but in reality we grew woozy from dehydration. I was the first one to tap out. I switched to water, and by the end of our session, even without more wine, both of us were spent. Our feet left sweat puddles on the floor as we stepped out from the sauna. Once we'd showered off, we sat for a moment to cool down. Then, on opposite sides of the booth, we laughed at how hard it was to put our clothing back on, skinny jeans on wet legs.

We carried our warmth into the cold night air. Steam rose from our bodies as we waited for a car. We ended the evening with a nightcap at the

Library, back at 11 Howard. I drank a green juice, while Anna had a glass of wine. What a bizarre and full Wednesday it had been, a day which otherwise, without Anna, would have been run-of-the-mill. I didn't know that much about her, nor she about me, but Anna and I had found our rhythm, and in the course of a single day, we had established the activities and places that would be central to our friendship in the months to come.

Chapter 5
Deluge

M y role at the twenty-third annual *Vanity Fair* Oscar party was to assist Justin, the magazine's staff photographer. Thanks to my colleagues in the fashion department, I would wear a borrowed navy-blue velvet A-line dress, made by Valentino, with a draped neckline and thin straps that criss-crossed on my back. I couldn't wait. I was in Los Angeles on Sunday morning, the day of the event, sitting in the spa at the Montage Beverly Hills hotel, when I heard from Anna.

Had a sauna this morning alone, she wrote, referring to the infrared spa we'd been to together. *Omg I just looked [it] up and you can buy the whole cabin for like 1k.* She sent a website link as proof.

Amazing, I responded enthusiastically. *I'm in the hotel sauna now!*

I didn't take Anna's discovery very seriously—she lived in a hotel; where would she put a sauna? Then her next text arrived: *I'll find out if I can put it in my hotel somewhere. It totally makes sense to buy your own.* Laughing out loud as I shook my head, I read her message twice before responding. (What was it she'd said about unnecessary stuff?)

Haha I wonder if they'll let you, I texted back.

I'm just gonna order it and say oh I didn't realize it's that big.

Asking for forgiveness, not permission. I knew that routine. But a thousand-dollar infrared sauna delivered to her hotel? I wasn't sure if she was kidding. Over time, I would learn that Anna often had ideas that sounded like jokes. She would laugh at them, too, before pushing them forward to see how far they could go. (In this instance, her idea went all the way. Four months later, 11 Howard would open a HigherDOSE location inside the hotel, thanks to her suggestion.) Anna's grandiosity, though sometimes confounding, had a tendency to work in her favor.

I carried on with my day. I walked to a salon and had my hair styled into a loose braid that fell over my right shoulder. Then, back at the hotel, I joined a couple of my coworkers to have our makeup done by a professional. Alone in my room for the finishing touches, I squeezed into shape-wear, strapped on my patent-leather Marni platform sandals (with a five-inch block heel), and finally slipped on my dress. Then came the tricky part: I sucked in and twisted around while attempting to fasten my zipper. Halfway up, it snagged. I battled with it for a few minutes but, already late, I was forced to give up.

Vanity Fair's party would be held in a pavilion connected to the Wallis Annenberg Center for the Performing Arts. Arriving at half-past four, I shimmied past colleagues to keep my back hidden. Ryan was the first friend I saw. "Help!" I cheeped, then spun around, inhaled, and stuck out my elbows. He gave the zipper a yank and it rose. Properly dressed and ready at last, I met Justin and we got to work.

The Oscars ceremony ended with a colossal snafu, an envelope mix-up that caused Faye Dunaway to mistakenly declare *La La Land*, rather than *Moonlight*, the year's best picture. The botched announcement resulted in an interrupted acceptance speech and a quick reversal that left more than 30 million television viewers cringing.

By the time guests arrived to the *Vanity Fair* party, full of adrenaline following the drama they had just witnessed, they were most definitely ready for a drink. White-coated servers holding trays of Dom Pérignon greeted them just inside the door. Movie stars, fashion icons, politicians, musicians, athletes, and moguls soon filled the room. The pages of the magazine came to life.

My job was the real-life, Hollywood edition of "Where's Waldo?: Spot the Oscars." They were in the hands of Emma Stone, Casey Affleck, Viola Davis, and Mahershala Ali, among others. I circled the room, scanning faces and nudging Justin when I saw a moment requiring a shot. The space became a dreamscape of celebrities—Mick Jagger, Scarlett Johansson, Matt Damon, Mary J. Blige, Tom Ford, Elon Musk, Jackie Chan—many of whom mingled in unexpected groupings, like Amy Adams with Vin Diesel, Pharrell Williams with Charlize Theron and Salma Hayek, Jony Ive with Katy Perry.

By two a.m., the party was winding down—here and there a few people still lingered, clutching their Oscars, riding the jubilant wave of a night's victory all the way into morning. When the room was nearly empty, I took off my shoes and walked barefoot to the car service line. Back at the hotel, I fell immediately into bed, and woke up hours later in a mess of bobby pins and fake eyelashes.

Anna didn't ask me about the party. Aside from our conversation about the sauna, she texted only broad questions, such as *How is LA* or *How is it going.* I liked that she didn't pressure me to divulge any of the gossipy details of my occasionally glamorous work life. Instead she focused on making plans together for when I got back. *I'm with Kacy at 6:30am next week Monday Tuesday Friday*, she wrote. *You're welcome to join.*

Determined to elevate her fitness regimen, Anna had done research and discovered that celebrity fitness trainer Kacy Duke had gotten Dakota Johnson in shape for her role in *Fifty Shades Darker.* Unfazed by a private session's $300 price tag, Anna had begun working out with Kacy while I was away.

I know you're only back Monday night, she said, *so [come] either Tuesday or Friday.*

Amazing, I replied. *I think I'll probably be too exhausted on Tuesday but would love to join on Friday!*

At first, I thought it would be a one-off, that I could join Anna for her session, which she was paying for regardless of my being there, and maybe learn a few exercises that I could repeat later on my own.

But upon my return to New York, my friendship with Anna would intensify and we would begin to see each other, and Kacy for workout sessions, on an almost daily basis. Nick was still away and our relationship was rocky. Coincidentally, I'd fallen out of touch with Ashley and Mariella while Anna had been abroad. Not for any particular reason—maybe just that during the winter I'd been feeling less social, wanting to stay in more than go out. Living in New York was like that—filled with phases. When you can have anything, at any time—restaurants, bars, clubs, museums, theaters, on and on, in the city that never sleeps—sometimes you go all out and sometimes you stay all in.

That Friday morning at six, Anna texted to make sure I was awake. Our session was scheduled for 6:30, and the plan was for her to pick me up on the way to Kacy's gym, in Chelsea. It was Anna who had decided that we should work out so early in the morning (partially because that was the time Kacy had available). Although she didn't have an "office job," like I did, Anna set lofty goals for herself when it came to kicking off her workdays. That said, she often missed the mark, and as time went on, I would learn that Anna was constantly late—even if her intention, to be an early riser, was sincere.

The morning air was frigid, so instead of waiting outside, I kept watch from a window in my go-to coffee shop, at the end of my block. Anna was already late when she texted to say that her first car had canceled. By the time she pulled up, at ten minutes to seven, I'd finished my coffee and a small bowl of oatmeal. We arrived to Kacy's forty-five minutes late.

Kacy's training sessions took place in a gym on the lower level of her luxury apartment building. Anna and I jumped out of the car and hurried inside, with Anna leading the way. Ignoring the building's doormen, we cruised through an expansive lobby straight to the elevator. When the doors opened, Anna walked in as though the people stepping out didn't exist. Downstairs, the double doors leading to the gym required Kacy's handprint for entry. Stuck on the outside, we were relieved to see a man approaching. When he pulled open the door, Anna waltzed through without giving him so much as a look. Trailing behind her, I quietly apologized, said thank you, and entered.

Despite our tardiness, Kacy met us with a smile. She was older than Anna and me—in her late fifties, although she looked much younger. She was in far better shape than either of us. "Come on, girls, it's time to get a move on," she said, which was a relief since I'd assumed we'd arrived too late for her to fit us in before her next client. Kacy brushed off my apologies and promptly put us to work. We began with arm exercises. After sizing me up, Kacy handed me a set of puny two-pound free weights, the same size she'd given to Anna. *She's underestimating my strength,* I thought to myself. Little did I know that after several rounds of small movements, with a dumbbell in each hand, I would barely be able to lift my arms the following day.

Next, we focused on our legs. Kacy would demonstrate an exercise (with impeccable form), then Anna would go through a set, and I would follow. I tried not to watch as Anna did her exercises. She rushed through them lackadaisically, and if we made eye contact both of us would laugh.

The morning's penultimate exercise—a "New York booty lift!" Kacy cackled—required us to assume a lunge position and then rock forward so that our rear ends rose into the air. Midway through my turn, just as I was getting the hang of it, Kacy interrupted. "Rachel," she playfully jeered, "how am I supposed to see your butt get into shape when you're distracting me with those awful granny-panty lines?" Anna and I burst out laughing.

Anna booked five sessions with Kacy for the second week in March. "You should come!" she insisted.

"Are you sure? I mean, it's *your* personal training session. I don't want to take up Kacy's attention. It's your time."

"I'm paying like $300 for each session, so it's kind of like I can do what I want with the time. Kacy is, like, pretty chill. I mean, she's fine with it. And it's more fun if we do it together. It's a little boring to do all those things by myself."

69

It was such a nice offer, and I was happy to accept. She and I went together on Sunday and again Tuesday through Friday. Every morning would begin with a *you up?* text from Anna. Then I'd head down to the end of my block and get us coffee while I waited.

Anna was always running behind schedule and seemed to have particular issues with car services. When drivers were assigned to her, they would frequently cancel. I attributed this to the rating that drivers give passengers after a trip ends. By then, I knew Anna well enough to understand and excuse her foibles, but to a driver she was liable to appear late, demanding, and rude. (She would never say, "Would you mind turning up the volume, please?" Instead, she'd say, "Can you turn it up?" or "Can you make it louder?" until the speakers crackled. Then she'd yank the plug and slam the car door without saying thank you.)

We'd ride to Chelsea with Anna's usual soundtrack playing loudly, jumpstarting the morning with songs like "Mask Off," by Future, or "Actin Crazy," by Action Bronson. The music would continue in Kacy's gym, where Anna would sync her phone to a Bluetooth speaker and carry it with her to each station. Kacy's other clients, who were also using the gym, would eye us with annoyance when the volume got too loud, so Kacy kept it in check. In fact, Kacy was generally the perfect counterbalance to Anna and me as a unit. Where we were flighty, she was grounding. Where we were late, she was patient. Where we were scattered, she kept us on track.

After wearing my workout pants for several days in a row, I upped my wardrobe game. Anna gave me a pair of leggings she'd ordered from Net-a-Porter and didn't like. They were cropped at her shins in an unflattering way, but since I was shorter, they came down almost to my ankles. With those, plus finds from a visit to T.J. Maxx, my beloved discount store, my new activewear supply would last just long enough to maintain weekly visits to the laundromat.

My Friend Anna

By this time, Anna and I were inseparable. The world was charmed when she was around—the normal rules didn't seem to apply. Her lifestyle was full of convenience, and its easy materialism was seductive. Our work-outs frequently ended with a visit to the infrared sauna. We'd rush from Kacy's to HigherDOSE and then back to Le Coucou for a quick breakfast, rounding out Anna's self-prescribed formula for healthy living. We took turns paying for HigherDOSE—not in a systematic way, just by whichever of us made the booking through an app—but when it came to workout sessions and Le Coucou, Anna insisted on covering the cost. "You work harder for your money than I ever have," she told me.

In isolation, these mornings might have whipped us into shape, were it not for our evenings. Anna would usually text me before I left work. *Want to stop by for a drink here after you're done?* she'd ask. And as March went on, two or three nights out of every week, I did. We'd begin in the Library. Anna did most of the talking. She held court, having befriended the hotel's staff, with me as trusted adviser and loyal confidante. As usual, she confided in me more than I confided in her, which made sense considering the magnitude of her day-to-day dealings (negotiating multimillion-dollar investments, for example) compared to mine (booking hair stylists and makeup artists for a photo shoot). I listened with interest as she spoke about her meetings with individuals connected to the hospitality world—people like Richie Notar (a managing partner at Nobu) and André Balazs. She also spoke about her financial dealings, about meeting with a managing director named Spencer Garfield and a banker named Dennis Onabajo from Fortress Investment Group. "We need to plan a dinner so you can meet them," she said, which I found a bit unusual but also kind of sweet. As far as I could tell, Anna wasn't close with anyone in New York aside from me, so it made sense that she would want to share news of her accomplishments and connections.

Over white wine and snapper ceviche in the Library, Anna was chipper when she announced, "Fortress did all this KYC on me and I passed—so anyone who's thinking I'm not legit should just look at that." Anna had taught me that "KYC" was an acronym for "know your customer," a pro-

71

cess through which a financial institution evaluates a potential client before doing business. Were Anna to have passed Fortress's KYC, as she claimed, it meant that the firm had verified her identity, assessed her suitability, and evaluated potential risks to determine she was credible.

The mere fact that Anna *understood* the hedge fund world was enough to impress me, let alone that she understood it well enough to navigate the paperwork and *god knows what else* necessary to satisfy potential investors. As for her concern that people might question her legitimacy, Anna was an oddball twenty-six-year-old—half fashion, half *foreign* (and I mean that intrinsically, as in: Anna had a quality that marked her as other, as outlandish—as *strange*). I completely understood why people would have doubts. She was like a fashion-girl/finance-bro hybrid trapped in a Botticelli body. It was confusing, but the effect worked in her favor.

The two of us made ourselves at home in the Library. We'd drop our stuff onto a couch and then perch on the stools in front of the concierge desk to gossip with whomever was working. Not everyone found Anna amusing, but no one could deny she was ballsy. She had a directness that could be off-putting to some people, and a sort of comical overconfidence that I found equal parts abhorrent and entertaining. She romped around with the demeanor of a spoiled, seldom-disciplined child, which was offset by her tendency to befriend workers rather than management and to let slip the occasional comment suggesting a deeper empathy. "It's a lot of responsibility to have people working for you. People have families to feed. That's no joke," she once said. It was reassuring to hear Anna make remarks of that nature, and she usually made them at just the right time, whenever I was finding it difficult to connect.

One evening, I caught her giving herself a pep talk in the mirror next to the concierge desk in the Library. "I'm so pretty and rich," she bragged. We'd had a few glasses of wine, but even still, my jaw dropped. Who says that? "Are you talking to yourself?" I asked. "Did you just say, 'I'm so pretty and rich?'"

She spun around toward me with a vulnerable smile, and then, noting my dismay, doubled over with laughter. She took delight in my astonishment, as if she were a kid who'd said a cuss word and gleefully discovered it was naughty. I laughed, too, stupefied by her oddity. At times it felt like she was putting on a show: the girl who fell to earth—grandiose, ingenious, one of a kind, and out of place.

Her behavior often landed in the ambiguous space between sincerity and jest. I remember one evening when she called someone a "peasant"— either to his face or as he walked away, I can't recall—but she said it with a theatrical scoff. I was appalled. "Did you just call someone a peasant?" I asked her, distrusting my own ears. Again, she laughed at my shock, except this time I didn't join her.

"Oh, it's not offensive in Germany," she explained.

"Well, it's offensive here," I said.

Now and then, we would banter with other hotel guests. Friendly to a fault, I sometimes chatted with them for longer than Anna seemed to like. She was fast with her appraisals, deciding within minutes whether a person had anything to offer—entertainment value, interesting conversation, and so on. If they didn't, she was liable to ignore them. Come to think of it, I can't recall Anna ever pretending to like someone or something she didn't. She was direct with her opinions, and she had them. "Get out of here with that garbage," she might say, only half kidding, if someone offered her some French fries or some other random thing she didn't want. She also loved to refer to people and things as "fake news." It might happen like this:

"Anna, no—it's *so* late! I need to go home."

"No, no, come back!" Anna called to the waiter, laughing. "Two more glasses, don't listen to Rachel—she's *fake news*!"

Anna knew where she stood on all things. Even her non-opinions were delivered with certitude. For example: if you asked Anna about her politics, she would tell you that she was decidedly nonpolitical. Politics had little to do with power, she professed. Money was the world's true governing force.

Even when I disagreed with her, or was embarrassed by her entitlement (she cut in front of people constantly), Anna's choosiness made me value her approval and feel privileged to be her friend. When it was only the two of us, Anna would tell me about her meetings and her frustration over delays with the lease for the Church Missions House. The art foundation was Anna's dream. She worked toward its actualization, but it was still in the conception phase, so I'd listen as she brainstormed.

Anna had a way of describing the world, its systems and power structures, so that anything seemed possible. In addition to the foundation's galleries, private members' club, restaurant, night lounge, juice bar, and German bakery, Anna wanted to curate experiential events that would blend art, food, and music. She mused about chefs she'd like to bring in (having watched rapper Action Bronson's TV show *Fuck, That's Delicious*, she eyed him in particular), artists she admired, and the contemporary art scene. She was savvy, and in the male-dominated world of bankers, lawyers, and investment professionals, she was unapologetically ambitious. I liked this about her.

After drinks in the Library, Anna and I would descend the spiral staircase, exit through 11 Howard's lobby, and walk around the corner to Le Coucou. Our first stop in the restaurant would be a nook to the left of the bar. You'd find us on a plush orange settee, drinking wine and distracting the bartender as he fashioned an occasional cocktail for other patrons awaiting their tables. The walls around us were covered with a hand-painted mural of a misty woodland. Its moody cool tones emphasized the romance of the warmly lit bar shelving and the room's crystal chandelier.

For most people, dining there was no small or daily affair. In 2016, the restaurant was at its buzziest, a destination for special occasions, with its reservations book always full. But Anna was a resident, like Eloise in the Plaza, and if the Library was her living room, Le Coucou was her kitchen. It was her choice location for meals, business meetings, and late-night shenanigans.

Because she came so regularly, we received preferential treatment. We'd enter unannounced, and after a drink beside the bar, the maître d', who knew both of us by name, would show us to our table. Anna, often wearing a Supreme brand hoodie, workout pants, and sneakers, would slide past the white tablecloth onto a mohair banquette, embodying a lazy sort of luxury. Her flippancy, in attire and comportment, sent a message to those around us: their big night out was her casual night in—except that instead of pizza she ate buckwheat-fried Montauk eel to start followed by the bourride. They were Anna's dishes of choice. She buddied up to the servers, the sommelier, and even the chef, Daniel Rose, who, upon her request, obligingly made off-the-menu bouillabaisse just for her. She drank Pouilly-Fumé like it was water, and I did my best to keep up.

The power dynamic in my relationship with Anna evolved in such a way that I was oblivious to its strangeness. The activities we did at the start of our friendship involved expenses that I could afford—the infrared sauna, for example, and the trainer we'd first booked through an app. Back then, when I committed to an activity, I assumed I'd pay my share. Anna would sometimes insist on paying for us both, but I'd return the favor on occasion.

The only problem was that Anna's taste grew increasingly expensive. She started in the shallow end and swam out fast. She invested in her appearance as if it were a business expense. She went to Christian Zamora for $400 full eyelash extensions, or $140 touch-ups here and there. She went to Marie Robinson Salon for $400 color and Sally Hershberger for $200 cuts. She wanted to try everything: cryotherapy, microcurrent facials, beauty-boosting IV drips, and on and on. When it came to material possessions, Anna was pared down, but when it came to indulgent experiences, she couldn't get enough.

This predilection is what led Anna to Kacy Duke, and kept her going back to Le Coucou. And since Anna liked to have company, she pulled me into the deeper water with her, where I knew my way around (thanks to my job and past experiences with wealthy college friends) but was not capable of floating on my own. Anna knew this. Yet, wanting what she wanted, she set our course and kept me on her raft. And I let her.

"What will it be this evening?" asked the server in Le Coucou. He held his palms together and inclined forward. He and I both looked to Anna, who ordered wine and hors d'oeuvres for the table. When it was time for me to order an entrée, I turned from the waiter to Anna, seeking her blessing. It's not like she required me to ask permission—she'd have told me to get whatever I wanted—but I operated with an excess of civility; because she was paying, I accepted my subservience and became increasingly deferential.

I had not noticed that, over time, the balance of our friendship had irreversibly changed.

Part II

Chapter 6

Hustle

The vacation was Anna's idea. She said she needed to leave the States again by mid-May, in about a month's time, in order to reset her ESTA visa. Instead of returning home to Cologne for boring countryside walks, she proposed we take a trip somewhere warm. It had been a long time since my last vacation, so after weighing her suggestion, I happily agreed, thinking we'd find off-season fares to the Dominican Republic or Turks and Caicos. I had already decided to spend some time traveling that spring—building in a few days' vacation around my planned trip to France, where I would join my colleagues for the opening of an exhibition of Annie Leibovitz photographs in Arles—so to factor in an additional week seemed doable. Thirty minutes after sending her first text about taking a vacation, Anna sent another message asking, *do you have [a] travel [department] at vf [?]* I responded to say that we used a travel agency. *Let me call you*, she wrote back.

Over the phone, Anna explained that she wanted to make a documentary film during the trip, and that she would be covering the cost of the hotel as part of a business expense. She wanted my help researching possible destinations, she said, so that we could make the most of the opportunity, since this trip out of the US was something she needed to do regardless. After a brief back-and-forth contemplating other places, Anna suggested Marrakech— she'd always wanted to go—and knowing that it was, in her words, "the hot spot," she chose the hotel La Mamounia, a five-star luxury resort ranked among the best in the world. A Google search later, I agreed it looked incredible. Four days after announcing that she wanted to go away, Anna reserved a $7,500-per-night private *riad* and forwarded me the confirmation email. This did not seem preposterous—after all, Anna lived in one five-star hotel after the other, whether she was on an island in Greece or in downtown Manhattan. And at the time, I fully expected to pay for my own flights and expenses.

All that was left to decide was whom else to invite. Finding a videographer for the documentary became Anna's first priority. That's where Neffatari Davis came in. As a concierge at 11 Howard, "Neff" was an affable go-getter with a pretty smile and a penchant for gossip. Conveniently, she was also an aspiring filmmaker. Anna and I spent time with Neff when she was on duty, and sometimes after her shift, when she'd join us for dinner or drinks. She was two years younger than Anna, making her five years younger than me. Her interest in talent, fame, and money was overt—if she was starry-eyed about this or that person, especially anyone having to do with filmmaking, it wasn't a secret. She wore her passion on her sleeve. For reasons unknown, she called me "Trachel," which stood for True Rachel—and I didn't mind.

As the obvious videographer for the Morocco trip, Neff was on board from the start. She and Anna had researched hotels before Anna settled on La Mamounia, and the three of us texted about plans for the film and whom else to invite.

Anna: The suite i booked has 3 bedrooms and can accommodate 6 people, assuming we all sleep 2 in each bed

Me: K that sounds great, we should meet to talk about who else soon right?

Anna: Throw me your suggestions for 3 other people we can invite.

Anna: We dont need to be 6 but we have the capacity.

Anna: I will ask my guys who work for me but most of them are married/have babies.

Neff: I'm so down with it.

Neff: I already have the people ready to cover my shift.

Anna: Cool

My Friend Anna

Anna: Making a movie

Anna: 🎥 🎥 🎥

Anna: Need 3 more props that would fit the narrative.

Neff: Ugh I'm so excited 🎬 🎬 🎬

Under New York State law, an occupant who resides in a hotel room for thirty consecutive days or longer is deemed a tenant rather than a guest, making him or her harder to evict. To avoid this, hotels usually set a maximum length of stay, after which guests are required to check out for at least one night.

As a result, 11 Howard required this of Anna every time her stay approached the thirty-day mark. She hated the inconvenience. Adherence to policies and procedures was her nemesis; she saw protocol enforcement as arbitrary. So, in mid-April, when she'd been at the hotel for nearly thirty days, Anna came up with a solution. She made a reservation in my name at 11 Howard for one night. I'd check in and pick up a key as a formality, but all of Anna's stuff would remain in the room. She'd pack a bag and move to the Greenwich Hotel for twenty-four hours, where she and I could have dinner and a spa night. She would take care of the billing for everything.

I didn't see anything wrong with the plan, so I went to 11 Howard around five p.m. on Tuesday, April 11, as instructed. Just as I entered the lobby, Anna walked by me without stopping. Had she not seen me? How could she have missed me? It was weird, but when Anna's eyes were fixed on an objective, it was like the rest of the world didn't exist.

Where'd you go? I texted, confused by her sudden departure. Our massages were scheduled to begin in one hour.

I need to pick up some luggage, she replied, *back in 20.*

Neff checked me in. The process didn't take long. She gave me a key card, but with no reason to visit the room, I waited for Anna in the lobby and called the spa to say we'd be late.

An hour later (ten minutes after our appointment start time), Anna finally returned to the 11 Howard lobby. Again, she flew right by me, pausing only to grab the hotel key from my outstretched hand before shlepping her giant new Rimowa suitcase into the elevator. Because Anna was the one who'd made the spa appointments and would be the one paying, I was perfectly calm waiting for her to go upstairs and pack. Nevertheless, I was taken aback—and not for the first time—by her erratic and somewhat mysterious behavior.

The front-desk staff at the Greenwich Hotel expedited Anna's check-in— we flew through the lobby and took an elevator down to the spa. We were so late that the duration of our services was cut in half. Still, the spa visit was an extravagance and I was grateful to be there, especially since I'd been stressed lately, working through tension with Nick about the on-and-off status of our relationship and also worried about my grandma Ruthie, in South Carolina, who was in her nineties and had come down with pneumonia. Not that Anna knew it; I kept my sadness and anxiety to myself.

After her shift, Neff joined us. While she and Anna chatted and laughed in the steam room, I stepped into the gym to take a call from Nick. When I found them in the changing room, Anna and Neff could tell that I'd been crying. Without asking for any details, they sweetly tried to cheer me up. Neff took the lead, telling me that I was too strong to cry over a guy and too nice to be in the wrong. Anna tried to comfort me, too, but in a different way. "He must be *stupid*," she said, smiling—having pulled the word "stupid" from a song we often listened to while working out: "Got It Good," by Russ.

It was rare for me to let anyone see that I was upset, so for it to happen now, in front of Anna and Neff, made me feel exposed. But their support made me feel closer to them, so I wasn't entirely sorry about it.

By the time we got to dinner, I was feeling much better. We ate in the Drawing Room, a cozy den that was exclusively for guests, where we spoke about Neff and her boyfriend (a rapper she knew from growing up in the Washington, D.C., area), other staff at 11 Howard, and our plans for Morocco. With her interest in film, Neff studied every detail in the Greenwich Hotel as if it had been chosen by its owner, Robert De Niro, himself. After dinner, I went home, feeling excited about the vacation to come and happy to have Anna's and Neff's friendship.

My Friend Anna

The trip was approaching, and Anna was determined to invite more guests. She asked me to suggest people, especially anyone who could help make the film alongside Neff. It struck me as odd that, as the host, Anna wanted *me* to pick her guests, though I did work in the photo industry and her connections to that world seemed limited. I casually asked a few friends, people who could potentially take a week off for a trip—but I didn't push very hard. My hesitation was definite but undefined—something just didn't feel right. Part of it was that Anna was so out-there and I wasn't sure if my friends would understand her. Was I trying to protect her? Trying to protect them? Maybe both? Anna also appealed to a certain part of me, and not necessarily the best part. Because of her, I was often late for things, I drank too much, and I neglected other friendships. I felt proud that Anna liked me, but was it possible, at the same time, to feel subconsciously ashamed?

Feeling a need to reconnect with my family, I spent Easter weekend in Spartanburg, South Carolina, at my grandparents' house. My mom and I planted flowers in my grandmother's garden. We also picked a few, which we brought to Grandma Ruthie in the rehab center, where she was "through the woods" of pneumonia but still recovering. I also spent time with my grandpa Fletcher, went on a hike with my dad, and, on Sunday, dyed Easter eggs on the back porch with my siblings and cousins. It was a calming and uncomplicated break. It felt good to be surrounded by loved ones.

Anna hung out with Neff while I was gone, which had become a bit of a pattern. Even though it felt like I saw Anna every day, I had traveled a fair amount throughout March and into April. I had gone to visit my sister, Jennie, in Baltimore, traveled to Stillwater, Minnesota, for a bachelorette weekend, and been to Washington, D.C., for an engagement party. I'd also had a visit from my college roommate, Kate, who'd come to the city for her wedding-dress fitting.

Neff later told me that Anna had seemed lonely while I was gone. I had noticed that Anna didn't seem to have many other friends, and I knew that she'd had a falling out with Mariella (and by extension Ashley) before leaving town in 2016. The details were blurry, something to do with Anna's lack of sensitivity—apparently she'd called Mariella to deliver some upsetting news but had relayed the message as though it were a fun piece of gossip. Even though the way Anna's friendship with Mariella and Ashley had ended made me wary, it didn't entirely surprise me, and I continued to give Anna the benefit of the doubt. Yes, she could be tone-deaf, I reasoned, and she lacked social graces, but she was well intentioned.

While I was in Spartanburg, Anna and Neff had dinner at Gramercy Tavern, went shopping at Rick Owens, and tried cryotherapy—an anti-aging beauty treatment that requires you to stand in a freezing-cold chamber for two to three minutes. Anna bought a new pair of sandals during their outings, and she sent me a photo: *I think they are so you with [their] pearls,* she texted.

Over the weekend, Anna brought Neff to work out with Kacy. During the session, Anna invited Kacy to come along on the Morocco trip. When Anna told me that Kacy had agreed, I was glad, and felt relieved to have a genuine adult joining our ranks.

I'm getting so excited for our adventure, I replied.

Yes we'll focus on the movie and working out 👽 , Anna said.

My flight back to New York was early on Monday morning, and I landed to a text from Anna. *How about inviting Mark Seliger to Marrakech?* she asked. Mark was a famous portrait photographer—also a friend and client of Kacy's—but I knew him strictly through my job. I told Anna it would be too weird and awkward for me professionally. I believed she was serious about her film project, but asking Mark, an older man with whom I worked, to come on a trip with four women to a private Moroccan villa? No.

Would make sense though since he knows you and [Kacy] and does film, Anna maintained.

He's a very well known/busy photographer, I replied. *I'd be surprised if he were free.*

The conversation shifted and Mark's name wasn't brought up again. I told no one that Anna had even mentioned the idea. It felt too off base. It was clear to me that Anna was becoming increasingly vexed over her indecision about whom else to invite, and what had started out as a fun idea was turning into a more stressful project than I had expected.

To make matters worse, by the end of April, Anna's friendship with Neff had become strained. Looking back, I can see that this was bound to happen given the nature of their relationship—Anna expected Neff to be both employee and friend. At the same time, it was easy to see how, for Neff, it might have been hard to gauge the sincerity of Anna's offer. Here was this girl operating in extremes, party nights and power lunches, making bold proclamations and grand gestures. What was Neff supposed to take seriously?

Despite Neff's enthusiasm, Anna told me, Neff was not getting back to her with the dates she was available for the trip—information that Anna needed in order to confirm her booking at La Mamounia—and the hotel's cancellation window (after which point Anna's deposit would become non-refundable) was approaching. Anna had given Neff a clear deadline and was annoyed that she had to follow up for an answer.

When the dates were finally set, Neff tweeted, *I'm going to Morocco in a few weeks to direct a film. Two years ago I was a manager at Starbucks. You can't tell me God isn't real.* In the comments section, Neff also responded to a person's congratulatory message by asking her if she'd like to come. When the girl said yes, Neff said she'd check to see if all the PA positions had been filled.

Anna sent me a screenshot.

That's a bit much, no? Anna asked.

I couldn't have agreed more. Part of my job on photo shoots had always been to make sure everyone respected our closed-set policy—social media wasn't allowed. It detracted from our collective mission, which was to make something great for the magazine to release. Travel, sets, locations, and talent were not booked so that a photographer (or anyone else for that matter) could take and instantaneously share shoot details or iPhone pictures that killed our exclusivity. It was a sore spot for me, which made my reaction uncharitable, especially since Neff did not have my experience with closed sets.

Considering i had to chase to get her vacation dates one day past the cancellation deadline, Anna continued.

Yeah. That's annoying, I said.

Thats my problem with all these ppl, Anna complained.

I interpreted her statement as a broad missive against people who were more talk than action.

Anna also wished that Neff had waited to actually make the film before posting about it. *It would be so embarrassing [for her] if this trip [doesn't] happen,* she wrote. *Then inviting randos from twitter when you 100% know you aren't in a position to invite anyone. I mean i like her in real life. She seems like she works hard. [But] this psychotic desire to show off is such a turn off for me.*

She went on to say that she'd offered to pay for Neff's rental equipment. According to Anna, Neff had said that she'd go to the camera store to look at lenses, but it never happened. *I mean what am I supposed to be doing that now[?]* Anna fumed. *I'm not the one who wants to be the filmmaker here. Plus i have better things to do. I'm also not supposed to be chasing you when you are invited for a free vacation. You cant really have that attitude in any of the creative jobs.*

You have to be scrappy, smart and self-motivated, I agreed.

I guess she wants to come across as someone like this, Anna said, *but there are so many discrepancies between talk and action. It's hard to look past it. I get it, she has this job for money, but no one has it easy.*

———

On the evening of May 1, I joined Anna for dinner at Le Coucou. Kacy and her friend, who happened to be a Swedish pop star, joined us, too. This was a dinner that Anna had actually made a reservation for. There was an air of expectancy in the room, and the waiters were preemptively giddy as they awaited news from the James Beard Awards, in Chicago. When they got the call, a huge hurrah exploded from the kitchen: Le Coucou had been named the year's Best New Restaurant. The staff hugged each other, joined in a circle to applaud, pulled down the top-shelf alcohol, and toasted in celebration. By the evening's end, Anna and I were the only guests left, unofficially part of the family. It was one of those rare occasions that I experienced as if from above: swirling in ephemeral revelry, I knew then that it was special, to be with these people, gathered by chance, for this moment in time.

In the back of my mind, I also knew that in less than two weeks Anna and I would be in Morocco. This evening in Le Coucou reminded me that, despite any misgivings, Anna had a magical way of looking to the horizon, understanding potential, and knowing exactly when to be where.

———————

Anna didn't dwell on her frustration with Neff, who removed the offending tweets as soon as she'd been asked. But exactly one week before the trip, Neff had a change in plans. It was the day before Anna was traveling to Omaha for the Berkshire Hathaway Annual Shareholders Meeting. Anna had invited me to come with her for the weekend, but I was attending the 53rd Annual SPD (Society of Publication Designers) Awards Gala with my colleagues from the magazine's photo and art departments on Friday and an engagement party on Saturday.

Neff sent a text to Anna, which Anna forwarded to me. If we were still going to Morocco, Neff said, she could be there only from Friday to Wednesday, not for a full week like the rest of us, because she needed to travel to Los Angeles for a video shoot with her boyfriend. Neff was going through a hard time in her relationship, so I wanted to cut her some slack. Anna did, too, at first, but the more she texted me, the angrier she sounded. She told Neff that it probably didn't make sense for her to come, since we would be arriving in Morocco on Saturday afternoon, and staying only until Wednesday didn't seem worth the expense. Neff backed out without offering an apology, and Anna was upset.

The situation ended strangely. Since Anna was preoccupied chartering a private jet for her travel to Omaha, she asked me to speak with Neff, to explain that her feelings (or was it pride?) had been wounded. *It'd be great if you could call her tomorrow,* Anna texted. *I feel like she doesn't understand how big of a deal it is.*

The trip aside, I knew that Anna was unlikely to handle such a conversation gracefully. Still, the triangulation was awkward. I spoke to Neff on Monday morning. While sympathetic to her situation, I did as I was bid. To Anna, this trip was a big deal, I explained. Even though she seems unbothered, she's actually pretty upset. Anna's more sensitive than she seems, I said.

Neff was lovely. She totally got it, and she promised to follow up with Anna to express her gratitude and regret. The conversation itself actually felt perfectly normal. I think I was the only one who experienced discomfort at having been thrust into the middle of tension between friends. (To me, it felt like a scene from *Mean Girls*—Anna was Regina George, and I was her pawn.)

But there was something else about the situation that didn't feel right. When I hung up with Neff, I paused to reflect. It was something about Anna, the way she appeared neutral with Neff, even when angry. She had forwarded me their text exchange, meant to show that she was annoyed:

Anna: It might not make sense for you to come out for 3 days . . .
Neff: You have a point.
Anna: So you're out?
Neff: Hmm I guess so.
Anna: Ok good luck with your shoot.

In sharing the exchange with me, Anna was hoping I'd affirm that her messages to Neff came across as clearly hostile. But they didn't seem that way to me. If I were Neff, looking at those messages without knowing that Anna was upset, I wouldn't have guessed it. Anna's words were too subtle to reflect the depth of her annoyance.

Anna sent me Snapchat messages from Omaha, including video of a rowdy, drunken visit she paid to the Henry Doorly Zoo and Aquarium in the company of some businessmen who were attending the shareholders' meeting. When she returned from the trip, she and I spoke on the phone. Our departure for Morocco was only days away. Now that Neff was out, Anna was struggling to find a replacement videographer. It seemed like she'd be happy with anyone who knew how to work a camera as long as we filled the space. Anna brought up the idea of inviting Nick. I asked him, but he declined, ostensibly because he was a still photographer and did not shoot video. This was true. It was also true, however, that he had become uncomfortable with the dynamics of my friendship with Anna. The last time I'd invited him to join Anna and me for dinner, he'd asked, "Where?"

"At Le Coucou," I told him.

"Let's go somewhere else. Maybe the Odeon," he suggested.

"I don't think Anna will want to."

"Why? Doesn't she ever leave her hotel?"

"Not really."

"Don't you think that's weird? She chooses the restaurant. She chooses everything."

By that point, I'd accepted the idea that because Anna paid for almost everything, she got to make all the choices, and I became defensive. I figured it was just the way some relationships were structured. I fended off his concerns, arguing that my friendship with Anna was real, and blaming anything he saw as weird as a harmless by-product of her hard-to-explain character.

Anna and I met up that evening for a drink and continued our conversation about who else to invite to Morocco. I was due to have dinner with a friend who was in town, but when it was time for me to leave, Anna was suddenly clingy. "I'd invite you, but I haven't seen my friend in forever," I explained. Jesse and I had become friends when he was working as a photo assistant and living in Brooklyn. He had subsequently bought a Winnebago and driven it across the country to Los Angeles, where he had been living for the past couple of years. It had been a long time since we'd seen each other.

Anna didn't take no for an answer, so minutes later I sent Jesse a warning: *I stopped by to say hi to my friend Anna who lives in 11 Howard . . . She asked if she could walk over to grab a bite (when I head over) and I felt awkward saying no . . . I told her I really want to catch up with you as it's been forever (!!!!) She should get the hint and not stay long. You'll like her though. She's a bit crazy but actually very sweet and fun.*

Love crazy. All good, he wrote back.

We met at a taco place called Tacombi, in Nolita. Anna did not leave after "grabbing a bite to eat," like she'd promised. She stayed for the entire meal and I let it happen. She and Jesse got along. Before I paid the check, without asking me, Anna invited him to Morocco. He accepted on the spot, granting Anna credibility based on her relationship with me. Apparently, my consent didn't matter to anyone; all around it was viewed as either irrelevant or implied. This bothered me, but I couldn't think of a way around it: I didn't want to stand in the way of Jesse's free trip (I'd be glad to have him with me), nor did I want to complain about Anna's inclusiveness. I could only let it go.

Having invited Kacy and Jesse, Anna looked to me for insight about what they'd expect her to pay for—aside from the hotel, which, according to Anna, was already a done deal.

"Well," I explained, "since you're essentially hiring each of them to do a job, they will expect you to cover their flights and expenses."

Anna processed this information quietly before graciously offering, "And I'll pay for yours, too"—as though this had always been her plan.

"Oh . . . ," I replied. "Thank you, Anna. You really don't need to. That's a very generous gift."

"I'm happy to take care of it," she said.

But the day before our departure, Anna had yet to book our flights. Her procrastination hardly surprised me. I'd seen Anna leave arrangements to the last minute time and again. Flights to Marrakech weren't sold out, and Anna didn't care about getting a reasonable fare. Anna's trip, Anna's rules. If she wasn't worrying, why should I?

She wanted to leave late in the evening, she said. She had a lot to wrap up before we left. This was fine by me; I had a lot to do, too. After Marrakech, I'd be traveling on my own directly to the South of France. It was something I'd always wanted to do. When I studied abroad, I had planned to visit Provence in late spring, but when late spring arrived, I didn't want to leave Paris—so I put off the trip for later in life, and the time had finally come.

It was a mad scramble to prepare for two weeks out of the office. Probably even more so for Anna, since many of her meetings seemed to take place in person. I had played it cool when flights weren't booked earlier in the week, but on the day we were scheduled to leave, it was time to nudge things along.

I wasn't the only anxious one. Kacy and Jesse both sent me texts that morning. Jesse was heading to set, to assist on a photo shoot during the day, and needed time to get to the airport well in advance to park his Winnebago in long-term parking. I was the Anna whisperer, an involuntary intermediary. Aware of her characteristic aloofness, everyone texted me instead of her.

I sent her a text at eight a.m.: *We could leave tomorrow if getting out today is too stressful. I do think people are slightly anxious about knowing the plan/flights being ticketed.*

Wanting to make the process as easy for her as possible, I looked up different flight options. Booking travel was a big part of my job, and since Anna struggled with logistics, I was happy to take on that responsibility. I took screenshots and sent her two itineraries that could work, one that evening and one the next day.

What happened next is puzzling: Anna's moves were smooth and fast. She and I texted back and forth with various flights and thoughts on what was available. Then she found the perfect option: a TAP Air Portugal flight departing from JFK at 11:25 p.m. The departure was late enough that everyone would have time to get ready: Kacy could pack and Jesse could park his Winnebago. The itinerary involved a long layover in Lisbon, but what did it matter? We'd finally be on our way!

Looks good to me! I texted, followed by a few dancing-girl emojis.

Will need to change the pick up from the airport as well, she replied, confirming she'd take care of it.

Good call. I'm sooo excited, I said.

Then, five minutes later, I received another text.

You busy? Anna asked.

I can talk, I replied.

I get interrupted all the time and about to get into meeting. Could you finish our flights booking? Just one way economy for everyone.

With what card? I inquired.

She texted two images: the front and back of a J.P. Morgan debit card belonging to "ANNA SOROKIN-DELVEY."

K! Yes I'm happy to help. Just forward me Kacy and your info. I have Jesse's.
She sent through a photo of Kacy's passport and then a scan of her own.
They left out 'delvey' on my esta [visa] so maybe just leave it out on the tkts as well. Billing is 11 howard st, 10013 ny.

Her passport, issued in Düren, Germany, said "ANNA SOROKIN-DELVEY," but I did as she asked.

Got it. Booking now, I told her. *Funny that her billing address was the hotel where she'd been living,* I thought to myself, *but what else would it be?* I guessed that's how it worked living the way she did, full-time in a hotel.

Thanks. It kicks me off the site after 1min, she said.

Right after I booked the one-way tickets using Anna's card, I received a phone call. It was a man from the travel agency, telling me that Anna's card had been declined. Fair enough. The flight total was around $4,000 for the group, so I assumed she'd need to call her bank for authorization. He asked me to call him back once Anna approved the transaction, so I took down his number and messaged Anna.

Hi Anna, card was declined. Can you call your bank to authorize the charge?

Will do, she replied.

Text me when done. Sorry for the hassle, I told her.

I'm on hold with bank, she replied. *They say they will call me back once the block is lifted and I need to raise my limits since Mamounia preauthorized today as well.*

At this point in the conversation, it was exactly 1:45 in the afternoon. We'd been texting about travel since early in the morning. I was impatient, ready to get things sorted out and move on with my day. That said, I have trouble in hindsight understanding why Anna's next text seemed plausible, but at the time it did.

Airline ppl calling me saying they are leaving in 10, she told me.

I wasn't sure what to do with this information, but I felt the urgency.

Should I put on my card and you pay me back? I asked.

And that's how it started, the beginning of the end.

Chapter 7
Marrakech

Travel is telling: the way different people like to pack and plan, or how early they leave for the airport. I've traveled so frequently for work that I've developed my own tried-and-true routine. I'm a proud member of the too-early club. I leave loads of time. TSA PreCheck (shoes stay on), headphones in, Hudson News for snacks and a bottle of water, and then a leisurely stroll—maybe I'll read a book while I'm waiting to board. The alternative is stressful to me: rushing in, carsick from a speeding cab, cutting in line, and jogging the umpteen miles to the gate. No, thank you. That sort of intensity makes me more vulnerable to the rudeness and bad moods of strangers in airports—and people can become unhinged in airports; stress does funny things. So I hide in my little bubble, going at my own speed.

I wanted to leave for JFK on my own that Friday evening. Anna's habitual tardiness was more than I could handle. I'd heard her talk one too many times about the six-minute helicopter flight that she could take as a last resort, if she were too late for a car. That kind of stress was unappealing to me—as was the unnecessary expense (although, as Anna put it, one day her time would be so valuable that taking a $700 chopper ride would be more cost-effective than wasting an hour in traffic). As for me, I'd rather leave wildly early and take the subway than rush and take a helicopter.

I may leave for the airport quite early so I can finish work when I get there, I told Anna.

Ok let's go together, she replied.

It was a nice try, anyway.

I went home to finish packing and told Anna that I'd pick her up around seven, thinking that if I booked the car we were more likely to stay on schedule.

Of course, it wasn't that easy. Anna had been butting heads with the management at 11 Howard for days. They had asked her to start paying for her reservations in advance, and she was infuriated by this irregular treatment. ("No one else must do that," she had complained.) Her retaliation was twofold. First, she canceled her upcoming bookings. Then, having made note of the general managers' names, she proudly declared that she had purchased the corresponding Internet domains.

She sent me a text around five p.m. *Fucking assholes,* she complained. Without a reservation, 11 Howard was now refusing to store Anna's belongings.

Will the Mercer let you? I asked.

Yes, she said. *Booked a month at Mercer. Fuck them.*

We would pack up all of Anna's stuff and drop it at the Mercer en route to the airport. We made plans to meet at 11 Howard around seven p.m., but when the time came, Anna was busy getting her hair done. I needed an extra half hour to pack anyway, so it made no difference to me.

Beneath my open suitcase and a mess of clothing, my bed was hardly visible. I took stock of each garment as I folded it: pajamas, stuff to wear with a bathing suit, shorts and pants, tops, and dresses. Once my large suitcase was zipped, I would go through a similar process for my carry-on. I was tugging a mini roller bag down from the deepest corner of my crowded closet when I got another text from Anna.

Shall I email them I bought their domains or not yet? she asked.

I wouldn't do that yet, I replied. I had tried to talk Anna out of buying the domains in the first place. Real estate developer Aby Rosen owned 11 Howard—along with the building that Anna wanted to lease for her foundation. If the managers told him about Anna's bullying tactics, it wouldn't be

94

a good look. But Anna had insisted that Aby would condone, maybe even applaud, her behavior. Without sincere interest in my opinion, she had done exactly as she pleased.

Why not? she asked.

It's a bit much, don't they have a relationship with the Mercer? I just don't want them to talk shit about you before you get there and settled and meet people for yourself. Her spitefulness was excessive. I was trying to talk her out of it by pointing to potential consequences.

No it's André [Balazs's] hotel, she argued. *There is no shit to be talked about me. I didn't do anything.*

I only mean that you bought their domains, I explained.

It's not illegal to buy anyone's domains. I didn't publish anything on them yet.

It was pointless arguing.

How would you tell them? I asked.

Email each of them the screenshot of ownership. I'm never going to do anything with them. I like the idea of them knowing that I might.

———————

When I pulled up to 11 Howard, Anna wasn't back yet, so I waited in my Uber.

I will get the big car, so come out of yours and we'll switch everything to mine, she said.

My car is pretty big, want to just stay in this one? It's an SUV, I answered, conscious of the time.

Ok if you don't mind circling around, she said. *Can add [the cost] to my invoice* 😀 .

Thirty minutes later, there was still no sign of Anna. With every passing minute, my anxiety increased. She asked me to have the bellhops load her bags, which I was glad to do since it would hurry things along. I exited the vehicle and orchestrated the packing as she'd requested. Two gold suitcases

95

and bags from Net-a-Porter would come with us; the rolling rack and a large cardboard box would stay behind. When it was all done, Anna came scurrying down Howard Street, shuffling faster than a walk, slower than a jog. Her freshly blown-out hair billowed as she moved.

Our SUV soon hummed along the cobblestones of Crosby Street. The bellhops at the Mercer helped us off-load Anna's bags and checked them to store until her return. Our errand complete, we climbed back into the car and set off for JFK. It felt like a small miracle—that I'd overcome the luggage obstacle and gotten Anna into the car, not as early as hoped but early enough to still be on time. I had always imagined that getting out the door, away from our busy Manhattan lives, would be the hardest part. And now we had done it. All that was left was to enjoy the journey—and we were ready.

Two hours before our flight, we were Marrakech-bound.

————————

Kacy arrived at the airport first and went through security on her own. Jesse was waiting for Anna and me at the entrance to Terminal 5. I gave him a hug. The three of us gossiped and cracked jokes as we stood in the check-in line together. When we reached the front, I went first, on my own. The agent took my passport with a warm smile. We made small talk as she clicked away at her keyboard. To my pleasant surprise, she turned a blind eye to my overweight checked bag, sparing me a hefty fine. I thanked her and then joined Anna and Jesse, who were checking in together with another agent.

Jesse was a seasoned freelancer, so from the outset he expected Anna to pay for his expenses, including the cost of checking his gear. But there was a hiccup in the process. Although she had her passport in hand, Anna had mistakenly checked her black clutch, the one containing her credit cards. She turned to me, since she already owed me money, and asked if I'd mind covering the $200 cost for now. As she was paying for the trip, of course I didn't mind; it was a relatively small favor to ask. Until Anna could recover her clutch, this pattern would continue: I paid $120 for sushi in JFK and $80 for lunch during the layover in Lisbon.

Finally, we landed in Morocco. It was Saturday, May 13. Marrakech Menara Airport was crowded, but La Mamounia had arranged for VIP airport assistance. Two men in coffee-brown uniforms met us at our arrival gate and led us through an expedited immigrations process. They left us before the baggage area, where the four of us collected our checked belongings and made our way to customs. The line was so long that we stood for a moment looking for its end.

That's when Anna did something peculiar.

She walked ahead, disassociating from our group as though she had arrived in Morocco alone. She moved briskly to the front of the line, and then she slipped right through, leaving the rest of us behind. When we realized she was wandering off, we called her name and followed in her direction, but the guards took notice of us somehow, not her, and blocked our way—directing us to the end of the queue.

Anna looked back as though she hadn't realized what was happening, and then her face broke into a smile. Given the length of the line the rest of us had to wait in, I understood why she had decided to test her luck—but I also realized, in a small but significant way, that Anna did not operate with a "one for all and all for one" mentality. She was on her own. Had she been like this in New York, too? It certainly wasn't out of character, but it struck me differently now that we were so far from home.

We reconvened on the other side of the checkpoint, in a large terminal with white walls and a ceiling that reminded me of the latticed foam sleeves that sometimes come on bottles of wine or shipped fruit. A driver met us there. We followed him outside, into the dry, warm air, where two Land Rovers were waiting. Anna and I rode in one car, Kacy and Jesse in the other. After a ten-minute drive, we pulled up to a palatial compound and entered through its gates. At the front entrance, we were welcomed by a host of men wearing fez hats and traditional Moroccan attire. We had arrived at our singularly opulent destination. Miss Delvey, our host, opted for a tour of the grounds for her and her guests. We proceeded directly, not having any need for keys or a traditional check-in procedure, since our villa was staffed with a full-time butler and, according to Anna, all billing had been settled in advance.

Our private *riad* was the size of a small house, and our butler, a nice man named Adid, met us at the front door. We entered through a foyer, then walked down three steps into the center of an elegant living room with a zellige-tile floor. There was a seating area to our left, containing a sofa, two chairs, and two ottomans—upholstered in saffron-gold velvet brocade. To our right was a dining space, anchored by a round, dark wooden table, on top of which white roses, chilled wine, and an assortment of fruits and pastries awaited us.

Two of the *riad*'s bedrooms were directly off the living room. Kacy took the room to the left, through a doorway in the seating area. Jesse claimed the room to the right, through a door in the dining space.

There was another door to the right of the dining space, leading to a long, dark hallway with crimson walls and a carved cedarwood ceiling. The corridor turned left and ran behind the living room, past Jesse's room, to a master suite featuring a private drawing room, a fireplace and desk, and the *riad*'s largest bedroom. I shared the suite with Anna. All three bedrooms had doors that opened directly onto the patio, where we could take a dip in the villa's private pool, sunbathe in a lounge chair, or pass through an ornate wrought-iron gate into the resort's idyllic gardens.

The hotel had four restaurants: French, Moroccan, Italian, and the Pool Pavilion. As it was our first night in Marrakech, we opted for Moroccan. We sat at an outdoor table and kicked off the night, and our vacation, with a round of Aperol spritzes and a bottle of dry white wine. The four of us had the satisfied glow of freshly arrived travelers.

Each of us brought something different to the group. Vacation-mode Kacy was sporting colorfully patterned pants, a white silk blouse, and an energetic smile. She was vocal about her excitement at being in such a luxurious place, but her enthusiasm stayed within measure. She seemed invested in our discussion of possible group activities—going to the souk and the Jardin Marjorelle, for instance—but also content to do her own thing, which I would come to find out meant lounging by the pool. Upbeat but always balanced, Kacy was our ballast.

Jesse was wearing a light-blue oxford shirt and dark pants, his long hair tied into a messy high bun. He played the role of amused observer, regardless of whether or not he had his video camera in hand—which he usually did. In conversation, he would often chime in with facts, stories, and opinions. He would have the idea to make a day trip to the Atlas Mountains, for example, because he'd done some research and spoken to a friend. Jesse ruled with his intellect. At times, he inclined toward cynicism. He would confide in me with his observations or complaints, but after voicing them, he was usually quick to let them go. He and I sometimes fought like siblings. The rigidity of his opinions could make me crazy, and my occasional tendency to rule with emotion over logic could drive him nuts.

Anna Delvey, international woman of whimsy and mystery, was wearing head-to-toe black, as was her norm: black skinny jeans, a black shirt, and her feathery black coat draped over her shoulders. It was as though she had summoned us, and now that we were all here, it gave her pleasure to sit back and watch. She giggled mockingly as we processed the fanciness of our surroundings. She was just as jubilant and wide-eyed as the rest of us, only she was much faster at making herself at home. Above all else—and at this first dinner especially—Anna looked *happy*.

Me? I filled in the seams, gluing the group together and doing my best to please. Sitting at dinner, in the cool night air, I wore an irrepressible smile. I was surrounded by people whose company I enjoyed, in a country I'd never been to, in a hotel grander and more extraordinary than anything I could have imagined. I was invested in making sure the others felt as happy as I did, both in this moment and throughout the trip.

A funny thing happened during our meal. One cat at first, and then another, appeared on the restaurant's terrace and moseyed over to our table. Marrakech is filled with feral cats, so their presence wasn't a mystery. But both of them came right up to me—only me—and stared until I gave them some food (which of course I did because I couldn't help myself). Cats would single me out for the rest of the week, wherever we went. It became a running joke that I was their master. So maybe that was my role: pleaser of people and of stray cats.

After the boozy meal, on the heels of our travel day, we returned to the villa feeling tipsy. Kacy turned in for the night, while Anna, Jesse, and I hung around. I think it was Anna who first decided to get in the pool. In a city roughly fifteen hundred feet above sea level, the evening air was chilly. Despite the thick sweater I'd worn to dinner, I had shivered on the walk across the gardens back to our *riad*. I had no interest in a swim, but Jesse gamely joined our host.

Anna's music played from a speaker in the courtyard while they swam. Meanwhile, I crawled under the covers in the master bedroom to get warm. Minutes later, I heard Anna's voice: "Let's get Rachel to come in the pool, too." *Not happening,* I thought. I'm a miserable person when I'm cold—I hate it. Dinner had been fun, I was in a good mood, but I really, *really* did not want to get in the pool. Not for all the tea in China—no way, no how.

I don't remember the exact sequence of events, but I do remember being chased. It was only Anna at first. She came toward me with a mischievous sparkle in her eye, which was enough to make me run. I darted around the bedroom, down the long hallway, through the living room, the courtyard, and past the pool. At first I tried to laugh off what was happening, but as the chase continued I could feel myself getting mad. "I *mean* it!" I yelled. "I am *not* in the mood!"

With Anna running after me, I sought refuge, through the rear door, back in our room. When I leaped onto the bed, she followed. I remember her grabbing my wrists. We tussled. She was laughing; I was not. I can still picture the look on her face when she realized that I was stronger than she was. I broke free from her grasp, rolled away, and kept running. At some point, Jesse joined in the pursuit.

I would not let them pull me in. If it was going to happen, I would do it myself. I made a dash for my suitcase, threw on a bathing suit, marched to the pool, and jumped in without hesitation, pulling myself out just as quickly. "There. Are you happy?" I said. They cheered. Dripping and cold, I stormed off.

Okay, I know—poor me, right? Chased by two friends who only wanted me to get in the pool of our private villa, on the grounds of one of the world's nicest hotels. But alone in the bedroom, I was so hot with anger that tears burned in my eyes. Sure, we were all a little drunk. And so what? The stakes were low.

Anna and Jesse? Only horsing around.

But they had inadvertently hit upon one of my trigger points.

I gave Anna so much leeway—I abided her bossiness, her rudeness, and her lack of boundaries. This was one thing I had said clearly: I did not want to get in the pool. Why couldn't she let me have that? Not only did she override my agency, she sucked Jesse in, too, using my friend against me. Anna knew that I was serious and still she hunted me for sport. I felt bullied, alone, and sorry I'd come.

I sent Jesse a text message and an email, just to be sure he got the point: *Please do not gang up on me with Anna. It's not fun. I do not find it amusing.* He responded within minutes to say that he was sorry and that it wouldn't happen again. Just before I put down my cell phone to go to sleep, Anna walked into the bedroom looking sheepish, her head lowered and eyes raised. I glanced up from my phone just long enough to make eye contact before looking back down. For a minute, there was silence as she walked into the bathroom to change. When she re-entered the room, she ventured a few words.

"You were really mad, huh?" she said, her tone soft.

"Yeah," I answered. I waited a beat before adding, "That was *not* fun."

"I'm really sorry—we got carried away," she said.

I felt something tight within my chest begin to loosen. "It's okay," I replied.

There was a pause. "I've never seen you get that *angry*."

To my surprise, I felt myself begin to smile—and then laugh. Anna started to laugh with me.

By the time I fell asleep, the air had cleared.

———————

The next morning, I decided to put the incident behind me. We had drunk too much wine, were overtired, and I'd no doubt overreacted as a result. Moving forward, I would make an effort to be less uptight. Anna took a private tennis lesson in the morning. We met her afterward for breakfast at the poolside buffet. We would spend the rest of the day exploring all that La Mamounia had to offer. We roamed the extensive gardens and relaxed in the hammam (a Moroccan steam room). Between adventures, Adid appeared, as if by magic, with fresh watermelon and chilled bottles of rosé. We luxuriated in the hazy bliss of a day without obligations. Lounging in the sun, we lost track of time. When we were hungry, we ate. When we were tired, we napped. By day's end, we were fully relaxed and all getting along.

Early the next morning, we did a workout with Kacy. Thankfully, we had the gym to ourselves. Jesse was there with his camera, and while Anna may have liked for others to see her being filmed, I was reluctant. Afterward, Anna and Kacy both took a nap. That afternoon, we decided to go for a walk around Marrakech. We all agreed that La Mamounia was beautiful, but at this point we were ready to venture out.

Anna wanted two things: piles of spices worthy of an Instagram photo and a place to buy some caftans. La Mamounia's concierge arranged everything, and within minutes we had a tour guide and had set off with a car and driver. Our van came to a stop, and we stepped out one by one, fresh from our sheltered resort life into the dusty warmth of the mysterious maze known as the medina—an ancient walled metropolis.

The tour guide knew what our priorities were; nevertheless, he made an unscheduled stop at an antiques store on the way. Next came the rug shop, which was something we'd wanted to see. Drinking hot tea, as was the custom, we sat on a couch and watched the workers unroll their wares.

Anna got on her knees to feel the texture of a one-of-a-kind, hand-knotted wool rug, made by the Berber tribes of the Middle Atlas Mountains. Quietly, she said to me, "I'll buy you one if you want it." The rugs cost thousands of dollars. It was a generous offer—typical of Anna. I thanked her but passed. After finishing our tea, we moved on.

We were quite a sight, walking through the narrow alleyways of the marketplace, led by our tour guide, a chatty, round-faced man in blue jeans and a baseball cap. Kacy trailed a few steps behind him, dressed in all white and carrying a blue woven tote bag in her left hand. Anna walked beside her, in a coral-colored dress that tied behind her neck, leaving her arms and upper back exposed. Her sunglasses were on top of her head, and she carried the black clutch that she'd accidentally checked when we were leaving New York. Then there was Jesse, wearing a backpack, floating behind Kacy and Anna with his video camera lifted in front of his face. I walked behind everyone, stopping here and there to photograph alleyways with my phone. No one spoke much as we wandered—we were too busy marveling at the mystical people and places that surrounded us.

"Can you make this dress but with black linen?" Anna asked a woman in La Maison du Kaftan Marocain. Before the woman could reply, Anna continued, "I'll take one in black and one in white linen and, Rachel, I'd love to get one for you."

I scanned the store's racks as Anna tried on a bright-red jumpsuit and a range of gauzy sheer dresses. I tried on a few things, too, but wary of the iffy fabric content and high prices, I soon joined Jesse and Kacy in the shop's seating area for glasses of mint tea.

When Anna went to pay, her debit card was declined.

"Did you tell your banks that you were traveling?" I asked. "No" was her reply. In that case, I wasn't surprised that such a purchase would be flagged. Anna asked to borrow the money, promising to reimburse me the following week. I agreed and charged the $1,339.24 purchase to my credit card, careful to keep track of the receipt. We wandered around until dusk. Then we went directly to La Sultana, a five-star luxury hotel nestled within the medina, where we sat on the rooftop terrace, bathed in lantern light and the mesmerizing sound of the Islamic call to prayer, echoing from minarets across the "Red City." Pleased with our expedition, we ate dinner in high spirits. I paid for that, too, adding it to my "tab" with Anna.

When we got back to our resort, we stopped for a drink in the Churchill Bar (within La Mamounia's main building). We were talking about what else we could do that evening when someone mentioned the hotel's Grand Casino. "I've never been to a casino," I said. That sealed the deal. We finished our drinks and walked straight over. We stayed only a short while, but within that time Anna helped me play roulette, explaining how it worked as she stood by my side. But my favorite game was the slot machines, and they seemed to like me, too. I won a little money in a lucky streak, and then lost it just as fast. We left when I ran out of cash—all of it except for one chip, which I held on to as a keepsake.

That night in the *riad*, Anna and Jesse got back in the pool. Jesse shot video while Anna swam around, wearing a black dress that she'd gotten in the medina. Eminem's "Rhyme or Reason" played in the background. Anna was deliberate with her poses: she lifted her dress so it floated around her, revealing her legs. The performance was artificially sensuous. She was playing to the camera, clearly loving its attention, and grinning nonstop.

Kacy wasn't feeling well. She had a stomachache that had started on Monday afternoon. So when it was time for our first outing on Tuesday, she stayed behind in the villa to rest. Anna, Jesse, and I were heading to the Jardin Majorelle. The hotel booked our car and driver—and the same tour guide from the previous day. We were walking through the lobby to meet them when a hotel employee waved Anna to a stop. "Miss Delvey, may we speak with you?" he said, tactfully pulling her aside. "Is everything okay?" I asked when she rejoined the group. "Yes," Anna reassured me. "I just need to call my bank."

Anna wore her new red jumpsuit that day, in the hope that it would photograph well. Jesse shot video, and I snapped a few pictures, as we walked together through the garden. We went from there to lunch at a poolside restaurant in the Dar Rhizlane hotel. After a successful search for photogenic spices—which we found in the Mellah, the city's Jewish quarter—we returned to La Mamounia contented.

We were walking out of the lobby, toward our *riad*, when a hotel employee approached Anna once again. She quelled his concern with assurances: "Okay, I'll just need to call my bank, it's because of the way you are trying to run the card over and over." Then we carried on with our day.

La Mamounia is surrounded by an ochre-colored perimeter wall, part of the city's twelfth-century ramparts. We were walking along its bougainvillea-covered interior when Anna approached a guard at the entrance nearest our *riad*. "Can you tell us—is there a way to get on the wall?" she asked. At first, I thought I'd misunderstood her. But she asked again, trying to explain that she wanted a way to be *on top* of the wall. The question was nonsensical, as was the idea. The wall was high and narrow. There were no ladders or platforms in sight. Moreover, the top of the wall was uneven— if Anna somehow managed to get up there, she wouldn't be able to sit.

Standing back, I watched the interaction with bemusement. When the guard looked to me for a translation, I shrugged and shook my head. Either Anna was suffering from confusion—faced with something impossible but looking for a loophole—or she was asking the question for the sake of entertainment. I wagered the latter and stood transfixed.

———————

On Wednesday morning, en route to breakfast, I was also stopped as I passed through the lobby: "Miss Williams, have you seen Miss Delvey?" When I joined the others at the poolside restaurant, I told Anna that the front desk wanted to see her. She was agitated by the inconvenience. You could always tell when Anna was agitated: she made almost comically huffy noises ("Ugh, why!") and typed furiously on her phone. She left the villa and came back shortly after, ostensibly relieved that the situation was being resolved.

Not long after, Anna, Jesse, and I were in the back of a van, drinking a bottle of rosé, on two bench seats facing each other, speeding through the desert toward the mountains. Kacy, still feeling ill, had stayed in bed for the second day in a row. As usual, Anna blasted music, as loud as her phone would allow. An hour later we arrived at Sir Richard Branson's Kasbah Tamadot, a destination hotel—with only twenty-eight guest rooms—situated in the remote foothills of the High Atlas Mountains. We'd come for lunch.

The hotel radiated a serene energy as its inhabitants lounged in the breeze, which was fitting since Kasbah Tamadot means "soft breeze" in the language of the Berbers, an indigenous people of North Africa. We sat around a table on the terrace, absorbing a sweeping view of the adjacent valley and mountains, before studying the food and drink menus, bound in beautiful handwoven casings. Anna and I ordered mojitos to start. Jesse went for a mimosa. The table would soon become a medley of flavor and color. We sipped Perrier from vibrant orange glasses and ate freshly baked Berber bread dipped in rich local olive oil. At some point, we switched to white wine. My vegetable tagine arrived so sizzling hot that I made Anna and Jesse look to see how it was bubbling. Not wanting the meal to end, we ordered dessert: raspberry and lemon sorbet, an Eton mess, and a round of espressos.

The bill came to $236.24, which, once again, I paid.

After lunch, Anna asked the front desk for a tour. We saw a sampling of the hotel's twenty-eight bedrooms, from suites to Berber tents, each decorated in a unique style blending traditional Moroccan furnishings with antiques from all over the world. We passed by the turquoise swimming pool—the property's centerpiece—and, at Anna's urging, we strolled through the fragrant, manicured gardens to see the two tennis courts located within the greenery. I couldn't tell if Anna was acting interested just for fun, if she was doing research for her foundation, or if she was sincerely curious. She toyed with the idea of making a reservation for the following week, but dropped the discussion when I reminded her that I was leaving for France.

Back in Marrakech, we went directly from our excursion to Dar Yacout, a restaurant situated within a former medieval home, where we began the evening with a glass of wine on the roof. Beneath a cobalt-blue sky, Gnawa musicians in bright-red costumes sat cross-legged on a rug, playing their instruments for a crowd of appreciative listeners, many of whom took photos and videos, like Anna, Jesse, and I did. We were exuberant. Anna, especially, looked joyful—maybe the most relaxed I'd seen her during the whole trip. She and Jesse had struck up a nice rapport, each making comments and jokes to make the other laugh. All three of us, in fact, were getting along very well. Once that silly drama from the first night passed, it had been smooth sailing.

Dinner at Dar Yacout was a drawn-out and heavy affair, a luxurious five-course feast, with huge serving sizes and plenty of wine. We sat in a salon, tucked within a cushioned booth, with a view of the courtyard and tables scattered with rose petals all around us. The meal went on for ages. It was the type of rich food in the type of cozy place that makes you feel almost too relaxed to remain in public. Once we finally finished, we decided to relocate to the courtyard for tea before calling it a night. I can't remember anything we talked about, but I do recall laughing about the day and feeling glad that we'd gotten to cover so much ground: driving through the Atlas Mountains, seeing Kasbah Tamadot, and now eating in this over-the-top restaurant. The vacation hadn't been quite what I expected. We had fewer activities planned than I had imagined, and we were working without almost any structure. But looking back on it now, I felt lucky to be there, a jillion miles from home, and filled with gratitude to Anna for having invited me.

It was late when we got back to La Mamounia. We entered through the hotel's main lobby and immediately two managers stepped forward. They pulled Anna aside, and she sat down to make a call while Jesse and I lingered awkwardly nearby. At first neither Jesse nor I paid the situation much mind, but as we stood there, the hotel employees around us were growing visibly flustered. Jesse began to talk with one of them. I couldn't hear their conversation, but Jesse later told me that someone had been fired because of the trouble with our villa's payment.

After about a minute, Anna, who was out of earshot but appeared to be speaking clipped phrases into her cell phone, began walking through the lobby in the direction of our *riad*. Jesse and I followed. So did the two managers, who, once inside our villa, stopped ominously at the edge of our living room. I offered them chairs, but they declined. Anna sat in front of them, intensely focused. I excused myself and went to bed, acutely embarrassed and sure there was nothing I could do anyway.

The next day was when it all went wrong. A panicked morning that turned into the perfect storm. The hotel managers in the living room, demanding a card. Me, caving to the pressure and giving them mine. When I packed my bags and climbed into bed that night, I was hoping to leave before Anna got up.

But the next morning, she woke up when I did. She floated behind me like a sleepwalker while I gathered the last of my belongings. Trying to put some distance between us, I rolled my suitcase into the living room and went out into the courtyard, where Adid brought a plate of fruit and some coffee. Soon, Jesse emerged from his room, groggy and shirtless, and the three of us sat around the table, Anna with her legs crossed, tugging at a hangnail with her teeth, while Jesse was perched over his phone. No one said much. Like kids after a stay at summer camp that had lasted just a little too long, we were ready to go.

"Don't have any fun without me," I said to Anna and Jesse, as I passed my suitcase to the driver in front of our *riad*.

Jesse hugged me. I hugged Anna.

"Thank you *so* much," I said to her.

Goodbyes were exchanged, and I climbed into the back seat. Looking out at Anna and Jesse, I made a sad face showing how sorry I was to leave. In truth, I was relieved to be saying goodbye after the chaotic and stressful billing situation that had occurred—but I was also grateful to Anna for inviting me on such a lavish vacation. I had enjoyed a lot of the trip: the luxurious *riad*, the incredible meals, the private guides. It was an extremely generous gift, and I viewed it as such.

At this point I thought that Anna would pay the hotel bill when she checked out—and, worst-case scenario, if the charge on my personal card were to stay there (without a credit for the same amount, as the hotel promised), Anna would repay me the following week when she wired reimbursement for the flights and expenses from outside the hotel. This was not an arrangement I had agreed to in advance, but considering the way things had played out, it felt as though I had no choice but to go along with it. Sure, I was annoyed by Anna's cavalier disregard for logistics, but this is just how she was. How she had always been. A rich girl disconnected from the mundane stressors of monthly billing cycles; who'd gone on an expensive vacation and not told her parents; who'd blown through her allowance and been forced to stall for time; who'd backed herself into a corner but could easily sort things out. And I trusted that she would. I believed in her.

Chapter 8

Reprieve

Eager to leave Anna and the *riad* behind, I arrived at the airport early, checked in, and flew through security. I used my downtime to write two postcards (featuring pictures of camels in the desert), mementos from Morocco: one to Nick and one to my parents. They were handwritten highlight reels: "Hello, isn't this card cute? I love you, see you soon." Neither included any mention of Anna. Lacking postage stamps, I slid the postcards into the book I was reading (*White Teeth*, by Zadie Smith) and went on my way.

I had taken two whole weeks off from my job at *V.F.*, a record for me, since vacation days were scarce and there was rarely a good time to be away from the office. (Print magazines operate on a relentless cycle.) It had felt like a stroke of luck to find this window in mid-May. I would go from Morocco to Nice, where I planned to rent a car and drive through Provence, before meeting colleagues for the Annie Leibovitz opening in Arles.

When I touched down in Nice, I switched on my cell phone and immediately received a text from Anna. It was the day that she and Jesse had originally planned to return to New York. I say "planned" because Anna had kept her itinerary flexible by design, booking only one-way flights to

Morocco so that her return travel could be decided at a later date. (*I'll deal with return flights later,* she had texted.) She eventually chose to extend her trip by a few days to stay at Kasbah Tamadot, the resort that we'd visited earlier in the week. Jesse, who was relying on Anna for his flight home, was along for the ride. It was from the Atlas Mountains that Anna was texting me.

I'm catching up on emails now, will forward you your confirmation as soon as I get it, she assured me. She then told me that, before she left La Mamounia, the tall manager had stopped by our *riad* one more time.

I gave him your contact he said he'd like to email a thank you note, Anna said.

I puzzled over this statement for a good two minutes before her next text arrived.

Will you rather have the whole total wired to your chase [bank account] and you decide what you want to take off your amex? That way you can email them directly with all instructions?

The question didn't make sense. Email who with instructions? Of course I wanted Anna to wire the money to my checking account. Was it even possible to wire money directly to American Express? Yes, maybe, but the idea confused me. I'd already sent her my bank account details, along with an itemization of expenses.

Yes, whole bill wired to chase is best thank you so much, I replied. *I'll just apply it separately to the Amex.*

She seemed to understand. *That way you can decide what works best for you and also get all points,* she reasoned, incentivizing the transaction with her mention of Amex reward points. Another text quickly followed: *Thanks again for stepping in, greatly appreciated!*

It was then I understood that Anna intended to apply the full hotel bill to my account, to add it to the total she owed me from expenses we incurred outside the hotel. I wasn't sure how that would work—I didn't think it was actually possible. How had she left La Mamounia? And how did she check into another hotel?

I sent three texts in rapid fire:

112

My Friend Anna

I don't know if the whole bill will go through.

You're welcome, thank YOU for the trip.

Just hoping we can get the wire etc. sorted today because I'm nervous about my cards not working for the weekend. Sorry to be a bother.

It seemed like a foregone conclusion that the entire hotel bill would be on my credit card. We were both already gone from La Mamounia, but I trusted Anna to reimburse me as she'd promised. What else could I do?

I'll wire you 70,000 [USD], that way everything's covered, she wrote.

That was more money than I made in a year.

Thank you so much, Anna, I replied.

Minutes later she copied me on an email to the hotel:

. . . following up on my last email. Can you please send me the total bill
and the summary of all charges that have been put on Rachel's card.
Appreciate your assistance - Rachel was nice enough to provide you
her card but it's my responsibility to make sure all parties are covered.
Looking forward [to] receiving it before the EOD today. Thanks, AD

Even though I'd never been to the South of France before, it felt familiar and welcoming. My aunt Jennie—my mom's oldest sister, a world traveler and fellow Francophile—had given me recommendations that I'd dutifully recorded and mapped out. I'd picked a route, booked a rental car in advance and lodging for each night, and loosely planned for each day, leaving ample room to wander.

I settled into a small guest room at Hôtel Nice Beau Rivage, which was simple but lovely, and in a great location—only a block from the sea, and a short walk from the city's charming old town. Since I had only one evening and morning scheduled in Nice, I rested briefly after my arrival before setting out to explore. The narrow roads were lined with colorful storefronts, drenched in the yellow of the warm evening sun. I carried a camera around my neck and with it a sense of purpose: taking pictures was an activity that I could do alone, which encouraged me to take in and engage with my surroundings.

Over the course of the day, Anna kept in touch via text message. During the night, she sent an update on the wire transfer: *I've initiated everything today, will forward you the FedRef [Federal Reference Number, used for tracking wire transfers] as soon as they email it to me. Hope you're having fun.*

The next day was the third Saturday in May, a market day. The sky was clear blue and the air was cool in the shade. I left the hotel early to revisit the Old Town for breakfast and to explore the open-air antique market in Place Garibaldi. I admired the furniture and bric-a-brac, content to collect photos in lieu of things.

My time in France was quickly becoming the opposite of my time in Morocco: modest lodgings and full cultural immersion replaced the decadence of La Mamounia and the lack of meaningful exploration. Marrakech was already feeling far away and long ago.

As checkout time approached, I made my way back to the hotel through the Promenade du Paillon, a park that separated the newer parts of Nice from the historic Old Town.

Along the walkway, geysers erupted at seemingly random intervals: spouts of water that shot upward, sometimes high, sometimes low. Drenched children dashed through and around the fountains, testing their bravery and trilling with laughter.

———————

The wire with my reimbursement had been initiated, Anna said; I only needed to wait. But at the front desk of Hôtel Nice Beau Rivage, I was abruptly reminded of my financial strain. American Express had raised my limit just enough for me to safely leave Morocco, but when I tried to use my credit card in Nice, it wouldn't go through. Fortunately, the day prior had been a Condé Nast payday, so I'd received two weeks' salary via direct deposit into my checking account, as usual. I used it to pay for the hotel.

My Friend Anna

I collected my suitcase from the front desk and went outside for a taxi. I sent a text to Anna: *Hi Anna - my Amex isn't working, I have enough cash for the weekend but hoping the wire can be processed on Monday so I'm able to make a payment to Amex.* Pause. *I hope you guys are off riding donkeys.*

It shall be credited on Monday first half of the day, she replied. A relief.

I took a taxi to pick up my rental car. I'd never driven a car abroad before, but I tried not to overthink it. At least in France they drove on the same side of the street as in the US.

Driving was calming and intuitive, and I made good time to Aix-en-Provence, where I spent the first part of my day just wandering around. Then I drove ten minutes north to Paul Cézanne's art studio, Atelier des Lauves, where I was excited to see the light, landscapes, and vignettes that inspired a painter I'd admired since childhood. The furniture in his studio was pushed to the perimeter, where it supported still-life subjects: skulls, bowls, fruit, and canvases, arranged in familiar tableaux. It was a pleasant but odd experience to "see behind the curtain" of his paintings—Cézanne's studio felt almost quaint compared with the artistic magnitude of his work.

Afterward, I drove another twenty minutes north to Château La Coste, where I traipsed along winding paths, toured two art exhibitions, and rambled through a sculpture garden. The grounds were modern and imposing after the more subdued elegance of Cézanne's atelier.

I arrived at Lourmarin just before dinner, pausing as I neared the walled village to photograph fields of poppies set afire by the afternoon sun. A man named Adam, about my age, checked me in for a two-night stay at Le Moulin de Lourmarin, an olive oil mill from the eighteenth century that had been converted to a boutique hotel.

Early the next morning, I walked a short way to the Cimetière de Lourmarin, taking photographs as I passed through town. The outing felt appropriate for a Sunday morning, and I went through the motions with a certain spiritualism, thinking of Patti Smith and her pilgrimages to sacred old places. I circled the small cemetery twice before finding Albert Camus's austere grave, set within a small plot of fading daffodils.

115

At ten o'clock the next morning, my phone buzzed with a text from Anna.

Hope you are good, she said. *Will make sure the wire gets settled today.* Like clockwork, she chimed in with an update before I'd even asked.

Thanks you thanks you, I replied.

I departed Lourmarin for a day packed with activities. I perused a market in Lauris, marveled at the views of Bonnieux, toured a monastery in Gordes, retraced Aunt Jennie's footsteps in Venasque (where she'd once rented a house), and at last arrived in Villeneuve-lès-Avignon. My hotel for the night was the fanciest I'd booked: Le Prieuré, a Relais & Châteaux property that had been converted from an old priory. I'd made the reservation through a discount website for less than $200.

It was heavenly. Ancient, ivy-covered stone walls, turquoise shutters, large windows with white trim, and, best of all, a cottage garden, perfect in its overgrowth. After a walk through the medieval town, I went to the hotel's restaurant for dinner. My table was outside on a terrace facing the garden, so I watched its blooms and branches like a show. Birdsongs mixed with the murmur of neighboring conversations. Sunlight turned the scenery from a bright yellow-green to gold. I was spellbound, and deeply glad to be there. The past few days had marked the first real vacation I'd ever taken alone, and it was drawing to a close. Even though I was staying in France for the rest of the week, I'd be with colleagues. As I sipped Côtes du Rhône between bites of cheese, I felt pleased with the decisions I'd made and the sights I'd seen, and proud of my self-sufficiency.

The day ended just as it began—with a series of text messages from Anna.

One: *Hey.*

Two: *All good?*

Three: *Let me know once you see the wire from your side. Hope it didn't cause you too much trouble this weekend.*

I checked my bank account. Nothing. *Hi hi! Haven't seen it yet. Maybe tomorrow. I'm good!! Not too much trouble thank you, just using my debit card but I'm at my last 1k. Meep. You guys leaving tomorrow?*

Yes trying to get a helicopter to go straight to Casablanca and not have to sit in a car for 4h.

Whoa, I replied.

Getting to know local cops to get the permits haha.

jeez girl. you a mover and a shaker.

The next morning, I returned my rental car in Avignon. My colleague Kathryn and her husband, Mark, were picking me up in their car later that afternoon so that we could ride together to Arles, where we would share a large Airbnb. While I waited for them, I visited the Pont d'Avignon and then walked into Avignon's *centre-ville,* or town center, where I spent a few hours roaming.

Anna texted that afternoon, but only to complain again about Neff. Neff had bragged on Twitter about having heard *Tha Carter V*—an unreleased Lil Wayne album that had come into the hands of Martin Shkreli, who shared some of the tracks with Anna, who in turn played them for Neff.

Anna had spoken about knowing Shkreli, the infamous "Pharma Bro," on occasion. The first time was when she had bragged about having met with him over lunch at Le Coucou. "After my meeting, all of the employees at 11 Howard were, like, coming up to me and saying, 'Anna, why are you meeting with one of the most hated men on the planet?'" Anna had told me. She had been annoyed by the hotel employees' nosiness. ("I had Martin sign an NDA. What, do I need to have everyone else sign one, too?") She hadn't realized how many people knew who Shkreli was—nor how strongly everyone felt about him. "Well, yeah, Anna," I had replied, "he's a pretty notorious villain." She had been quick to defend him by arguing that he was just making decisions based on business, that he was taking advantage of the system in a way that cost insurance companies, not individual people, and that what he was doing wasn't illegal. To me, Anna's logic demonstrated that she was able to willfully separate business transactions from their moral and ethical consequences. Observing her coldness, I had supposed it was a mentality that she'd had to adopt in order to hold her own in the world of finance. I didn't agree with her, but she left me no room to argue.

I told her not to mention it to anyone, Anna continued to text, venting about Neff, *and she's like of course not, I'd never.*

I sympathized with Anna's frustration. *You're joking,* I replied.

Its so easy for anyone whos not completely stupid to put two and two together. Like she works at the hotel im staying at. What a coincidence, Anna said.

Yeah. Not cool. You should ask her to take it down.

She's just fishing for attention, said Anna. *She removed that tweet but never texted back. Uh whatchu gonna do* 🙄

Furget about it, I replied.

Kathryn and Mark picked me up and we drove together to Arles. The trip took less than an hour. It was Tuesday evening, and our return flights weren't until Saturday. The opening of the Annie Leibovitz exhibition would take place on Friday, so we had a couple of days to do as we pleased. With Kathryn and Mark, I happily relaxed my producer brain's need to make plans and was content to go along with their agenda. As a group, our dynamic was much like that of a niece traveling with her aunt and uncle. What's more, they'd been to Arles before; Kathryn had traveled there for photo shoots. She shared its haunts and stories—tales from the Grand Hôtel Nord-Pinus—like cherished folklore, and I felt lucky to be along for the ride. I looked and listened, wide-eyed and thankful.

On Wednesday morning, we went by the Luma Foundation, where Annie and her team were readying the show. The works were still being installed, but the scale was already staggering. The exhibition was entitled "The Early Years: 1970–1983: Archive Project #1." More than eight thousand photographs, printed and unframed, were being pinned to freestanding walls inside an expansive industrial warehouse. The prints didn't feel precious: they felt raw, and granted intimate access to their subjects. The collective impact was astounding.

Afterward, on our way to lunch at La Chassagnette, a restaurant and organic farm a few miles outside of Arles, I received a text from Anna.

How is it going? In arles? she asked.

Got here last night, it's good!! Haven't received the wire yet, maybe I should call chase? Are you and jesse still in Marrakech?

An hour passed. Mark, Kathryn, and I sat in the dappled sunlight that came through La Chassagnette's vine-covered trellis. We sampled wines and devoured small tasting dishes the moment they arrived at our table.

Anna kept texting.

I will forward you the FedRef so your bankers can track it. They called me yesterday to confirm.

perfect thank you, I wrote back. *You guys traveling today?*

Yes. My friends are coming for one of their wives birthdays this weekend to marrakech so i might stay a night or two longer to see them but jesse has to return.

Friends? I'd not heard her mention them before, but I didn't give it much thought. Given my response, it was possible I'd misread her text. *Bon voyage!!!* I replied. *I hope the settling into Mercer goes smoothly.*

Anna's texts kept arriving over the course of the afternoon. She wanted to try a new personal trainer, she said. Someone to see on days when we didn't work out with Kacy: *Maybe they have some empty room at mercer that we can use for the workout, otherwise im not sure where.*

After lunch, Kathryn, Mark, and I drove through the Camargue to Saintes-Maries-de-la-Mer. The seaside town was filled with caravans thanks to the Gitan Pilgrimage, an annual event when Romani people from across Europe come together in honor of their patron saint, Sara-la-Kali, or "Sarah the Black." We watched from the car as we slowly drove through. I saw bare feet on asphalt, a blend of colors and people. "Eternal pilgrims on the world's roads," as Pope Paul VI is said to have called them.

Back in Arles, we met up with colleagues who had gathered in anticipation of Annie Leibovitz's opening when Anna resurfaced. *Jesse just left, im staying here till fr night,* she texted.

This was good news. When I left Marrakech, I had wondered how he and Anna would get along. In their company, my presence had often served as a buffer. Once I left for France, Jesse kept in touch with me via text message. At first, he seemed okay. He and Anna rode mules on a trek through the Atlas Mountains. He said hi to Richard Branson when he saw him on the property. Like in Marrakech, Anna asked the hotel for private tennis lessons. Eager to accommodate her request, Kasbah Tamadot brought in a coach from La Mamounia each day. The coach became friendly with Anna, and his company outlasted their tennis lessons. He joined Jesse and Anna for dinners and a hike. I imagined a third party was good for their dynamic. But Jesse's tone quickly grew restless: *FYI- anna tried to book flights today for tomorrow. Can't book under 24 hrs for US flights out of here,* he said.

What happened? I replied. Remembering that I'd booked a flight for Kacy without any issue, I wondered if he was mistaken, but assumed he'd done his research.

I've been asking everyday what flight we got. She just didn't buy them. I dunno why.

Par for the course amigo, I answered.

It's driving me nuts inside, he said.

Jesse was clearly ready to leave. He was relying on Anna for a flight home, but she kept avoiding buying a ticket. I was relieved when Anna said that he had finally gotten out.

Kathryn, Mark, and I returned to our apartment. As we went about our evening, Anna kept rambling by text. She was going to stay in Morocco for a few days to celebrate the birthday of one of her developers' wives, she confirmed. And from there, she would fly to Los Angeles to attend Recode's annual technology conference. Her focus ricocheted: Morocco, LA, New York. She forwarded an email from Peter Bracke, who was involved in reservations at the Mercer. It confirmed her new arrival date and included information about the hotel's relationship with a nearby gym. She wanted to know if we should suggest that gym to the new personal trainer.

Anna: Next week 3 times?

Anna: I think if we say we're from mercer they let us do anything

Anna: So i can plan kacy on other days

Anna: Ugh i forgot i might be going to California

Anna: Maybe let's start with key [the new trainer] the week of the 5th

Anna: Unclear how tolerating he is to last minute schedule adjustments
we dont want to throw him off from the start 💀 💀

I was feeling refreshed and centered after my alone time, and was beginning to think that it was time to slow down my friendship with Anna. Our travels had shown me just how different we were as people—and although I still found her engaging, I was ready to give the relationship some space. I wasn't in the mood to make plans.

I joined a group of friends for a late dinner: Kathryn, Mark, Annie's studio manager, the executive VP of an image licensing company, and her husband. Annie stopped by briefly, too, to say hello before going to bed, in preparation for tomorrow's big day. Seven of us huddled around a small table in the courtyard of Hôtel du Cloître.

At midnight, I heard from Jesse. He was stuck in Casablanca. He had insisted that Anna confirm his return ticket before he got into the car at Kasbah Tamadot. Despite her assurances, he arrived to the airport four hours later without a reservation.

He was incredulous. Jesse was accustomed to traveling for photo shoots, which meant that it was usually a producer's responsibility to make sure that his travel went smoothly (to make reservations in advance and to troubleshoot issues, should they arise). He had little tolerance for poorly made plans, and it was not usually *his* job to be involved with fixing them. He expected days to be filled, flights to be ticketed, and hotels to be booked—reasonable expectations, and ones that I shared, but clearly with Anna there were no guarantees.

When confronted with the mishap, Anna told Jesse that her assistant had mistakenly canceled his booking when she adjusted *her* plans to stay. Stranded at the airport and determined to leave, Jesse managed to book

121

his own flight home, but by the time he bought the ticket, it was too late to board. He spiraled, venting to me as he sparred with Anna. Reading his texts, I felt sorry for him. He spent the night in a hotel.

That night, unable to sleep, I checked my bank account for any sign of an incoming wire. Then I logged in to American Express. The La Mamounia charges were still on my account, now totalling $36,010.09. And there were new charges, this time to my Condé Nast corporate card—two lines from La Mamounia, which totaled $16,770.45. It was the balance of our bill, an amount the hotel had been unable to put on my now-frozen personal card. Evidently, they'd kept my corporate card on file.

My stomach did a somersault.

If I received Anna's wire promptly, I could put the money toward payment of my corporate statement before anyone noticed. And yet, Anna was becoming increasingly unreliable. Her tone with me was unchanged, but her empty promises were cause for concern and her treatment of Jesse was cause for dismay. In New York, Anna's flakiness and lack of attention to detail had few consequences, but in Marrakech it was dangerously problematic. Still, she made us feel as though we were under her umbrella. Even when I'd had to front the money, she had been physically there beside me to assure me that it would all be okay. She was our generous host, after all. But letting Jesse get in a car for a four-hour drive and stranding him at the airport without a flight or a plan was something different.

I started to see Anna's behavior as negligent, and it worried me.

Chapter 9

Re-entry

I t was Saturday, May 27, when I flew from Marseille to New York by way of Paris.

Text messaging with Anna about repayment had become part of a new routine. We took turns starting the conversation each morning.

Sometimes I'd go first: *Hi A, the wire still hasn't come through. Do you have that ref so I can call chase to check on the status?*

On other days, she'd beat me to it: *Do you see the incoming wire in your account? Still waiting in remittance letters that I'll forward you once i get it. If the wire still hasn't arrived, your banker can use it to track it.*

The delay weighed on my nerves, but since I had faith the funds would arrive any minute, I didn't tell anyone about it. It didn't seem necessary, and I'd always been taught that financial matters were private. If I were Anna, I'd have been embarrassed to put such a strain on a friend. By not blabbing about it to others, I was being respectful. Besides, I thought I understood Anna better than anyone else, so there wasn't much point in asking for outside input. I rationalized her delay by considering the way she often put the cart before the horse—like booking a *riad* before deciding who to invite, or making a dinner reservation for four people and then scrambling to fill the seats. Where logistics were concerned, Anna was simply ill-equipped, but somehow, it always worked out. The same principle applied to sending a wire transfer. She set the plan in motion, and even if it took a while—and she couldn't find the reference number—I was sure the rest would fall into place. Though the situation was stressful, I was happy to be home, reunited with my little rascal of a cat, Boo, and spending time with Nick. I also got to see my brother, Noah, who had moved to New York and was living in Grandma Marilyn's spare bedroom—a rite of passage. The first weekend after my trip, Noah's girlfriend came to town, visiting from Knoxville. We joined Nick in Brooklyn and romped around the borough together. I carried my camera and took pictures like I'd done in the South of France, pretending I was still in tourist mode. Monday was Memorial Day, so we embraced the long weekend. I continued to remain silent about my financial situation. I'd always been very private—not only about finances but also about my feelings—so it wasn't unusual for me to keep this sort of information to myself. Although this time around, it felt like I was entering a sort of denial as I tried to shrug off the stress and keep moving forward.

Anna said she was stopping by London and then going straight to Los Angeles: *No one is in ny and everything is closed for memorial, i dont want to go to mercer for 2 nights and be gone for the rest of the week.*

Coincidentally, I would also be in Los Angeles that week, on Thursday. I was to attend a site visit at the Wallis Annenberg Center in Beverly Hills to prepare for a group portrait which Annie Leibovitz would photograph in October, during *Vanity Fair*'s annual New Establishment Summit, a conference Anna once again hoped to attend. Though my scouting trip would be brief, its timing seemed convenient. If the wire hadn't arrived by then, Anna and I could meet in person to settle our accounts.

And then what? Would I continue being friends with Anna? Would I fault her for relying on me when her cards weren't working? She'd been generous enough to invite me on a trip like that, I reasoned, and even though the way she'd required my help had been frustrating, there would be no lasting damage once the debt was repaid. It had always been my impulse to aid a friend in need.

But the situation had pushed me to my limits. Did Anna expect me to overlook the inexplicable delay in repayment and ignore what had happened with Jesse? My feelings toward her had irreversibly changed, and I was trying to understand how. Traveling with Anna had revealed a previously undetected riskiness beneath her idiosyncratic behavior. In New York, when she tested the limits the stakes seemed low, but not in Marrakech. Her recklessness was hard to fully excuse.

When this was finally over, I would want space. Perhaps Anna and I could resume a more casual friendship after a time. I didn't want her as a close friend, but I didn't want her as an enemy, either. Burning bridges was not something I ever did—and I hated the thought of having someone mad at me. It takes a lot of nerve to completely cut off a relationship. So I thought perhaps I could keep Anna as a friend, but at a distance. She could be a person I saw once in a blue moon. And this time around, I would do a better job of defining and fortifying my boundaries. I would better know what to expect and to limit the degree of my involvement. A friendship less close, but a friendship just the same.

Still, for now, it seemed wiser to lean into my relationship with Anna than to pull away, at least until the reimbursement arrived. We continued communicating, mostly through text messaging and, occasionally, by phone. When we weren't discussing the wire transfer, we spoke as though nothing had changed. The normalcy of our dialogue was reassuring to me.

As usual, Anna was propelled by grand notions. She swung from one plan to the next using her fantastical dreams as fuel. We looked ahead to California, and she eyed her next move.

Right now im planning on being in la Tuesday afternoon. The conference is over on Thursday lunchtime, Anna said, referencing Recode's annual technology conference, which she wanted to attend.

I would arrive on Wednesday night, I told her, and be done with work by five p.m. the next day.

K sounds good, Anna texted, *maybe we can meet up on thursday night then. Yes exactly, would be fun,* I responded.

Anna wrote back, *Maybe we can go to doug aitken's mirage thing in palm springs on [Thursday] Its a 2h drive. Last thing that's still open from desert x*

Anna had mentioned this art piece before: Doug Aitken's *Mirage,* part of "Desert X," a site-specific exhibition in the Coachella Valley that opened in 2017. *Mirage* was a life-size replica of a suburban American house, nondescript in shape but covered in mirrors so that each of its exterior surfaces reflected the landscape it faced. You could read about the project on a corresponding website:

> MIRAGE is reconfigured as an architectural idea: the seemingly generic suburban home now devoid of a narrative, its inhabitants, their possessions. This minimal structure now functions entirely in response to the landscape around it . . . Its familiar architectural form becomes a framing device, a visual echo-chamber endlessly reflecting both the dream of nature as a pure uninhabited state and the pursuit of its conquest . . . Like a human-scale lens, MIRAGE works to frame and distort the evolving world outside of it . . . There is no fixed perspective or correct interpretation. Each experience of this living artwork will be unique.

I understood Anna's interest; the installation ticked all of her boxes. It was popular with the right crowd, its impermanence made it timely, and its location made it exclusive—it was the ideal destination for a stylish excursion. We would drive to Palm Springs on Thursday and see the installation on Friday. There were rooms available at the Parker Palm Springs.

    Anna: There isn't much going on there usually if not a wedding or
           Coachella.
      Me: Could do two nights and fly back Saturday before redeye around 4.
    Anna: K me too im running out of contact lenses after next week so
           gotta return to ny.

Did she want me to pick them up for her? I offered.

No, but I should bring my Polaroid camera.

We went through familiar motions as we planned our journey, only this time I was more skeptical of Anna's schemes.

Anna: We can also rent a cute car. Something classic?

A rental car would have made sense for the two-hour drive from Los Angeles to Palm Springs, but Anna suggesting a "cute car" further reinforced my disbelief that the trip would happen at all. From there on, I engaged in the fantasy as a sort of test—letting her dream up whatever she wanted, just to see what she would do.

Three minutes later, a link appeared: a black Porsche 356 Speedster Tribute with red leather seats.

Next up: a white 1971 Pontiac LeMans.

Anna: Haha they actually are available. Not sure you are supposed [to]
       drive them for long distances though.

One last link: a 1928 Ford Model A—bright blue.

Anna: Pull up with the squad hahaha.

We were going through the motions, all right. Anna approached possibilities from the top down. The grandest options always came first, affordability be damned. We were striking matches in the rain, and we both knew it.

———————————

On Wednesday of that week, a few hours before I was leaving for the airport, Anna sent me a text, from London, I presumed.

I will try to catch a flight to la later assuming im done with everything. I missed over half of that conference now, she said.

Two hours later, she wrote me again.

Not going to la unfortunately, too much to do. . . . But lets still go to doug aitkens thing in a cute car sometime this summer.

Okedoke, I replied.

I flew to LA that afternoon, as planned, and took a red-eye back home the next day. My rent was due, I was stressed, and there still was no sign of a wire transfer. My anxiety was no longer something I was able to bear on my own.

Buckling under the pressure, I confided in Nick.

"Nick, I gotta tell you something."

"What's that?"

"For some reason, when we were in Morocco, Anna's credit cards stopped working."

He waited for me to continue.

"And I got stuck putting my cards down—"

"Okay . . ."

"It's a lot of money—a lot of money," I stammered. "I mean, she promised to reimburse me, but the wire hasn't come through yet and it's *really* stressing me out."

"Well, that's not good," he said.

"Yeah, I know—I mean, I'm sure it will be fine." I started to choke up. "It's just a lot—and I don't get why there's a delay, and she's still traveling, and—" I was full-on crying now. We sat on the couch and talked through the details. "I trust her. It's just *a lot—it's a lot*," I said.

He got up to get me a glass of water, and I followed him into the kitchen. Turning away from the refrigerator, he saw me crying, put down the cup of ice, and held me in his arms.

"It's only money, Rachel—it just happens to be *a lot* of it."

The way he said this made me laugh. We both knew it was enough money to have real consequences for my life, but still, in this moment, it felt like the kindest thing he could have said.

My texts to Anna grew increasingly desperate. *Hey lady, do you really think the wire will come through today? I need to mail my rent. Could you do quick pay for 2k so that I can send a rent check w/o it bouncing? . . . My Amex bills are also due, but they can wait until Monday.*

To help resolve the issue, Anna put me in touch with Bettina, a woman based in Germany whom Anna described as a family accountant. Bettina would help with an advance on my reimbursement while Anna was still on the road. I initiated a Chase QuickPay request, as instructed. On June 1, Anna emailed Bettina about my QuickPay request, cc'ing me.

> Bettina - has this been finalized? Please also follow through on the wire transfer that's been overdue almost 2 weeks now - Rachel is a personal friend and was kind enough to extend her credit to cover my expenses.
>
> Confirm cc'ing us both asap.

I emailed a few hours later.

> Hi Bettina, Following up on Anna's note. Can you please advise?
>
> Thank you,
> Rachel

Anna responded right away.

> Bettina, it's almost EOD in NY - make sure this goes through asap and forward the successful confirmation to everyone. You have all access to verifications for my accounts, and there are no more reasons for delays. As i mentioned many times before, this is not an invoice that can wait, it's a personal transfer - contact whoever you need to to make this happen now. I am available on my 917 us phone any time if anything further is needed from me personally.
>
> Thx,
> AD

One and a half hours later, Bettina finally wrote back.

Anna- apologies for the delay, we submitted everything from our side and I shall be receiving the bank confirmation shortly. There are no further steps needed to complete this.

We will be in touch with all parties as soon as possible.

Kind regards,
Bettina Wagner

I went through that day and the following as if nothing were wrong.

With her wedding only two weeks away, my college roommate, Kate, came into the city for a weekend visit from Amherst, Massachusetts, where she lived. There were no bridesmaids in her wedding, but I served in an unofficial capacity—as what she called a "can't do this without you" friend. The two of us sat for lunch in the front of Café Mogador on St. Mark's Place, eating Moroccan food and drinking a bottle of French wine. Morocco and France: was a pattern really there or was I just seeing things? I suppressed my anxiety. Kate was like a breath of fresh air. Not in spite of my strain, but partially because of it, my time with her felt special. I dove deeper into the joy of our friendship and gave her my full attention. We mapped out the order of her wedding processional. *This is a time for Kate,* I thought, and I was glad. I held on to my secret. It was beginning to eat me up inside, but I hid it.

Aunt Jennie and Janine were in town soon after Kate left, visiting from D.C. and upstate New York. Janine was essentially part of our family; she and Jennie had been friends since they met during a college semester abroad in England, and I'd known her my whole life. She wore silk scarves, red lipstick, and a profusion of sterling-silver bracelets that jangled on each arm.

The three of us met for dinner on Monday night on the Lower East Side. They were eager to hear about my travels—especially Jennie, who had helped so much with planning my trip in France. I looked forward to filling them in, but at the same time, I made a mental commitment *not* to tell them about Anna. There was no reason to cause alarm, and I felt uncomfortable disclosing the vacation's cost.

That was my intention, anyway.

Somewhere between the second glass of wine and the last piece of duck, I casually let it fly.

"Yes, Marrakech was great, but a weird thing happened . . ."

And there it was. Next thing I knew, I was on my way. I worked overtime as I told the story to instill faith—to give some optimism with all of the dread. And then came the question . . .

"How much?" asked Janine.

I told them, and they went silent.

"Do you think there's any chance she could be a con artist?" asked Aunt Jennie.

I laughed. "Who? Anna?" I said. "No, not a chance. Looking from the outside in, I get why you'd ask, but no—she's just a mess. I think she's probably distracted, but she'll be back from London anytime now—so, I'm sure it'll be soon."

I swore Jennie and Janine to secrecy, adamant that no one should worry.

Anna had been in touch with me that very afternoon. She was still traveling abroad. Someone who had worked for her family for thirty years had just died, she had told me, and she needed to stop by the ceremony in Germany.

Cant wait to get back to ny back to normal, she said.

Hang in there!! 💕 , I told her.

Calm as I seemed, my brain worked in overdrive to rationalize the delay and scan for solutions. On the Tuesday after that conversation with Jennie and Janine, I woke up tired. As if completing a thought from an interrupted dream, I started my day with a plea to Bettina for news:

Rachel DeLoache Williams

Dear Bettina,

Can you please share an update? I am late in my payments as a result of this delay. Please let me know if there is anything I can do to ensure remittance of this payment in the first half of today.

Thank you,
Rachel

And then a text to Anna for good measure: *Anna, I'm really anxious about money. Is everything ok? Can we ask Bettina to make sure it goes through today? My rent check will bounce and I cannot pay my outstanding bills.*

Following up now, she wrote. *Sorry im in a bit of stress my wallet got lost/stolen i need to get everything replaced and get on a flight. Your wire has nothing to do with it though, I will call Bettina again. Sorry for the delay.*

After sending the texts, I asked Nick for a fast two-thousand-dollar loan so that I could avoid a bounced rent check, and he generously provided.

Later that same morning, I heard from Kacy. *Anna's had a rough go of it in Casablanca,* she texted. In Casablanca? I thought she was in London. Kacy told me Anna had been at the Four Seasons in Casablanca for four nights with no way to pay her bill. When hotel managers came to her room demanding payment and threatening to call the police, Anna called Kacy distraught. Kacy spoke to the managers and tried to send money, but they were already out of patience and wanted Anna gone. They escorted her from the property, Kacy managed to order her a car, and Anna was on her way to the airport.

Oh shit, was my reply. I told Kacy about La Mamounia. *In the end I put everything on my credit cards and am still waiting on a wire—which I need desperately at this point.*

Kacy: Something's not right here.
Me: She won't ask her parents for money.
Me: Her accountant has been in touch with me. Allegedly everything will go through today but I don't feel good about it.

132

My Friend Anna

Kacy: Why did she stay in Morocco so long!? And alone?!

Me: No idea. I thought she was going to London . . .

Me: She told me her wallet was stolen. What is this girl doing?

Anna was having a problem, that was obvious, but why? And what could be done? Kacy and I saw a friend in distress and we were natural helpers. We agreed that the best course of action was to contact Anna's family, and yet neither of us knew how. *She's talked to me about her family,* I told Kacy. *It's just hard to understand the way she speaks sometimes . . . it can be vague.*

Early that afternoon, I received an email from Bettina.

Dear Rachel,

I am awaiting for bank's wire room confirmation that I can forward you. You shall be able to track the transfer from your side using it.

Regards,
Bettina

I wrote back:

Dear Bettina,

It has been over two weeks. Do you expect to receive the wire room confirmation today?

You did say that I would have it yesterday, along with the successful remittance of payment.

I cannot afford any additional delays.

Thank you for understanding,
Rachel

Two hours later, with no further reply from Bettina, Anna began texting me about the difficult time she was having.

Anna: Literally hell of past days.

Anna: Never traveling again haha

Me: Yikes I'm so sorry sounds awful. I'm in a tough situation until this wire goes through. Is everything ok? I don't understand what the delay is with Bettina.

Anna: Will call them again. Sorry craziest day, im still at the airport trying to catch a flight and replace all my cards.

Anna: I feel horrible for putting you into this situation.

A few hours later, I heard from Kacy.

Kacy: Did Anna wire u the money yet?

Me: No not yet.

Kacy: She wants me to buy her a ticket back in business class for $2500! Have you spoken to her yet? This is madness!

Me: I texted to be sure she was ok.

Kacy: AND?

Me: She's embarrassed about not paying me yet so wouldn't ask me for help right now (bc I literally can't pay).

Me: I do think she'll pay you back.

Me: Did you suggest she ask her parents?

Me: I don't know what to say.

Me: I hope this is a wake up call for her.

Kacy bought the ticket, and Anna arrived to New York the following afternoon. Barely through customs and bound for the Beekman, she texted me: *If you feel like stopping by after work for a bite you're welcome.*

We'd come a long way from those days. Didn't she realize? Her nonchalance was astounding. *The stress is getting to me,* I told her. *Let's do tomorrow if you're free?* I was pushing off the commitment, with no real intention of following through. *Ok sure. I will do Kacy tomorrow probably if you wanna join.*

Was she testing me or missing our routine? Texting was all I could manage. To see her in person felt like too much. Even so, I was glad that Anna was back in New York and staying in a hotel near my office. Though her connection to my reality seemed tenuous, her physical proximity gave me reason for fresh hope that restitution was on the way.

Chapter 10

Unraveling

I continued to guard my secret closely, but as the puzzle grew more complex, I couldn't help but share my story in as vague terms as possible with the three female colleagues who sat closest to me in the *V.F.* office. They were flabbergasted. I asked for their feedback as I worked to navigate my friendship gone awry. They had heard about my antics with Anna back when dinners at Le Coucou, infrared sauna visits, and early-morning training sessions had been our norm. She'd always been enigmatic—that we knew—but where this had once been fun and intriguing, it was now alarming.

With Anna back in the US, and closer to her banks and employees, I imagined it would be easier for her to get her finances in order. There had been an issue with her taxes, she told me; working on behalf of the Anna Delvey Foundation, she hadn't realized she needed to pay them. In response to her delinquency, the IRS had frozen her accounts, but, she said, the situation had been redressed. *I have a team of lawyers who confirmed everything is resolved,* she said. *There is no reason for the wire to be delayed.*

I believed her. I imagined that she hadn't taken the time, or didn't have the ability, to keep in touch with her lawyers while she had been traveling. Now that she was back and had a handle on the situation, I had faith the repayment would come through, just as she told me it would.

By this point, the number for Chase Customer Service was on speed dial in my phone. I called them at least once a day hoping for an update. The money

137

I had borrowed from Nick wouldn't last very long. I gave up on my communication with Bettina altogether, convinced that she wasn't getting the job done. Nick and I joked that "Bettina" was probably just Anna, replying from a fake email address. It was an amusing idea, but I didn't imagine it was true.

American Express had begun to call with increasing regularity, asking if and when my payment would be made. I tried my best to explain: *It will be any time now.* Stuck in the liminal space between promise and fulfillment, I waited.

Around noon a few days later, my cell phone buzzed. It was Anna. *I have a wire reference nr G0871010031505. Not sure if that helps.* I spun away from my desk and sprung to my feet. *Eureka!* I thought. I'd been begging for so long.

Nick came to join me. I had been up late the night before in a panic, and he was worried about me. We met in Westfield World Trade Center, the underground shopping mall beneath my office building, and walked straight to my bank. We watched as a banker carefully entered the reference number, but it wasn't in a format the system recognized.

My pulse quickened and my spirits dropped. This was not a good sign, and I knew it, but I held on to my willful optimism. Over the course of the afternoon, down but not defeated, I repeatedly asked Anna for a Federal Reference Number, instead of whatever it was she'd given me.

I really don't understand why the wire transfer hasn't happened already, I texted. *I've been waiting for this Fed Ref # since Marrakech. Every day it's processing. This cannot keep happening. Can you please send me the [tracking number] to show that this wire transfer is actually going through[?]*

Forwarded, she at last confirmed. *Sorry again for getting you into this situation, I should be more organized moving forward. I sent you a bit more than owed as a thank you and apology for the delay.* I checked my email and saw that Anna had forwarded a message from someone named Ryan that included a Federal Reference Number. I logged into my Chase account every few hours that evening to see if the money had arrived.

Me: No luck with the wire yet, I'll keep checking and will keep you posted.

My Friend Anna

Anna: Ok. It's been debited from my account.

I woke up before five o'clock the next morning, unable to fall back asleep, my mind racing. I was queasy with a feeling of dread. I texted her back.

Me: You've said that before. Still nothing. I'm really losing sleep over this. So sick to my stomach. This must post to my account this morning or something is seriously wrong.

Anna: Anything I can do to help with this?

Me: Can you check the status of the wire from your end using the Fed ref #?

Anna: Not that i know of, i will call my bank again once they open.

Anna: What did they say from your side? Its not unusual for transfers to take a while, especially for higher amounts.

Me: My bank said domestic wires usually happen same day and almost always within 24hrs.

Anna: If the wire takes longer for some reason, im sending you PayPal.

Me: Thank you, anna. I'm sorry for texting in the middle of the night. Just so stressed.

Anna: No problem, I understand it's no fun being in this situation, and I caused it, you have all reasons to be upset.

It was comforting to hear her claim responsibility for the circumstances. She validated my feelings and made me think she understood them by acknowledging I had good reason to be upset. For an hour or two, I felt lighter. But by lunchtime, my fear had resumed.

Me: My job is on the line here. And I'm being told that the Fed ref number is not valid.

Anna: Give me a moment, im in a meeting.

Me: Anna, what is going on?

Me: ?

Anna: Just finished here.

139

Anna: Will call them now.

Anna: They are in a meeting, im getting a call back by 2:30pm.

Me: Why is it always something? I feel like you've been stalling on this for weeks and it's finally gotten to this point where I can't cover it any more. Im out of backup options.

Anna: Im really trying here.

Anna: Not everything is in my control.

Me: it feels like there is a problem. something is holding this up—obviously everything is not ok. A wire does not take weeks. A wire does not take days even. I feel like you're not being straight with me and I can't afford to keep chasing you like this.

Anna: Also if you'd like me to confirm to your employer's accounting that i assume the responsibility for the outstanding balance and confirm what led to it, i can do that

Anna: I resolved any outstanding issues this Wednesday.

Me: I just don't understand why it can't be as we discussed: I've yet to receive a wire confirmation and it's been two business days since Wednesday.

Anna: Wire just got sent yesterday. Im sorry i dont have the confirmation in the format you want it, so i cannot forward it.

Me: I don't care what format confirmation is in so long as it proves a wire was sent to my name and account yesterday.

Me: Please just be straight with me. I do not understand why this should be so complicated.

Anna: Ill send you the proof once I get it.

Anna: PayPal let me send 5k, I had to submit my address proof to send more

Anna: Did you get [the 5k] ok?

Me: Yes thank you.

I had received an email from PayPal with the subject line: "You've got money." The body of the email read: "Anna Delvey sent you $5,000.00

USD." Anna had never sent any money to me via PayPal before, and I almost never used my account, so I wasn't entirely sure how it worked. I logged into PayPal to double-check that the message was legitimate, saw the funds, and immediately transferred them to my checking account.

Anna: [The wire] shall be there by monday, if not they have permission to escalate this and reimburse for damages.

Me: And did they not send you a confirmation of any kind?

Anna: No not yet.

Me: Then I don't think your bankers actually processed the wire yesterday. That Fed ref number isn't valid and they can't provide you with any receipt from the transaction? Do you expect a receipt today? When a wire transfer is initiated then a receipt is produced. And then it can take 48hrs (if not more) for it to show up in my account.

Me: You said it'd be here yesterday so hearing now it will be in on Monday just feels like pushing it back another day again and even then there is definitely no guarantee because we don't have any proof the wire has been initiated.

Me: I don't know what escalate means because I feel we should already be past that point.

Anna: It will be there by monday.

Anna: If not ill send another one from a different account/ get out cash/ check or another form of payment.

Anna: Its not a big deal.

Me: Ok. It's a huge deal to me.

Me: But you know that.

Me: My job and finances are on the line, as was my apartment until you sent the 5k today. I'm not sleeping. I've been waking up at 4am in a panic. My life is completely distraught right now. This is a huge deal - actually one of the most traumatic experiences I've had. I don't understand why you would say it's not a big deal.

Anna: I only said it to say that I have multiple other options to settle this
       payment with you.
Anna: Not like I sent you my last money.
Anna: That's the way I meant it.

This back-and-forth became a dizzying and nauseating routine. Every night a panic and every morning a rush. When the money from PayPal appeared in my bank, I finally paid the "minimum payment due," $1,922.66, for the May statement on my personal American Express card. My June statement would close at the end of this same week, with a minimum payment due of $32,879.60. I was glad to have received the money from Anna, but it did very little to alleviate the stress of my financial situation. And Anna was unmoved by my intensifying pleas and accusations. Each message I flung at her merely bounced back in a perverted echo. She fired off wave after wave of text messages—riddles on which I might trip, or even choke. Delay tactics. My despair grew steadily worse, but Anna evidently misjudged my tenacity.

And so we carried on, business day after business day, week after week. Still, I showed up for work. Every photo-shoot detail, phone call, and conversation seemed to take twice the effort. I booked a photographer and a studio space for a portrait of the musician Beck. I went back and forth with a London-based agent for a shoot with Clive Owen. I'd been doing my job for so many years by this point that it was intuitive, even when it was demanding, but now I was barely holding it together. Even as I went through the motions—"Are you the stylist's assistant? Okay, great: you can set up in this part of the studio"; "Are you all getting hungry? Lunch is scheduled for noon. I'll see if the caterers can come any earlier"; "Hi, I'm just calling to see how early you'd like me to schedule your car to the airport?"—my brain was somewhere else. I tried to use weekends to alleviate stress, but instead they became the days when my panic was at its worst, because Anna's bankers weren't working and there was no hope of the money arriving.

Almost all of my energy was devoted to Anna—to rationalizing her delay, and chasing reimbursement.

"Nothing yet, but it will be fine," I kept saying—to Nick, Jennie, Janine, and most of all to myself. But no one was convinced. My anxiety peaked at night, as I lay awake in bed. Nothing felt real and anything seemed possible. *What if she never pays me?* I had waited so long to give voice to those words—afraid that in doing so, I would lend them more power. Now, at last, unable to sleep, I said them to Nick, and felt their truth for the very first time. It wrecked me.

Nick rubbed my back as I struggled to breathe. I choked out fear in rhythmic bursts: "I . . . won't . . . be able . . . to make . . . it back . . . I'll . . . never . . . save enough . . . to buy . . . a house . . . I won't . . . be able . . . to have . . . kids."

Morning came before sleep. But Germany, where Anna's bankers were located, was hours ahead. Maybe today—it must be today. I had to keep moving forward. One puffy eye focused on my cell phone, the other closed under a cold compress. My fingers shot flares in the dark. Texts at five a.m. How to convey the urgency? Could I make Anna *feel*, understand, and act? I put my hair back, makeup on, and made it to work on time. I smiled at colleagues in the hallway, wondering if they could tell. There was a pinprick in my protective bubble, and I felt the oxygen escaping fast. It'll be there this morning, this afternoon, by end of day. *Everything should be on track now,* Anna had said.

Mid-June and still no wire. On the Thursday before Kate's wedding, I made a decision: Anna had taken enough; she couldn't have this moment, too. My energy redirected, and I handled my responsibilities with loving care: I picked up Kate's wedding dress from a tailor in Brooklyn and had my rental car ready to go. I would leave at six a.m. the next day to be in Amherst by noon for a celebratory lunch with the bride.

Anna: When are you back?

Me: Sunday evening sometime.

Anna: Haven't seen you in like a month.

Me: We keep traveling at opposite times.

Anna: I did nothing fun the whole time since im back.

Anna: Lets plan something monday.

Anna: I shall be at mercer then.

Me: I really need this to be over with before I can have fun. I'm too stressed out.

Fun. That's how our unlikely friendship had begun: nights out, fancy dinners, white wine, and glamour. Now the party was over, and yet we were still bound together, against my will. I wanted her gone but couldn't let her go. Had she trapped me in a room with her and locked the door on purpose? Was she afraid that I would leave? Did she want me to need her? Was this the power she craved?

Aside from Nick, no one in Amherst knew anything about my Anna problem. I could tell them, of course, and they'd be there for me, but it wasn't the time or place for that. Besides, their mere existence—*my people*—was support in and of itself. I needed them. Nine of us, a sisterhood forged in college, not because of a sorority or club but by choice. Anna had no place here. She had no lasting friendships that I had ever seen. She was too insensitive, antisocial, and detached by nature. She would have needed me as a conduit, as someone people could relate to. My acceptance of her would have encouraged others to do the same. Now I understood.

My friend Liz officiated the ceremony in a white tent on a grassy hill: "We are wrapped in the arms of the Connecticut River Valley," she began, "where Kate and Russell have chosen to make their home, for this grand celebration of love. Let the magnificence of this place hush your soul." Everyone was calm; everything was still. "Russ and Kate, turn away from each other for a moment, if you can, and look out at these faces . . . you have chosen to surround yourselves with this fellowship of people quite deliberately."

In times of trauma, life unfolds in a chiaroscuro of peaks and valleys.

You feel the highs and lows with amplified intensity. Overcome with love for my friends, I wept.

Back in New York, the nightmare resumed and intensified. "Can't you see that something's not right?" Nick fumed. I had been keeping Nick abreast of my efforts, and shared some of Anna's text messages with him as I struggled to find a way forward. He had grown increasingly angry with her indirect responses. At times, faced with his pessimism, I actually found myself trying to defend her.

"If she sent a wire, where is it?" he asked.

"I called Chase to check and they said it's not in the system yet, but if it's not here tomorrow, Anna will take out cash or find some other resolution," I said.

"Nothing this girl says is true!" he replied.

That possibility concerned me, of course. But what else could I do? I was trying to be as firm with Anna as I could without scaring her away. At least her constant contact was a comfort; she hadn't simply gone silent and disappeared.

Quite the opposite: on and on she communicated. More than one wire had been initiated; surely one would arrive. Or maybe she could transfer the balance to a credit card of her own. Would Bitcoin be okay?

Mm no thank you! Don't know how to pay Amex with that 🐷, I responded.

Anna wrote: *So the wire from yesterday is on the way, and the first one will be sent once they get certificate of good standing from my lawyers. Whichever comes first today.*

And yet, one day passed and then another, with no sign of the money in my account. *Did you get confirmation?* I texted. Three hours went by. I texted again: *Still nothing on my end. Did they send you anything? It's getting close to EOD. I thought it'd be today?? Anna?*

I dont have the swift [code], im in a meeting, she replied. *I have couple missed calls I cannot speak right now. No one emailed me about any delays. If its not there by Monday morning we can meet and do cash deposit.*

Ok, I wrote. I'd learned that SWIFT codes were commonly used for international wire transfers.

She continued. *I provided everything they ever asked for from their fraud prevention dept etc, i made it first priority for everyone involved. Im sorry for this whole thing and you are rightfully frustrated, it doesn't come from my negligence, everyone's demanding more and more absurd things and throwing sentences around like 48-72h processing time. I just got a voicemail from person who was supposed to get back to me on Wednesday.*

I'm sorry, I texted. *I know it's frustrating for you, too.*

Yes like nothing can be easy for me, she replied. *For every one thing that goes well there are 99 that dont.*

Another Monday came and went and still there was nothing—no wire, no cash, and no clear explanation. Anna continued to make excuses: *Im waiting for my lawyers to forward [the bankers] one last thing. After that everything shall be cleared right away; they had to verify more info and i wasn't aware it was federal holiday in Germany last th-fr, so they just got the stuff they needed today; Im driving ill text you shortly.*

Driving where? I texted in response. *Anna—this is so urgent and has been for so long!! We need to make a plan to meet for the cash deposit today. I can't keep waiting for this wire. I'm extremely stressed about this.*

Back to the city, she wrote, claiming to have been dealing with some sort of a work-related "emergency" upstate. *I was up all night working with europe.*

I typed out a response. *Ok - will you go pick up cash and text me? I'll meet you at chase- or I can meet you at citi. Either way.*

But Anna was still "in a car" and then "in a meeting" for the rest of the day. She texted at three o'clock in the morning: *Just got back, i have to go upstate tmro again for the first half of the day. Im supposed to leave around 7-8am. If i catch a bank thats open i can drop an envelope off with security at otc [One World Trade Center]. That or wire will go thru, or ill be back in the afternoon.* Almost two hours later, she texted again. *Still* up working, *I probably wont be in town till afternoon, but promise to settle this today.*

When I woke up that morning, I replied right away: *Please keep in touch. There is nothing in my account. I have not received any email with a swift code etc. I do not expect the wire will come through. Please plan to get the cash before banks close today.* Except by that afternoon, it began to sound like Anna wasn't coming back to the city before banks closed. Her texts went on. *Can i do it myself [deposit cash to your account]? There are [chase banks] here,* she said. I called Chase to ask if this were possible and learned that Anna could deposit a money order, cashier's check, or a regular check on my behalf—*not* cash—but they would go through a clearing process that could take up to seven days. Anna insinuated that a cashier's check would work best.

Fine, I wrote her, *if you're not going to make it back today, which I'm guessing you're not?? will you withdraw a cashier's check and deposit into my chase account today?*

Ill let you know when I stop by at the branch, she replied.

One hour later, I checked in. *Are you heading to the bank yet? Please leave enough time to make sure this is done.*

Yes, she promised.

What's the status? Did you get the cashiers check?

Im at a branch rn, she wrote. Then, a few minutes later, *They didn't have enough cash at that one, omw to the next one.*

For a cashiers check??? I asked. That didn't make any sense.

Cash cash, she replied. *Cash is available right away. Cashiers check takes at least a day to clear . . . I can't be responsible for clearing times, and it will be my responsibility to cover it . . . I meant if they place a hold on [the] check for x days you'd be equally frustrated.*

Hadn't we just decided on a cashier's check? Hadn't I just told her that she wouldn't be able to deposit cash on my behalf? Was I going out of my mind? Was she?

Just do the cashiers check if they do not have enough cash, I told her. *At this point I'd rather wait for the cashiers check to clear than wait for the wire . . . at least my bank will be able to track it.* More than two hours later, I asked, *What's happening?* She didn't respond. *It really feels like you're just stalling. What's the deal?*

I did get everything from my bank, fell asleep in the car sry for not responding, she finally wrote, almost an hour later.

. . . what did you get? I asked.

Check from citi, she said.

———————————

The next day was Thursday, June 22, one month and two days since I'd left Morocco. If Anna had picked up that check, I wanted to make the handoff as easy as possible, before she had time to encounter any additional obstacles. It was time to confront her in person.

Unexpected and unannounced, I walked into the Beekman hotel at quarter to eleven. *Hey - I'm here. What room #?* I texted. No response. I called from my cell phone. No answer. Unfazed, I found the concierge desk. "Hi, is it possible for me to call up to a guest's room?—Anna Delvey. Thank you." I wasn't nervous; I was angry. My words and actions were pointed and firm.

She answered with a groggy "Hullo?"

"Hey, I'm here. What's your room number?"

It was the first time I'd seen her since La Mamounia. She looked disheveled, her hair matted from sleep. She wasn't wearing any makeup and her eyelashes were jagged, missing extensions here and there. Her small bedroom was full and messy. Papers covered the surfaces. Her suitcases lay open and overflowing. The black linen dress she'd had made in Morocco hung in dry cleaner's plastic from an open closet door.

"Where's the check?" I asked, trying to make the transaction simple. She shuffled through piles of papers, looked under clothing, and dumped out various bags before claiming to have left it in a car. After working upstate the day before, she had ridden back to the city in a Tesla loaner with one of her lawyers, she explained. The check must be there.

Of course it couldn't be easy. Of course there was a problem.

My Friend Anna

First she called the Tesla dealership, and then her lawyer's office. ("He must have it," Anna proclaimed.) I refused to leave. Anna assured me that the check would be dropped off. First she said it would be delivered to me at my office, but when she was unable to provide me with her lawyer's cell phone number, I decided not to leave her side. I shadowed her to Le Coucou, where she had a lunch meeting with a different lawyer, who was introducing her to a private wealth manager. The wealth manager seemed unimpressed by Anna's art-foundation summary. Compared with the other times I'd seen her describe the project, Anna's presentation today had lost some of its shine. She seemed juvenile as she spoke, vainly fussing with her hair, as she disjointedly relayed the key components. We finished our food, and one of the men picked up the tab. I followed Anna back to the Beekman. She told me that she needed to take a conference call.

"By all means," I said, unmoved. "I'll wait."

She didn't make a phone call. Instead, we sat side by side in the clubby bar beneath the hotel atrium. Our table was patterned like a chessboard. True to form, Anna ordered oysters and a bottle of white wine and signed the bill to her room. I sat in silence, sending work emails from my phone, largely ignoring Anna but keeping a watchful eye on her and asking periodically for an update. Aside from our waiter, I didn't see her interact with anyone—no hotel staff, no more phone calls or meetings. To prove a point, I stayed until eleven p.m., when I finally left in anger, telling Anna that I would be back in the morning at eight a.m. so that we could go together to the bank. She agreed. "I hope you had fun, at least," she chirped, with an impish grin.

"No, this was *not* fun. This is not okay," I stammered, incredulous.

The next morning, I arrived at the hotel on time and texted her.

Me: Hey I'm here.
Anna: Im not there.
Me: I told you I was coming. . . . where did you go???
Anna: Im picking up all stuff.

149

Me: I'll come meet you where are you. This needs to be over with this morning before I go to work.

Anna: I thought you'd text me before showing up.

Me: I thought you'd be sleeping. Where can I meet you? I'll come up town. Doesn't matter. Need to get this done.

Anna: I woke up like at 6 to get this done.

Me: Then why isn't it done? I'll meet you.

Anna: I'll text you once I have everything.

Me: No anna. If you woke up at 6 let's do this now. I have plans today. And I must make sure this is done. I don't feel I can trust you to do it. It's been too long. Come on. I'll meet you and make it easy.

Anna: I'll drop it off at OTC.

Me: Or I can go pick up the items . . . This is shady. Come on.

Anna: I'm out picking it up whats shady?

Me: Then let me come meet you now. I'm not going to the office to wait. Too much waiting.

Anna: I'll text you once i have it.

Me: I will come meet you now. Where are you? I can't wait for you to text me. I will not be in the office. I can't believe you're not here. Anna. You said we'd go to the bank this morning. I am losing my ability to trust you.

Anna: Im not at my hotel, I'm picking up things from my lawyers.

Me: That's great then I'll come meet you now. Just tell me where.

Anna: I thought you'd at least text me before showing up.

. . .

Me: Then I will come meet you to get it. I do not trust that you're on it.

Anna: I thought you'd ask me first.

Me: I told you very clearly last night when I'd be back. And now you won't tell me where you are. And I do not trust that you're doing what you say.

. . .

My Friend Anna

Me: I want to come meet you and we wait or we go to the bank. You're stalling. I will come meet you now Anna come on. Do not ruin our friendship over this it's fucking stupid. Step up and deal with this now. Let's go to the bank. I feel like you're just sitting in your hotel room avoiding me. What am I supposed to think. Do you even have the money? Anna??????? Did you ever even get a check? What ever happened to the wires? Why am I having to chase you? This is not how this should work. You should pick up the phone and have a conversation with me.

Anna: If you don't believe I'm not in my room you're welcome to wait for me there, and I'll come pick you up once I have everything.

Me: I have better things to do with my time. Just follow through and stop making excuses.

Chapter 11

Gear Shift

E nough was enough. Patient to a fault, I had tried for so long to find logic in what, by design, was nonsensical. I lost all faith that Anna would solve this problem on her own. It was time to look elsewhere for answers. One of the benefits I had as a Condé Nast employee was limited legal coverage, and on Friday, June 23, I finally got up the nerve to request a list of in-network attorneys. I began investigating what was really happening with Anna. I reached out to anyone who might know something about her I didn't.

I contacted Ashley first. After she and Mariella had stopped hanging out with Anna, Ashley had told me that Anna was "crazy." I thought I had understood what she meant, that Anna was slightly *off* socially, and I'd made an effort to overlook it. Now, thinking back, I saw I was mistaken. I should have taken Ashley at her word.

Ash. Of course I've gotten into a shitty situation with anna and she owes me money. You mentioned once that someone knows how to reach her parents? I'm getting to that point. It's been over a month and she hasn't reimbursed me and it's an absurd amount of money (long story) . . . I'm considering legal counsel but don't want to go there unless I have to. Such a fucked up situation. Can't say you didn't warn me.

Ashley suggested I contact Tommy Saleh, who was at Happy Ending the night I met Anna. Apparently, he had once loaned Anna money and might have a way to reach her family. Tommy was someone I had often encoun-

153

tered in the New York party scene but didn't really know. I sent him a text, and he and I met in a beer garden in Williamsburg on Saturday afternoon.

He was German, like Anna was, and he'd known her since she was an intern for *Purple* magazine in Paris, where he also used to live. In Paris, she had a big apartment and lived a lavish lifestyle, he said, full of fashion shows and parties. In vivid detail, he described the Anna that I, too, had known. But then he told me something new: Anna received around $30,000 at the start of each month and quickly spent it on shopping, hotels, and food. That's when she'd ask friends for loans, he said—friends like himself. She'd always had problems with money in this way.

"And did you get your money back?" I asked.

His response was alarming and reassuring in equal measure. After weeks of pestering, he had gotten his money back by threatening to involve her father. "Her dad is a Russian billionaire," he said. "He brings oil from Russia to Germany." Anna had once told me that her parents worked in solar energy. Tommy went on. Anna had stood to inherit $10 million on her twenty-sixth birthday, which was the previous January, he believed. But because she was such a mess, her father had arranged for the inheritance to be delayed until September, just a few months away.

Aha! Well, that would explain her stalling tactics, I thought, clinging to hope. But why couldn't she have just said so? Had she been embarrassed? I imagined she was battling with her family to gain early access to her trust. Perhaps the postponement had been a result of mental health issues (I'd begun to suspect she had a personality disorder), or maybe her general recklessness was to blame.

I worried that Anna was using her bankers and lawyers to negotiate disbursements, rather than going to her parents directly. Could she not see I was in a state of emergency? Maybe this time she had so drastically exceeded her means that fear of her parents' retribution outweighed any concern for my well-being. Would her overspending be reason enough for her father to again postpone her inheritance? Would he cut her off altogether? I didn't care. It had all gone too far! If there was a pattern to this behavior, she needed help.

My Friend Anna

I would need to convince Anna that there was only one option: to come clean. And if I couldn't convince her, I had a list of lawyers who could.

The evening after I met with Tommy, I decided to tell Anna I was considering legal action. I really didn't want to involve lawyers—I assumed the process would be costly—but I hoped the threat alone might spur her to finally pay me back. At the same time, I didn't want to spook her, and was wary of her potentially leaving the country. So while I took a firm approach, I tried to be compassionate as well.

> Me: Anna I will need to have a lawyer involved next week if this is not resolved on Monday. I literally cannot withstand anymore delay. I don't want to go that route (at all) but you're leaving me very little choice. I'm running out of options. I don't know if you need to talk to your parents or what but this is a huge deal in my life and I cannot keep on this way forever waiting for you to sort this out. I'm just fundamentally unable to support this debt for any longer.
>
> Anna: K.
>
> Me: I really, really hate this. I'm sorry. I hope we can sort it out.
>
> Me: I wish you'd just be honest if you don't have or can't access the money. By making excuses or stalling it makes it impossible for me to trust what you're saying. And I feel completely powerless to actually get through to you to convey how serious this is for me.
>
> Anna: [It] makes little sense for me not to have any money and [get] myself into this position on purpose.
>
> Anna: I assumed that [it] was almost done with [the] check, and I have a lot of things going on. One thing came on another at the same time, especially yesterday.
>
> Anna: What did I gain out of this?
>
> Anna: You think im that stupid.

155

Me: I am not calling you stupid and I don't think you did this for personal gain. I am only trying to convey the severity and urgency of the situation . . . This needs to be resolved on Monday.

Anna: K.

Monday morning on the forty-first floor of One World Trade Center, I sat at my desk, distracted. There were conference calls ("Yes, we have talent from noon to three thirty") and emails ("Are you attending the meeting this morning?"). Photo department business as usual. I ducked out to meet Kathryn at Annie Leibovitz's studio, where we would review plans for the New Establishment Summit—Annie would look through the Wallis Annenberg scouting shots from my recent trip to LA and select an area for her group portrait.

The minute the meeting was scheduled to begin, Anna called, but I didn't pick up. Her text messages affected my composure, each one striking with a jolt, and the idea of a phone call seemed even worse. Either she'd fixed the situation or she hadn't. *I'm in a meeting - can text,* I told her, an invitation she quickly accepted. Despite my legal threat, Anna continued to make empty promises. She also wanted to meet me for lunch. The Beekman was sold out for the night, she said, and she was waiting to hear if there was availability at the Mercer. I couldn't understand the relevance of this last information. What did her hotel have to do with me? I was too busy to pause for lunch, I told her, but I could pick up a check whenever it was ready.

My problem with Anna was only getting worse. By threatening legal action, I had hoped to instill a sense of urgency—I had agonized over telling her that a lawyer might be involved—but she batted away the threat as though it were nothing. She appeared completely unperturbed. There were no desperate pleas or offers of apology from her, only more of the same.

Back in the office, I weighed my next move and turned to Kathryn for

156

support as I'd done countless times before, though never for anything of this magnitude. I don't remember if we were next to her desk when I explained the situation or if we stepped away for more privacy, but I'll never forget the unflinching way that she looked at me as she immediately offered a loan. With tearful gratitude, I told her I expected the wire to come through any day; there was no need for a loan quite yet. But knowing that it was an option was of immense comfort, second only to knowing that I was not alone.

Anna called me crying the next day to say that the wire would be coming from a German account. I wondered if she was crying because she'd finally told her parents. Her next move made me think that perhaps I was right. She sent a screenshot of a Deutsche Bank wire confirmation, which I forwarded to Kathryn's husband, Mark, who speaks German, to translate. Everything appeared legitimate. So, once again, I waited for the funds to arrive.

When I was seven years old, I went with my family to Kiawah Island, South Carolina. I was building drip castles by the ocean when I noticed a girl around my age walking across the beach straight toward me. Shy and introverted, I'd kept my eyes down and prayed in silence that she would pass. But the friendly, freckle-faced girl came right up to me and landed at the water's edge with a plop. We sat side by side in the surf, two tiny dots against the horizon. We reclined, legs outstretched, cradled in the sand. Then all at once she flattened out.

"Lie all the way back," she instructed, eyes squinting in the sun.

I paused and studied her carefully. "But my hair would get sandy," I said.

She propped up on her elbows to look at me. "Well, whaddya come to the beach for?" she exclaimed.

That afternoon I stood in the shower and watched lines of sand form in the tub. The warm water stung against my skin, but I was happy. I'd made a new friend. This sequence of events is stamped into my memory: an act of trust, letting go, full immersion, no regrets.

Twenty years or so later, Nick and I drove in a rental car along the oak-lined roads that led back to Kiawah Island, my happy place. It was the week of July Fourth and we would meet my family at the beach.

Without question, I knew that I could tell my family anything and count on their support. But I wasn't willing to do so. It has long been my style to box up my emotions and work out my problems privately. It doesn't make me easy to be close to, but it's part of my nature—a way I've found of holding myself together under stress. I've learned from experience that when something bad happens, like a breakup or a car accident, I can keep it together until a loved one gives me a hug. That's when I break down and cry. So that's what I was trying to avoid. The emotions I was feeling about my experience with Anna were packed so tightly inside, I was afraid that opening myself up to them would induce a sort of hysteria.

On a more practical level, even if I wanted to explain the situation to my parents, how could I? How could I explain Anna? They would listen to my attempts, and they would come out feeling sad for me and stressed about what I should do next. It would just make me feel more vulnerable. I'd also need to keep them updated from that point forward, which I didn't have the energy to do. Getting through each day without losing my mind was taking all the strength I had.

They were busy enough as it was, and keeping my problems to myself would spare them the worry. My dad was running for Congress as a Democrat in a district that had been Republican since 1855, before the Civil War. Though he'd never previously held public office, having worked in health care for more than thirty years, he saw the effects of policy on people's lives and he wanted to help. As for my mom, she was working full-time, helping with campaign events, and frequently driving back and forth between Knoxville and Spartanburg to be with her parents, who were both in their mid-nineties and still living at home. My mom and dad had enough on their plates. I knew they would be there when I needed them, but I hadn't hit a wall yet. I still had options. I was finding ways to contain my emotions, and move forward.

Swallowing my secret, I swam in the ocean, played games on the sand,

and tried to regain my balance. Between activities, I snuck glances at my cell phone. Monday, July 3, was overcast. I walked to the middle of the empty beach and took a photo of the soft, low-lying clouds. When I got back to my folding chair, I logged in to my bank account. Still nothing.

Were you able to get tracking info? I messaged Anna. My sister saw me holding my phone. "Hey, Rach, will you take my picture?" she asked. I walked with her and her boyfriend out to the ocean and shot a few frames. A half hour later, Anna responded: *Yes, getting back to you this afternoon.*

Yeah, right. I tried to beat my brother in a ball game. He'd met Anna once, when she tagged along to a family get-together, joining Noah, my uncle David, and me at the Westville on Hudson Street for a casual dinner. They had liked her, they told me later, even though we all agreed she was quirky. After Morocco, I told Noah the same true (but incomplete) thing about Anna that I had said to my parents and sister: "I don't think we're going to be friends anymore."

After losing the ball game for a second time, I rested on a beach towel and turned my attention to the book I was reading, *All the Light We Cannot See.* Leaving our stuff behind, we put on sandals to walk through the hot sand, up the boardwalk, and back to our bicycles. We then biked down the road to our rental house, made sandwiches for lunch, applied a fresh coat of sunscreen, and biked right back to the beach.

> Me: Still nothing.
> Anna: Im getting on a call with your and my bank.
> Anna: I requested tracking from german side since its been so long and your bank doesn't see it - they will reach out to me with response
> Anna: Sorry its such an unfortunate timing for payments to get delayed. It's supposed to be [a] one-time thing and shouldn't be happening in the future.
> Me: I can't imagine I'll be in this situation again so am just concerned about getting this settled.

Rachel DeLoache Williams

We returned to the rental house. Our sandy shoes and beach bags stayed by the door. Inside, my family showered off and then gathered in the living room. My sister had brought a Hula-Hoop with her, so we took turns doing tricks. (No one could do anything half as well as she could.) We worked on a jigsaw puzzle in the living room and snacked on chips and salsa before dinner. I continued to give no indication that anything was wrong.

The next morning was July 4. Across the island, kids were taping red, white, and blue streamers to their bicycles for a parade around the town. Others were on the beach, using shovels and pails to make mermaids, castles, and turtles that would be judged in the afternoon's sand-sculpting competition. I was in my bedroom, steeling my nerves to withstand another day of stress. I had checked my bank account the moment I woke up but nothing had changed.

I made it to the beach around noon, and sent a text to Anna.

Did you get tracking? Still nothing has posted, I wrote.

Banks are closed today, she told me.

Isn't the tracking # coming from Germany? I asked, wondering why Independence Day would affect European banks.

Yes, she responded, providing no further clarity.

We came in from the beach late in the day, showered off, and ate hamburgers and corn on the cob for dinner. My sister baked a cherry pie. Afterward, we went out to see the fireworks and played charades before bed.

On Wednesday, Anna went silent. I sent texts from the beach in the morning and from Charleston in the evening. They all went unanswered. I woke up on Thursday morning in a panic. I could hear my family in the kitchen. I stayed in my bedroom with the door closed. Anna had texted in the middle of the night: *Sorry just got my phone now. Checking tonight.*

What was she checking in the middle of the night? How did that make sense? *I can't believe I'm still waiting. It's shocking. It's been close to two months. I was stressed about it at the beginning. Now it's unbearable,* I told her.

No response.

Anna?

160

That's when I got a text from Kacy asking me to give her a call. *Hi Kacy - I'm on vacation with my family,* I told her. *Anna has not paid me back yet. I'm considering legal action. This situation has ruined our friendship as far as I'm concerned. Insanely stressful and frustrating. Are you ok?*

While I waited for Kacy's response, I resumed my conversation with Anna: *This has reached a point. I'm really out of options here.*

Im sending it, she said.

Sending what?

The tracking, she replied.

Why don't you have it by now? Why am I always chasing you for this info? If you were actually embarrassed or sorry about this situation you'd be on it every day until it was paid—much earlier than two months later when your friend is still having to follow up with you for every single piece of information. You're making this so hard for me.

I asked them for the reference, she replied, *they didn't provide any till now, am I supposed to invent one?*

Was she out of her mind? *Of course not,* I fired back. *You're supposed to keep on them until they give you what you need.*

I will get it sorted so you have it this week, she said.

You've said that so many times. It hasn't happened yet. Please see that it does . . . Today is Thursday. This week means today or tomorrow. Was that wire even valid? Did you cancel it or was it voided? Why can't you provide a ref # and why can't my bank see it? This has ruined months for me. And you keep failing to give any sort of tangible proof that money has actually been transferred. I'm in serious trouble, Anna!!!! What friend leaves another person in this situation for this long. I don't care who in your family or bank you need to talk to but YOU MUST FIX THIS IMMEDIATELY. I AM OUT OF OPTIONS AND OUT OF PATIENCE.

When I came out of the bedroom, Nick was waiting in the kitchen with our lunches packed. We rode our bikes to the beach to join my family. I pulled my chair off to the side and covered my phone with a towel to keep texting.

Kacy responded: *Not really. She texted me at 1AM and is on my couch! She has not paid me back yet!*

What was happening?! Did Anna not have another place to stay? *Oh. My. God. This girl is a nightmare. Maybe you can talk her into calling her parents for help. I met with someone who had been in financial trouble with her in the past and knows Anna's family. He said her dad is in oil and is extremely wealthy but they limit her because she obviously has major spending issues, etc. . . . He encouraged me to file a police report but I know that would have her deported and I'm not sure I'd get paid back if I were to do that . . . The girl needs help.*

I'm with clients so slow to text, Kacy wrote. *Omg! I think we may need to do an intervention! Can I tell her u told me? She is still in my house and needs to leave! Does she steal or do drugs?*

Not that I know of re: drugs. Yes you can say you know about owing me money but do not mention the attorney please.

Kacy headed back to her apartment while Anna kept in touch with me. *Please send ref or transaction #,* I insisted. *Call Deutsche Bank. This shouldn't take long.*

I'm talking to them now, Anna replied.

She just left! Kacy said. *I didn't say anything to her yet because I wanted to get her out first. I will meet her downtown and talk to her. She told me she was hanging out with you recently is that true?*

Oh, you've got to be kidding me, I thought. *We weren't hanging,* I told Kacy. *I was following her around for a day trying to pickup a cashiers check. She made up some story about it being left in someone's car and I was waiting like a sap for this nonexistent person to come drop it off to us!!!*

Do you think she's staying at a hotel? Kacy asked. *She said she's at the greenwich hotel. How can we reach her family?*

I'm trying to get contact info for her father, I said.

Great! Kacy replied. *Because she needs help! Is she really trying to open something or just trying to piss off her family? She is not close to her family it seems.*

Both would be my guess. Not close with her family at all, I confirmed. *I don't know what the full story is but I think she has some major psychological issues . . .*

. . . So she stopped communicating with you all together now? Kacy asked.

No. We text daily . . . Every day it's another excuse or delay.

Same here! Kacy said.

Yep. She's very good at stalling. Masterfully manipulative.

Masterfully!!!! Kacy replied. *That's why I was thinking . . . con artist?*

I sighed. *Yeah . . . I don't know. The fact that she's back in NYC and still in our lives without having disappeared. I don't think it's that simple.*

That's when Kacy noticed that Anna's laptop was still in her apartment in West Chelsea. Anna was asking if she could come back for it. To avoid letting her in, Kacy left it with her doorman and went out for the day. Six hours later, Kacy's doorman told her that Anna was still in the lobby. Kacy stayed away from her building until Anna finally left.

———

On the morning of July 7, our last full day at Kiawah, Nick sweetly agreed to take some photographs of my dad that he could use for his Congressional campaign. I tagged along. In one of the island's clubhouses, we found an empty conference room with ample daylight and neutral-toned walls that worked nicely as a backdrop. While doing my part to help—easing conversation and offering feedback—I was also busy texting with Anna.

Me: Can't you please call and get the tracking information??

Anna: Are you reading my messages? I called them million times.

Anna: I have so much going on right now, I am on two phones they have endless holds.

Me: . . . I don't care how much you have going on! I can't keep caring. I just need to be reimbursed! . . . Why do I bother continuously calling chase and checking my account if you know

163

funds aren't on the way yet. What an immense waste of my
time . . .

Anna: How do you come up with this info? I said multiple times that
payment has been issued.

Me: Then I don't understand why I haven't received it. I'm obviously
totally panicked. I'm in such a shitty, stressful situation and I
don't see an end in sight!!!

Me: Can you get help from your parents? It feels like you're in over
your head. Are you ok, Anna?

Anna: Idk.

Anna: Im being promised things that never happen and it makes me
look bad

Anna: Ive been working non stop for past weeks and its almost like
nothing's changing.

The following day, she had the nerve to ask whether anyone was staying in my apartment. *I forgot I'm supposed to leave my hotel for one night
tonight,* she said.

I wasn't going to be using it—Nick and I would be back late that night
but were going to be sleeping at his apartment in Brooklyn. For obvious
reasons, though, I didn't want Anna spending the night at my place.

*No one is there but I don't have a spare key that's in NYC and there isn't a
doorman,* I told her. It was true. For a real friend, I'd have figured something
out, but why should I keep bending over backward for Anna? Enough was
enough.

Did she really have nowhere to go? At what point would she call her
own bluff and admit to her family that she needed help? I figured if she told
her parents, they would make her come home. But if they did that, I wondered, would they also reconcile her debts?

On Monday, back in New York, I spent the day at the office putting together a small shoot that would take place on Wednesday—Gasper Tringale
was to photograph TV actress Carrie Coon. Time at the beach had been
somewhat restorative, but when it came to Anna, I remained completely

exhausted. My energy to confront her came in heated bursts, after which I needed a beat to recharge. The length and frequency of my text messages varied accordingly. On this day in particular, I had very few words. Attempting to extend the feeling of my vacation, I bought a peach after work and ate it as I walked north along the West Side Highway. I sat in a grassy spot next to the water and read Anna's text messages. More of the same.

After an hour, I went home to my apartment. I'd barely put my things down when Anna called. Her voice was broken and high-pitched. "I can't be alone right now," she sobbed. I offered to meet at her hotel. "I had to check out," she said. "Can I come to you?" I said no and hung up. Then my conscience got the better of me—she was clearly having a hard time. I called her back: "You can come by, but you can't stay here."

She was at my door within the hour, haggard, bleary-eyed, and disconsolate. It was the first time she'd ever been over. I didn't have the energy to engage, so I said very little. My tiny studio apartment was in terrible disarray, the physical manifestation of my mental state: piles of papers, boxes, clothing, and other stuff. I apologized for the mess. "You don't need to apologize to me," she said. She was right. Then she sat down on my couch and began to cry. "I've messed everything up for myself," she sniveled. She owed her bankers and attorneys $1.5 million, she told me.

"You need to tell your parents, Anna," I implored. "You need help."

She was quieter than normal, and looked profoundly sad. She weighed my appeal as though I'd suggested she tell the tooth fairy, but spotting the sincerity in my eyes, she responded, "They'd make me get a normal job, that's for sure."

That sounded perfectly reasonable to me, and I told her so, but she wasn't done feeling sorry for herself. A fresh round of tears began. I stood up as she blubbered, took four strides into my small kitchen, and came back with two glasses of water. She'd gone uptown looking for the suitcases that she left at her friend's house, she whimpered, but when she got there, her friend pretended not to remember the suitcases at all. I'd heard Anna mention this luggage before. She had told me that a ring her mother gave her was inside.

"What about your mom's ring?" I asked.

"Oh," gasped Anna, taking a sip of water to steady her nerves, "I forgot about that." More tears. I couldn't help but feel sorry for her. We both needed a night off. I made a conscious decision to turn the proverbial cheek for this short time. I ordered two salads from a restaurant down the block and put on *Bridget Jones's Diary* to avoid having to talk. I watched as Anna waited until midnight to begin half-heartedly "looking" for a hotel. Even though I'd already told her that she couldn't stay for the night (before she'd even arrived), I was hardly surprised when she asked to sleep on my couch. Too tired to argue, I relented. Still, my couch was small. It would be hard, even for a kid, to lie on it with legs outstretched. I watched Anna try to get comfortable for a minute before telling her, "You can just sleep in the bed." I let her borrow some pajamas—black cotton pants and a T-shirt. We went to sleep without any conversation, each hugging an edge of my full-size bed, with our backs to each other.

In the following days, Anna would send texts every now and then like: *I feel horrible for getting you involved in the first place, please know I appreciate you helping out, not everyone would do that. I owe you big time and if there is any way i can help you in the future (obv aside from getting this settled), let me know.*

It would tug at my heart and slow me down. She was my friend, right? Obviously, she wasn't okay, but her refusal to give me straight answers or a rational explanation was maddening. What was I supposed to do?

    Me: Anna????
    Me: Please Amex is calling me every day to schedule a payment.
    Me: I have no money.
    Me: I can't keep starting my days with panic attacks and tears.

It was July 17 when I finally telephoned a lawyer, almost two months to the day after I'd left Morocco. I was still worried that by going this route, I might lose direct communication with Anna, and that she might panic and disappear, leaving me with no way to find her. But at this point, what else could I do? Despite my best attempts, I hadn't been able to reach her family.

Tommy wasn't able to help, and I didn't know where else to look. I didn't want to ask Anna's other acquaintances, like Hunter, because I wasn't sure whom to trust. Taking the lawyer approach felt like a necessary gamble.

The lawyer returned my call while I was at my desk in the office. As succinctly as possible, I explained my situation. Before I could even finish, he cut in, "Did you learn your lesson?"

"Excuse me?" I asked.

"Do you want to pay for my son's medical school, too?"

What a jerk—could he not pause for three seconds to imagine how completely broken and lost I felt? I felt as though I'd been knocked out by a cheap shot in the first round, and I wanted to sit down for a while before getting back in the ring. When I did try again with another lawyer, I learned that my first course of legal action would be to send Anna a "demand letter," formally acknowledging the debt owed and establishing a deadline. That seemed simple enough, except that if Anna missed the deadline, my next course of action would be to sue. My Condé Nast legal coverage applied to a consultation and demand letter only, not to litigation. And even then, if I were to pay out of pocket to sue, there was a collections issue—could Anna even access the money? Even worse, I learned that under federal law Anna would have thirty days from receipt of the demand letter to dispute the debt. I feared that within those thirty days, her visa would expire again and she'd need to leave the country. If that happened, I'd have to travel abroad to file suit and my expenses would likely exceed the balance of the debt. Was there no lawyer who could help me think through this conundrum? None that I could find—or afford.

> Me: You come off like a fraud!!!!! I'm extremely panicked. I'm in trouble anna!!!!
>
> Anna: How so?
>
> Me: How am I in trouble???? I can't pay for any of my credit cards, for my rent, for my bills, for living expenses!!! Nothing you say contains clear information and every timeline you give turns out to be false. And it's been over TWO MONTHS . . .

Anna: What makes me a fraud here?

Me: I didn't say you were - I said all of the shifting and vagueness
comes off [as] fraudulent . . . I'm surprised you even have to ask!
I'm trying to keep the faith up, anna, I really am, but I'm unable
to work I'm so freaked out. I'm a total mess.

Anna: Im trying to be transparent and responsive. Im sorry i brought
you into this situation- was never my intent- and im doing
everything i can to settle the payment.

Anna: I have the money. Its just the administrative issues . . .

Me: I believe you every time you say I'll receive funds and every time
I don't I'm crushed. Im crying from stress I'm not sleeping and
I'm getting constant phone calls. I did not agree to this.

Me: Please anna, tell me what is going on.

Me: Do you have money in a checking account? Or is it just a trust
and you don't have access to the amount you need?

Anna: Yes.

Me: Yes to what?

There was no response.

Chapter 12

Operation Clarity

On the last Sunday in July, I took the subway to Brooklyn and walked along the broken pavement to Nick's building. He met me at the foot of the stairs, and together we walked the four or so blocks to my friend Dave's apartment. He was expecting us.

Dave was one of the first people I met in college. During our freshman year, he lived on the floor above me. We had been introduced during soccer pre-season, before the rest of our classmates arrived. He had bright-blue eyes and an LA tan, and made endearingly goofy jokes. After Kenyon, he attended NYU School of Law. He was a close friend, someone I trusted, who happened to have an excellent knowledge of the law. I had debriefed him via text message before we arrived. It was time to form a strategy.

Sitting on his couch, I managed to tell the story in full with only a few tears. Anna had gone silent a few days prior, but she'd gotten back in touch with me through Facebook Messenger, claiming to have lost all three of her phones. Next, she had called me from a strange number—her lawyer's office, she said. After she hung up, I looked at my call history and googled the phone number: Varghese & Associates, a law firm focusing exclusively on criminal defense. Red fucking flag.

"First things first," Dave insisted. "You've got to stop the bleeding. If there was ever a time to accept help from loved ones, this is it." American Express had been calling me about the past-due balances on both my personal and corporate cards. If I didn't issue payment in less than two weeks, I'd be reported to the credit bureaus. On the night of July 17—the day I first called a lawyer—I had received an email from Janine. She had been keeping tabs on me since our post-Marrakech dinner, back in early June. Like Kathryn, she generously offered to extend a loan. Dave encouraged me to take it. Navigating this situation would be hard enough without the burden of worsening financial strain, hefty late fees, and damage to my credit, he argued. I needed to plug the hole.

Next, I would send Anna a "friendly note" detailing the repayment terms. I hoped that since it was coming from me, and not from a lawyer, she'd sign it without objection. Regardless of whether or not she signed it, however, I would proceed with one of two options.

Option One: I call Anna out: "Your actions amount to fraud and if I don't have the funds in my account by _____, I will go to the authorities. (Maybe even the FBI!)" She wanted to stay in New York, I reasoned, so perhaps the threat of being reported (and potentially deported) would be enough to scare her into action. The downside to this approach, of course, was that she might disappear, and if she fled the country, I'd be effectively without recourse. Dave also had some concerns that this approach could be viewed as extortive.

Option Two: Since I still believed Anna might receive an inheritance from her family trust in September, I could offer her a deferment. I could say, "It's clear you're having trouble settling the debt at this time. I propose that we postpone the due date to September __, at which time you'll pay the original amount plus _____." I would make sure this agreement was properly arranged between lawyers.

We still had to decide which of these two next steps to take, but we all agreed that I would start by drafting the "friendly note" to Anna, as well as an email to Janine. Dave wanted to bounce our game plan off another friend, who regularly handled this sort of law, just to be sure that he was offering reasonable advice. In the meantime, I would get everything ready and await his go-ahead. For the first time in months, I felt hopeful and lighter.

Around one p.m. the next day—a Monday—I sent the email to Janine.

170

My Friend Anna

Janine,

I deeply regret that I'm not coming back to you with better news. My situation with Anna has worsened . . . She is clearly a deeply troubled girl and her actions amount to fraud though I do still hope that I will be reimbursed . . . I'm just not sure how quickly . . . Janine, it's really a lot of money. I want to be sure you know that—and if, in the end, it's not feasible to provide the loan I totally understand . . . God, I hope you're not on the floor and are still breathing if you've made it this far into the letter. I thought I'd rather come tell you in person, but I have no money to get upstate. Things are grim. And I wanted to call you on the phone, but this whole ordeal has left me so emotionally drained that my ability to maintain composure has really gone down the tubes.

Miraculously, my parents are still unaware - as are Jennie and Noah. You and [Aunt] Jennie are the only family in the know. I would like to keep it that way for the time being. It's just too stressful, and I don't think they'd be able to help. I'd rather spare them the weight of the knowledge. They all have so much else going on right now!

Janine, it's so important that you be frank with me. Do not feel obligated, please please please. Know that regardless of the money, I'm deeply grateful for the emotional support and the gesture that you'd like to help if you could. I really do understand if you can't.

I love you.

Janine was kind enough to offer a loan. But somehow I was still holding out hope that I would not need to resort to accepting it—either Anna would come through with the repayment or one of the approaches Dave suggested would work. I thanked Janine profusely and told her that this would be my emergency backup plan.

Reaching out for help made me feel both vulnerable and deeply supported at the same time. At last, things seemed to be falling into place. The forward motion was exhilarating after running in circles for so long. At the end of the workday, I telephoned Dave.

"What's the word?" I asked.

"Scratch the plan," Dave answered.

He'd spoken to his friend, who shared Dave's worry that if I threatened Anna with going to the authorities, it might be viewed as extortion. As for agreeing to let Anna defer the repayment until she received her inheritance, he'd decided that we shouldn't trust her, and that giving her an extension would only delay the inevitable.

"Your best bet is actually the police," Dave said. "Try to get an appointment with a detective unit. This could be the sort of thing they would find interesting."

The police? Although Anna's actions seemed criminal, I'd been trying to avoid going to the authorities. But now it did seem like my best option. Directive accepted. I would go to the police, and I'd show up prepared.

———————

That same night, I made a folder on my computer called Operation Clarity, in which I saved every text message, email, and file that seemed relevant. It was late that evening when I printed the last of the pages. While they were still warm from the printer, I slotted them into a three-hole punch before dropping them carefully onto the open metal rings of a black office binder. I closed the binder with a snap and slipped it into my backpack. I was so tired of waiting. Waiting for Anna to get back to me. Waiting to see whether her promises would come to fruition. Waiting for lawyers to return my calls. *Just one more night,* I thought, relieved to finally have a plan.

Before I went to sleep, I heard from Kacy. Once again, Anna had appeared in the lobby of Kacy's apartment building. Kacy had a date sleeping over when her doorman called and said that Anna, who was still without any of her cell phones, was in the lobby and needed to speak with her. When she got on the line, Anna was crying and told Kacy that she might kill herself.

Kacy, wanting to avoid a scene in front of her date, met Anna in the lobby to calm her down. They sat and talked for a while before Kacy encouraged Anna to leave and get a good night's sleep. That way they could regroup tomorrow, Kacy said, when they were both better rested. Anna took her advice and began heading downtown, allegedly bound for the Greenwich Hotel.

Was Anna really suicidal? It was hard to measure the veracity of such a claim. She had insinuated the same thing when I let her stay in my apartment. Was she being manipulative or crying out for help? Or, to Anna, were those one and the same? That evening, while gathering my Operation Clarity files, I noticed an article on The Real Deal website from the week prior: Aby Rosen's realty company had reportedly signed a new tenant, a Swedish photography organization called Fotografiska, to lease the entirety of the Church Missions House—the very building that Anna wanted to lease. She had been working toward it as long as I'd known her. Anna and her schemes were falling apart.

———

On Tuesday, August 1, 2017, I wore pearl earrings and a white shift dress. I felt focused, driven, and resolute.

"I'd like to speak with a detective," I said to an officer, who stopped me just inside the door of One Police Plaza.

"Do you have a police report?" he asked. I shook my head. I was in the wrong building. "You have to file a report at a local precinct first," he told me, "and then—*maybe*—you'll be referred to a detective unit."

Today was the day. I went straight there. I looked up the closest precinct on my phone and marched swiftly down to Chinatown. The building on Elizabeth Street was nondescript. Then I noticed blue lamps on either side of a door, above which it said "5th Precinct" in gold letters. Upon entering, I passed through a set of double doors and immediately found myself in a small wooden pen, waist high, and closed. From the other side, an officer asked, "How can we help you?"

Oh, this was not how I had imagined it. I thought I'd be in someone's office, or at the very least in a cubicle and maybe sitting in a chair. How could I answer a question like that while standing in a doorway? They really wanted me to deliver an elevator pitch to the open room? Where to begin? Maybe after I started, they'd let me inside. As I began to speak, the first officer was joined by a second. I continued. After a bit, the first officer left and the second officer was joined by a third. I kept telling my story. At last the second and third officers were joined by another, a man with gray hair who was introduced as a lieutenant. When I finished, I was breathless and still standing in my pen, and I hadn't even showed them my binder yet! I took it out of my backpack and made sure to point out the labeled dividers. By then, only the lieutenant was left. His nods were sympathetic, if a bit dismissive.

At last, he spoke. "I'm sorry this happened to you," he offered, "but since it happened in Morocco, there's nothing we can do."

My chin dropped like an anchor. "What?" I croaked. I had not seen that coming. "But the trip was planned from New York," I explained. "She and I are both in the city. The charges were made on American credit cards." Two rogue tears escaped from the inner corners of my eyes as they fixed on the lieutenant. Was there no way to approach this from a different angle? Was there really nothing to be done?

"With your face," he said, "you could start a GoFundMe page to get your money back."

That was not the advice I had been looking for. His only other suggestion was to try the Civil Court. "I don't know—maybe someone there could help you," he said.

Back down the front steps, on Elizabeth Street, I stood beside the station and, for a moment, I sobbed. The police had always been my last resort. I'd never considered they might be unable or unwilling to help. This came as a shock. Regaining my composure, I called Dave to tell him the news. Then I called Kathryn for a morale boost, and I kept on.

I walked straight to the nearby Civil Court. Did I really think I'd find answers there? No. After my experience with the police, my faith had hit rock bottom, but I was committed to trying everything possible, if only to check each stop off my list.

The Civil Court building was large, boxy, and metallic. Its entryway spanned a city block, with large windows and entrances at either end. The inside felt like a small airport with metal detectors placed at each door. I watched my backpack slide down the conveyer belt and pass through the X-ray machine. I walked through the archway and collected my backpack on the other side. Then, in the middle of the lobby, I paused. I'd come somewhat aimlessly searching for someone who might be able to help, but how would that work? That's when I noticed a sign: "Help Center," it read. *Perfect,* I thought. In the middle of the two entrances, against the entryway's longest wall, a man sat in a booth between two American flags. I approached.

"Is the help center open?" I asked. They were closed for lunch, he said, but would reopen at quarter past two. *Lunch.* I heard Janine's voice in my head: "And I know you're stressed; you better be eating!" I'd stop for lunch, too.

On Baxter Street, in a row of storefronts offering bail bonds, the Whiskey Tavern looked welcoming. Inside, I sat in a tall chair at the bar, next to a cop and a large man in a suit.

"What can I get ya?" the bartender asked. I ordered an iced tea, chicken fingers, and tater tots. "What brings ya to the neighborhood?" he inquired, returning with my drink.

"I think I've been conned," I blurted out. The two men beside me stopped talking and turned to face me. The bartender leaned forward on his arms. Before I even realized what was happening, the elevator pitch just spilled right out, only this time, in the height of my despair, describing the absurd futility of my efforts made me simultaneously laugh and cry. I couldn't stop myself. Oh, things were pretty bad, all right, and there was a dark humor to it all.

"Lunch is on the house," said the bartender. Fried food, comedic relief, and the kindness of strangers. I was done feeling sorry for myself.

Back in the Civil Court, I followed signs to the Help Center. It was a bit like the Department of Motor Vehicles. I waited in line for my turn. When the young man in front of me was done, I stepped up to a window and spoke with a woman through an institutional Plexiglas divider. "How can we help you?" she asked. Her question shouldn't have come as a surprise, but I laughed nervously at the notion of once again having to explain my situation in such an awkward setting. It wasn't the right day to ask for help on that sort of a topic, she told me, but then she turned to speak with a man who happened to be passing behind her. He nodded. "He's not usually here on Tuesdays, but come on back," she said.

I went through a door and followed a mousy man in khakis over to a small cubicle. "Okay, tell me," he prompted. Sparing no detail, I relayed my tale of woe. It felt like dumping a fresh jigsaw puzzle onto an empty table. *Here, here it is*, I wanted to say. *Tell me, what can you make of it?*

When I finished, he smiled a sneaky little grin and said, "Well, gee, I'm kind of jealous that you got to go to Morocco. How was it?"

Really? That's your response? I thought. "All I can tell you is it wasn't worth it," I answered. He tried to help by offering pamphlets on pro bono lawyers, but the money involved surpassed the financial limit dealt with in Civil Court, he told me. Another swing, another miss.

Back outside, I called Kathryn. She suggested we meet to strategize. Surely one of our connections through *Vanity Fair* or past photo shoots might be able to help. It was just before four p.m. and she was in the office. Since it was conveniently midway between us, we decided to convene at the Beekman. I arrived first and stood outside to make phone calls while I waited. I called Nick and Janine with my update. Then I sent a text to Kacy to ask whether she'd heard from Anna again. She responded almost instantly to say that Anna had reappeared in her lobby only moments before. *I think I or we need to sit her down and try to get to the truth*, I responded. *The situation is really bad.*

When Kathryn arrived, we stepped into the bar, the same place I'd been with Anna not long ago waiting for an imaginary check. We sat in a booth near the entrance. My world felt completely upside down. Before Kathryn and I could order, I got a text from Kacy asking if I had a moment to talk. "White wine?" Kathryn asked. I nodded and excused myself for a phone call.

"It's intervention time," I told Kathryn when I returned to my seat. Kacy had an idea. One of her clients, Beth, was a divorced mom in her early fifties who, according to Kacy, was a real straight shooter. Kacy would ask Beth to meet Anna in her lobby. Beth would then explain to Anna that Kacy would be meeting them nearby at an outdoor bar called the Frying Pan, on a pier off the West Side Highway. Kacy and I would join them, and together we'd ask Anna for answers. It was a Hail Mary play, but worth a shot.

"Go! Good luck," Kathryn said. I took a sip of my wine and left.

Part III

Chapter 13

The Frying Pan

Kacy was also wearing white. I met her in front of her apartment in West Chelsea. "We've got our power whites on," she said, smiling. We walked west toward the Frying Pan. "This has gone too far; something is just not right. We need to get some truth. We need to reach her family." I nodded obediently as she said what I already knew.

My stomach ached as we crossed the West Side Highway and found our way to the outdoor bar. As we approached the table, I tapped the record button on my cell phone. I knew this would be an important conversation, and I wanted to have every word of it preserved.

The table was on the far left-hand side of the pier, next to a fence. The bar was crowded, filled with men in suits with loosened ties and women in professional clothes who'd traded their high heels for after-work flats. Anna was sitting on the far side of the table, next to Beth, facing us, as we approached. She was wearing the same dress that she had for weeks, a loan from her night's stay in Kacy's apartment. Aside from looking more unkempt than I'd ever seen her—and a bit sulky—she was strangely calm, considering the circumstances. Anna seemed surprised to see me—not startled exactly, but taken aback. You could see her gears spinning as she realized that Kacy and I had been in touch without her knowing. She appeared to regain her footing quickly, readying for the confrontation that would follow. I sat down directly across from her. Beth stood up, introduced herself to me, and went to the bar to get white wine and beer for the table. Kacy sat beside me, across from Beth's empty seat. And so it began.

"We can't go through this anymore, darling," Kacy began. "Anna, we had to be here because something is just not right. We have to figure out what's happening, what's going on, and how can we make her stuff better, and get you better. Because if not, it's gonna spiral and spiral and spiral and spiral."

"I keep telling her that she's the first priority," Anna answered, nodding toward me. "I haven't really been taking care of my own stuff."

"I don't question that," I cut in, "but what is your own stuff? *What* has gone wrong? *What* is the truth of your situation right now?"

"Because there are too many lies, too many lies, no more lies," Kacy interjected. "*No. More. Lies.*"

"I didn't lie about anything," Anna said in a monotone voice, devoid of emotion.

Kacy jumped to my defense: "She has had—how many times?—her money coming to her from wires, from this, from that. It's just too much!"

Beth, back at the table, turned to Anna and asked, "Do they know about what's going on in September?"

At first I assumed she was talking about Anna's inheritance, but it quickly became clear there was something else Beth was referencing.

Anna looked to Kacy and me. "Have you seen what they wrote about me?" she asked, again without much emotion. I had no idea what she was talking about. Anna—with interspersed commentary from Beth—went on to describe an article that had come out the night before in the *New York Post* calling Anna a "wannabe socialite." Anna began to snivel. She lifted her glasses to wipe away tears. She had been portrayed unfairly, she complained. She had been sitting and working every day, not partying or acting frivolously. She wanted to be taken seriously.

Hungry to read the story for myself, I waited for a lull in the conversation and then searched on my phone. The *New York Post* article came up right away—and there was a second one! The *Daily News* published a piece of their own, just this morning. The articles described how Anna had stiffed the Beekman hotel for a multi-week stay, then did the same for a shorter stay at the W New York–Downtown, and finally tried to skip out on a lunch bill at Le Parker Meridien. She'd been caught as she attempted to leave Le Parker Meridien, was arrested and then released without bail, and was now facing three counts of misdemeanor theft of services. The total amount she was accused of failing to pay was more than $12,000. And the event that would be going on in September that Beth had referenced wasn't Anna receiving her inheritance: it was a court date.

I was in shock. How had she let things get this bad, and go this far? She hadn't come clean to her parents or admitted to us what was happening, and now her name and face were being disparaged in the tabloids.

Though I tried to keep at a remove, I couldn't remain unaffected as I looked at Anna. She was so visibly upset. For a moment, we tried to console her. "Nobody cares about that anyway," we said.

Then we snapped out of it: Why were we worrying about Anna's reputation when my life was falling apart? Why was *that* the cause of Anna's tears?

"You being in the papers, who cares?" cried Kacy. "Do you know what her life has been like?"

"But all I'm doing is, like, working on this," Anna whined. "I don't, like, sleep. I don't do anything. I mean—"

"Who gives a fuck about you sleeping?" Beth exclaimed.

Beth was dressed like a chic mom with a country club membership, but when it came to confronting Anna, she didn't pull any punches. I appreciated her forcefulness. She was voicing many of the things I wanted to say. This allowed me to stay focused on Anna's reactions.

"—what am I going to do? Am I going to *kill* myself? Like, what am I supposed to *do*?" Anna whimpered.

Oh, spare me the theatrics, I thought. "Do your parents know anything about your situation right now, at all?" I asked.

"They're not going to do anything about it," Anna said dismissively. Her tears had stopped.

Kacy jumped in. "What do you mean they can't do anything about it?"

"They're not *going* to do anything about it," Anna clarified. "They would want me to sort through this myself."

Beth stopped the conversation and pointed out the difference between my pain and Anna's pain. "Her pain is fucking real. It's not pain because 'my accountant didn't do this.' She's gonna be fucked, her life is fucked," she explained. "Just give us the truth, Anna, because once that opens up you can breathe."

Anna was completely calm now. "I never lied about anything; this is what's happening," she said.

"But we don't have any information!" I cried.

Kacy cut in. "I have a question. Why don't you want to tell your parents? Give me the reason why you don't want them involved, because you need a lifeline here."

"They know about it," Anna said.

"Are they pissed at you because you've done it before; because you spend too much money; because they're mean people; because they don't want to help? Give me a reason why they are not coming to your rescue," Kacy implored.

"They say [I] should be sorting it out with the bank, and this is their money in the end, so . . ." This was a classic Anna response—she blamed both her parents and the bank in one go.

"This is *whose* money?" Kacy asked.

"My trust comes from my parents."

"Why can't you access the money?" I asked.

"Because I have, like, monthly disbursement. All my trust is in the securities until eighteen months after my twenty-fifth birthday, which is supposed to be in September, and they just keep changing. They don't follow through. They were supposed to set up everything by April and they still did not."

She was like a malfunctioning computer spitting out words.

"What happened with your lease?" I asked, changing the topic of conversation. "That building got let to someone else."

"What's that?" Anna said.

"The Park Avenue South building, somebody else leased it."

"Who?"

"That Swedish photography agency."

"They did not," she said in disbelief. "It was Fotografiska? No."

Kacy said, "They just had an announcement—"

"Where?" Anna snapped.

"It was in the paper."

"Four days ago," I added.

When she asked to see it, I picked up my phone and paused the recording before showing her the article. For a millisecond Anna appeared crestfallen. I took my phone back.

"It's fake news," she said.

We refocused on Anna's outstanding debts. Kacy asked why Anna couldn't simply go home, sort out her finances, and come back.

"It doesn't help me going anywhere," she answered. "I need to resolve this. If I leave, I can't come back, like, never again. Not for a moment. Like *never*, ever again."

"Is there any other hotel that has anything against you?" Kacy inquired.

"I don't know," Anna sighed. "Just read the stuff that they [wrote] about me and you'll [learn] something new."

Kacy circled back to how little we cared about the article—although, inwardly, I did care. The article confirmed that *the Anna problem* was getting bigger. First me, then Jesse, Kacy, and the bankers and lawyers Anna had mentioned when she slept in my apartment. Now *this*. Everything she touched was falling apart. "You can change your image anytime," Kacy said, "but you still did things. You went above your head, Anna. You spent money you didn't have, and that's not good."

"I do have it," Anna insisted.

"But you knew you were going to a hotel . . . ," Kacy went on.

"You spent money that you *don't have yet*," I ventured. There was a pause. "Is that right?"

"I spent money that I've been promised to I'll have access this afternoon." Another jumble of meaningless words. Afternoon had come and gone; it was dark outside.

"But they say this afternoon. How many months has this been going on?" asked Kacy. "How many promises? The check, the this, the that?"

"Do your parents not realize that [this is] a problem?" I said.

"What are they going to do?" Anna shrugged.

"They can do anything," Kacy answered. "They could actually say, 'You know what, we'll give you this [money] right now, but then we're gonna take it out of your trust.' It's as easy as that."

"For them, it's not because of the amount or the money," Anna explained. She was totally composed now—no stress, drama, or tears—and described her parents' attitude as though it meant nothing. "They just want me to sort it out." Again, I thought, what needs sorting out? What was the problem?

"But they'd rather you go to *jail?* If they find you guilty, you're gonna be in jail. They're not gonna just say, 'Oh, here's a fine.'"

"There is no debtors' prison," said Anna, as if stating a fact. "No one is gonna go to jail."

"How are you paying for *any* hotel?" I asked.

"My family office," Anna said.

Kacy interjected to say she'd called the Greenwich and there'd been no reservation under Anna's name.

"My family office did that," Anna told her. "It's under their name . . . I dunno." How could one possibly check into a hotel without knowing the name on the reservation?

"So, Anna," Kacy resumed, "is there any way that we can at least talk to your parents?"

Beth cut in before Anna could respond. It was a jumbled interrogation. "You've never been in a situation like this?" she asked Anna.

"No" was Anna's response. Kacy spoke over Beth to remind Anna about the Four Seasons in Casablanca. "This is not the first time," she reminded her.

"This is like—I'm not, like, lying," Anna said argumentatively.

"You'd rather go to court with this [than talk to your parents]?" Kacy stammered.

"I don't have a choice!" Anna squeaked. "It's not like I'm choosing to go rather than do this or that, this is just what happens." She was irritated but still without tears.

"But, Anna, you could talk to your father and mother!" Kacy argued.

"But, Anna, then you're full of shit," Beth announced. "You could say whatever the fuck you wanted right now. We just need the truth to know how to move forward. That's it. We don't care if you didn't come from anything. I don't care if you came from fucking Serbia. That doesn't matter."

"It's like we're missing an essential piece of this puzzle," I said.

"There's something missing here," Kacy concurred.

"*We need the truth,*" Beth emphasized.

"What is missing?" Anna taunted. "What piece is that? What's missing?"

There was a pause.

Kacy filled the silence. "The truth is that I think that your parents should know about what's going on. We need to talk to your father and mother because forget this trust shit."

"My parents are going to buy me, like, a one-way ticket to Germany, and they'll tell me to go get a job," Anna said.

"Well, at least let them pay your bills first and then you can figure it out from there," Kacy quipped.

"They're gonna tell me to go get a job and pay my bills myself."

"But if they understand that somebody else is hurting," tried Kacy, "that this person is hurting here, that she really needs her money, and this is a good friend of yours, and you used her—"

I interrupted. "Do you *have* family? Like, living family?" I stammered. It suddenly clicked. There was a foundational lie.

"Yes . . ." Anna said quietly.

"What is your father's name?" Beth asked.

Anna hesitated. "I do have my father."

"What's his name?" Beth pressed.

"Daniel . . . Daniel." Anna pronounced the name slowly, and twice.

"Daniel . . . ?"

"Decker Delvey," Anna finished.

"Daniel Decker Delvey?" Beth parroted.

"Yeah," Anna said.

"So why don't we just talk to them?" Kacy said. "Let somebody talk to your parents and make them understand."

"*I am already doing all of that,*" Anna replied, getting agitated. "I *am* trying everything. I'm not just like sitting around all day and counting *stars*."

"What is going on that you feel like you wanna commit suicide? What is the reason for that?" Kacy asked.

"Because nothing is working out!" Anna answered.

"What's not working out?" Kacy pushed.

"Like *nothing* is working out," Anna whined.

"As friends of Rachel, we need to help her out," Beth insisted. I had only just met her—she was Kacy's friend, really—but I appreciated her advocating on my behalf.

"I've been in touch with Rachel every day," Anna replied.

"But you've been saying the same thing for two months," I objected.

"This is what they've been telling me," Anna alleged, "and I have, like, ten people who are witnesses." Her words were meaningless.

Beth went off on Anna, poking holes in her excuses. Beth had dealt with plenty of bankers and lawyers through the years, and there was no chance that they were responsible for the type of delay Anna was describing. "*It—does—not—happen,*" she said. "There's no fucking excuse, because I know."

I kept my eyes fixed on Anna, studying the way she moved, the way she fluttered her eyes as she decided what to say next, the way she had an answer for everything.

"You're not even aware of my situation," Anna said.

"That's what we're asking you," I cried.

"Because you're not telling us," Kacy said. "We keep asking you."

"Because you're just telling me, 'Oh, you are lying,' and I'm not," Anna said. "I have all these lawyers who are witnesses." She was dancing around the point—shifting, spinning, and deflecting.

"If you cannot hear what is going on that is *so wrong,*" Beth began.

"I see how that's wrong, but this is what I'm being told," Anna said.

Wondering how Anna would react, I decided to bring up Tommy. "Anna, you've obviously had trouble in the past," I started.

"Like what?" she said.

"Like Tommy."

"I never had any financial troubles with him," she claimed.

"He definitely loaned you money, and—"

"No, he didn't," she interrupted.

"—had to threaten you to get it back."

When she continued to deny this, I begged her: "I'd rather know you had no money, and just have truth, than hear these elaborate lies."

"What's your plan?" Beth asked. "To leave the country, not come back, and then do the same shit in another country?"

"And what are you paying a lawyer for?" Kacy asked. "He *cannot* do anything because you're guilty."

"She doesn't have the money to pay him," said Beth. "He doesn't have his retainer." Kacy and Beth spoke about the lawyer. I talked to Anna.

"Are your parents mad at you?" I asked.

"I don't know if they're mad at me. They'll tell me to sort it out myself."

"How do you know that they'll say that? What's the worst-case scenario, they'll tell you to come back?"

"Yeah, they're gonna buy me, like, a one-way ticket and tell me to get a job," she said again.

"But it sounds like things here aren't going very well. So don't you think at some point you're gonna have to?"

"I mean . . . I'm doing everything I can. Like, I'm literally staying up all night."

"But it's not doing anything," I said.

"I know, but it's like—what else could I be doing? I'm doing everything I can. I'm on the phone with everyone. What else can I be doing?"

"Is there a date in September when this will definitely be over?" I wanted a reason to believe. This was my last, pathetic, desperate attempt to revive my faith in Anna.

"It should be in September—you know, it's not like I'm taking care of everything but you. It's, like, I have all my other stuff—"

"Well, I know that. I don't pretend that's not the case. I just wonder if—is there a date in September you think—?"

"No, but it shouldn't be in September—it should be like tomorrow," she said.

"That's not the point. What was the original date in September?" I pushed, testing what Tommy had told me.

"It wasn't September," she said. And then, without explanation, Anna began discussing her trial date and the fact that it was set for September 5, one day before her ESTA visa would expire once again—three months after her return from Morocco. My head spun. She had completely dropped (or ignored) the thread of my question.

"She's got an answer for everything," said Beth. "Okay, so you know what I think? You are not being honest."

"I am being honest," Anna said defensively. She had no tears, no anguish; only scorn. How was she so calm?

"You're not fucking being honest, Anna. Because you've got so many fucking bullshit stories."

"Like what?" Anna asked, with a dare in her voice. "All my story's the same. My story is the same and consistent and I'm doing everything I can. I'm not, like, being out all every night!"

"You keep saying that," said Kacy. "It's not about you being out. You're not a child."

"It's about you having to pay somebody money," Beth said.

"It's about being responsible," said Kacy.

"She's full of shit. She's full of shit. She's got nothing," Beth declared.

"How can you say that?" Anna questioned.

"I know your story," Beth said skeptically. "Your story is—"

"Can you explain my story to me?" Anna interrupted, taking the bait.

"Your story is that . . . none of it's true," Beth replied.

"Can you explain to me why my story is not true?" Anna was spinning,

doing anything possible not to be the one having to talk. Her tone was defi-
ant, almost haughty.

"What the fuck are you questioning me for?" Beth snapped.

"Okay, everybody calm down," Kacy interjected.

"Just explain to me my story that you think I presented to you that's not
true," Anna persisted.

"How do you go to fucking Morocco? How do you do this? How do you
do that? How do you not have the right accountant? There's no explanation
because it doesn't exist," Beth said.

"Well, I did those things. It must exist." Anna was smirking now, gain-
ing confidence.

"No, because you're like a [transient]," Beth said.

"I think what Beth is trying to say is that all the roads are leading to—"
Beth interrupted. "No, listen, I've lived in Eastern Europe. I've lived
in Russia."

Kacy and Beth spoke over each other until Anna chimed in. "Can anybody explain what's wrong with my story?"

"Your story is a never-ending fucking story," Beth answered. I knew she
was right.

"She's too skilled at manipulation to have this conversation," I said,
crying but composed. "She doesn't work like that. I've seen this for two
months."

"You are not giving a straight story," Beth said bitingly.

"I'm German and I have a bank in Switzerland. How does Russia have
anything to do with that?"

"Because originally where is your family from?" Beth asked.

"Germany," Anna quickly answered. I thought about Tommy telling me
that Anna's father was a Russian billionaire. Something wasn't right here.

"Your family's from Germany?" Beth asked again.

"Yes," said Anna.

"And where are your parents from?"

"They're from Germany."

191

"Everything in her life has changed because of this shit," Kacy said, refocusing on me.

"How do you think my life is?" Anna asked.

"*It's not about you. You did it,*" Kacy cried. "You got what you wanted out of this deal. It's not about *you*, Anna. It's not about *you*. That's the problem. You've gotta step out of yourself and think about someone else. And it's not about you or your shopping or your hair or your nails or your massage or your whatever. This is about real fucking life. This girl is fucking working her ass off, just like you *maybe* are, but you borrowed money on her card."

"I didn't borrow like . . . I didn't get into her bank account and go shopping with it," Anna said.

"You went and fucking vacationed with it," said Kacy.

"I know, but that's why I'm not denying it—I'm trying to repay her."

"But it's not about *you*," Kacy said, again.

"But don't you . . . see the whole story?" Anna whimpered. "Do you see how, like, I'm doing?"

"Forget about you for a minute," Kacy tried again. "Forget about what you have to do or what you've done. Forget all that shit. Think of somebody else—someone else totally—not you. Not what you want. But someone else's pain. You need to detach from yourself, Anna. Okay? Understand something, because the minute that you pay it forward, that you can feel someone else's shit, that you can do something out of an unconditional loving place, your shit will change. You need to understand that. You . . . you . . . you keep looking at it as if, like, I'm doing the best I can. That's not brownie points. Because you already have overstepped your bounds."

While this condensed, live-action version of my experience from the past two months was happening—filled with misinformation, lies, and deceit—I texted Ashley, Nick, Dave, Kathryn, and Jesse with links to the articles. None of them had seen it.

Kathryn wrote back: *Per the article now you have [Anna's] attorney contact,* she said. *Let's reach out to him tomorrow.*

Ashley's response was: *Wow. I'm so sorry.* She also offered to connect me with a family member of hers who was a lawyer, if only for advice.

My Friend Anna

It's pretty dark over here, I wrote back to her. *[Anna is] a terror.*

Jesse texted me: *Omg. Rachel. That's insane. Did you talk to her?*

At a confrontation right now with kacy and one of kacy's friends, I told him.

And anna? he asked.

Yes.

Jesus, he said. *Does she owe Kacy?*

Yes.

Is she a con or is this a matter of spoiled brat doesn't have access to her family's money?

It took around ten seconds for me to type and send my reply: *I think she's a long-game con.*

No way, he said. *Fuck.*

I looked back to Anna, who was utterly devoid of compassion. She stuck to her story, claiming that everything she said was true—that nothing was her fault. I said little as I watched. I seemed to float outside of my body, while tears ran down my cheeks. Against the raised voices and direct accusations, Anna's face remained unsettlingly blank. Her eyes were empty. I suddenly realized that I didn't know her at all. With this epiphany came a sort of strange calmness and release. I understood Kacy's and Beth's anger and disbelief; I'd had those feelings for months. But I had finally come through to the other side, and I knew that there was only one answer.

After two hours, the intervention had gone as far as it could. Kacy was the first one to call it a night. She had given Anna enough energy and didn't want to look as tired as she felt during her scheduled appearance on a television show the following morning. Beth, Anna, and I soon followed suit. The three of us walked south along the West Side Highway beneath a waxing summer moon. Beth kept pace beside me, bound for her apartment in Tribeca, and Anna strode two steps ahead, on her way to the Greenwich Hotel. I watched Anna intently as we strolled, with her Balenciaga tote bag over her arm and large sunglasses atop her head. Was that all she had? Maybe to Anna, everything and everyone were disposable. Her feet fell quickly but with minimal impact, so that she almost seemed to glide. How had someone who had once felt so familiar become so hopelessly obscure?

I thought through the months leading up to this moment, and about the way Anna had responded to questions and accusations. I studied the framework of her explanations and tried to crack it with my mind. But that was the thing about Anna: she was all riddle, no solution—and that was an answer unto itself.

I stopped at Clarkson Street and waited to cross the highway toward my apartment. Beth said a quick farewell. Anna kept walking.

"Bye," I shouted after her.

She turned around abruptly, flashed a smile, and waved. "Bye!" she answered.

That would be the last time I saw Anna for a very long while.

Chapter 14

Penny Drop

Still reeling from the night before, I awoke on Wednesday morning to a text from Kacy asking if everyone had gotten home all right. *I think so,* I told her. She was also curious whether anything significant had transpired after she left—whether Beth, such a staunch caller of bullshit, drank Anna's Kool-Aid in the end. *No, she definitely didn't,* I assured Kacy. Beth was a firm nonbeliever. But even so, thinking of Beth and Anna walking into the night alone, I couldn't help but wonder if it was possible. I knew Anna's power.

I was irritable, distracted, and slow while getting ready for work. It was after eleven a.m. when I got to the *V.F.* office. My brain was burnt out and my spirits were down. The closer I got to the truth about Anna, the further I got from relief. The police weren't interested in my black binder. I was still out $62,109.29, and American Express kept calling. I could borrow money from Janine—she'd immediately responded to my email with an offer to help—but how would I ever repay her? And a corrosive idea was beginning to form: Had Anna betrayed me on purpose? Sitting at my desk, I felt pangs of a sadness so heavy that I was tempted to lie down on the floor. Could I go home? Get back in bed? What way forward was there now? It had been two and a half months. Was she toying with me all along? Seventy-five days! Morning apprehension. Afternoon effort. Nighttime dread. And for what? I'd been waiting on something that would never happen, right? Was any of it real?

Noon. A text from Kacy. Anna was asleep at Beth's house.

Of course she was. The brazenness. We all knew that she wasn't staying at the Greenwich Hotel, but why hadn't Anna said goodbye to Beth to protect her lie? Couldn't she have found some other place to sleep? Then again, the obvious path was never Anna's route. When she lit a fire, she stuck around to watch it burn. It's possible she really had *nowhere else to go.* But could it also have been that she was drawn to a challenge? Had she latched onto Beth in a ploy to win her approval? Poor Beth. Had she offered or did Anna finally ask? The newly paranoid part of me wondered if maybe they'd known each other all along.

Beth had given me her phone number. Taking into account her unexpected guest, I sent a message to ask whether everything was okay. Anna was still sleeping, Beth told me. She'd get her up and out in a little while and would check in with me afterward. *Don't let her toxicity get to you!* I cautioned. *I won't,* she replied.

I tried to bury myself in my work. I'd managed to hold it together for so long. Oh, how badly I wanted to crumble. Could I please just curl up into a ball and disappear under my desk? Would anyone notice? Would it all go away? I was struggling not to cry. But it was useless.

i'm so sick to my stomach today, I texted Kathryn, who was out for lunch, *i'm in the office but i'm not sure how long i'll be able to stay. i'm trying to keep my head up but i'm totally overwhelmed.* She returned within the hour and checked on me straight away.

The showdown at the Frying Pan had unfolded like a stage drama. I relayed its essential plot points to Kathryn, who absorbed them carefully. "Remind me how much money you owe?" she asked. Although she understood the situation's magnitude, she encouraged me to view the setback as surmountable. Resourceful as ever, she also thought of ways to help. "We could do a photo auction," she proposed. She had the idea to talk to some of the photographers we worked with, to see whether, knowing the situation, they might be willing to donate prints. Rattling off names, Kathryn reminded me that I was part of a community, that I wouldn't have to carry my burden alone.

Bolstered by this assurance, I refocused on how to move forward. Dave suggested I contact the Manhattan District Attorney's Office. Thinking it would help to have a connection, Kathryn reached out to one of our colleagues, who, assuming we were looking for a photo-shoot location, pointed us to the press office. I drafted an email, and we sent it from Kathryn's account.

Dear Emily,

. . . A dear colleague of mine . . . has been the victim of fraud . . . perpetrated by Anna Sorokin-Delvey, who was the subject of this piece in yesterday's Daily News: "Aspiring socialite Anna Sorokin accused of skipping out on $12G in hotel stays." . . . I am hopeful that you may be able to point us in the right direction, as we are eager to help our colleague and also feel that she has important information to disclose. Is there someone in the District Attorney's office with whom she could meet in person to explain the situation and to explore the best course of action?

Thank you in advance for any insight you can provide.

With gratitude,
Kathryn MacLeod

While we waited for a response, I sat at my desk picking at my memories from the last six months. I googled "Anna Sorokin-Delvey," "Anya Delvey," "Anna Sorokin," "Anna Sorokina." Was she German or was she Russian? Old party photos with random scenesters, crazy hair, and questionable fashion. How far back did the lies go? How had she gotten to *Purple* magazine in the first place? From what I could tell, that was when she broke into the social circuit.

So far, in the world of people who also knew Anna (not counting Kacy or Jesse), I'd confided only in Ashley and Tommy. I wanted to reach Olivier

Zahm, editor in chief of *Purple*, to see what, if anything, he might know. I contacted him through a friend we had in common, explaining the situation and hoping for insight. They were both in Europe, so with the time difference, I hoped to hear back the next day.

The DA's press office responded: they would pass on my information to the prosecutor on the skipped-hotel-bill case. With that, it was back to waiting. Waiting to hear from Beth, from Olivier, from the prosecutor. Maybe this time around I'd learn something new.

I had concert tickets to see Gillian Welch at the Beacon Theatre that evening. When I was feeling disconsolate, I'd unsuccessfully tried to sell them. I was too worn out, too depressed, and frankly in need of the money. I'd just skip it. But when Kathryn heard me say so, she intervened. She could tell I needed a boost. We would go together.

In the lobby of the Beacon, Kathryn bought white wine and Peanut M&M's. Inside the theater, everyone was seated and the lights were off. Two people holding acoustic guitars stood illuminated on the stage: Gillian, in a faded blue dress, hair down and parted in the middle, and her partner, Dave Rawlings, in a loose-fitting jacket and pale cowboy hat. The duo was on tour to celebrate the vinyl release of their 2011 album, *The Harrow & The Harvest*. Their set list was the album from start to finish, in order. I knew every word. Once, I had been in the Adirondacks without cell-phone service. *The Harrow & The Harvest* was the only album I had, so for several days I listened to it on repeat. Lines echoed in my head for weeks. It had country grit, and soul, and made rural melancholy sound beautiful. "We wouldn't normally lay so many minor-key songs on you in a row," Gillian told us from the stage, "but this is how the record goes." There was something powerful about hearing music that met me where I was. Slow. Sad. Tired but strong.

Beth called at intermission. She'd spoken to Anna's lawyer, she told me, and would fill me in more after she finished with dinner. When the show was over, I said goodbye to Kathryn in the lobby. She gifted me with a Gillian Welch T-shirt that she'd bought when I wasn't looking. She really was trying so hard to support me. It warmed my heart.

I gave Beth a call when I got off the subway downtown. She had spoken to Anna's criminal-defense lawyer—he sounded legitimate, but his twenty-thousand-dollar retainer hadn't been paid. I asked Beth how she'd gotten Anna to leave her apartment. She told me that she put Anna up in a hotel (the Hotel Hugo in Soho) for the night. Beth also said that after speaking with Anna and her lawyer, she thought if we could find a way to put money toward the lawyer's retainer, maybe he could retrieve Anna's cell phones from the police, who were apparently holding on to them. The reasoning was convoluted, but it seemed Anna had explained that she needed her phones to access her emails and contacts. Without those, she couldn't issue the outstanding payments she owed. And if Anna's lawyer received a portion of his retainer, he might take the necessary steps to negotiate getting the phones back. Beth was trying to help me. Anna was trying to help herself.

I thanked Beth sincerely and told her it was time for us both to disengage. I made a commitment as I said it aloud: From now on, we must operate under the assumption that Anna is a highly skilled con artist. No more doubt about that. Anna had upended my life and watched as I came undone. Now here was Beth, a new mark with an impulse to help. Her empathy had made her vulnerable, and Anna had seized the opportunity. I recognized the pattern now.

Understanding Anna as a fraud, one had to marvel at how widely she'd burrowed her roots. Details varied slightly from person to person, but the central story was always the same—you had to give her points for consistency—she was an ambitious German heiress with an interest in art and business. You could ask anyone else who knew her and they'd tell you the same story. Like, for instance, Tommy—did he really know anything about Anna's family? The information he gave me had lodged in my gears like a wrench.

I decided to ask him: *Hey Tommy, I'm beginning to think Anna is just a total fraud. Like there's not even a trust fund or rich parents at all. Is that possible? Are you positive she even has a family?* He told me that Anna had given him a family name from Munich, but he agreed it could have been make-believe.

The more I picked at the pieces, the faster they fell apart.

I did get a response from Olivier Zahm, but it was vague and brief—all he said was that Anna had been let go from *Purple*. I didn't fault him for his terseness. Anna's waters were murky, and it was hard to know whom to trust and how much information to share. Just the same, the pattern was clear: Anna's past was filled with ambiguity and discord.

Now I just needed to reach the prosecutor from the DA's office. I assumed their case pertained to the misdemeanor offenses reported in the *New York Post* and *Daily News*: stiffed bills at both the Beekman and W hotels, and an attempted dine-and-dash incident at Le Parker Meridien. Did the prosecutor know those offenses were just small pieces of a much bigger puzzle?

I followed up with an email: *If possible I'd really like to speak with someone today. I think this girl is a con artist. I'm happy to meet in person or to speak over the phone. I can be available any time.* With so much hanging in the balance, after such prolonged stress, I was fully committed to exploring every possible lead. I'd gathered as much information as I could. I had a scan of Anna's passport and an image of her debit card from when I booked the flights to Morocco. Everything was saved into my Operation Clarity folder, printed, and filed in the black binder.

As I waited for a response, I warned others to stay on guard. I sent a text to Beth: *Hi Beth, I hope you got some rest. I'm still working on gathering as much background info on Anna as I can. It's clear that she has a track record of sticking other people with bills or not paying them. I do think she's a fraud. I highly recommend that you distance yourself from her entirely. You clearly have such a kind and strong heart but she is masterfully manipulative and completely toxic. I do suggest telling your doormen not to let her in your building.*

She had already done it.

My cell phone rang. The caller ID read "United States." I answered as I stepped away from my desk. "We think you're right," a voice said.

My Friend Anna

It was an assistant district attorney from the Manhattan DA's office, who confirmed that Anna Sorokin (aka "Anna Delvey") was the subject of an ongoing criminal investigation. They wanted me to come in.

As I hung up the phone, I felt a rush of clarity. My brain skipped back and forth through time like a VCR tape gone berserk. Breathing slowly, I slipped the black binder into my backpack, logged out of my computer, and switched off my desk lamp. I had felt that I was right, but even so, that voice on the other end of the line, echoing with affirmation, rang loudly in my brain. If it was true, and Anna really *was* a con artist—then what next?

I don't remember waiting for the elevator, or leaving Condé Nast's headquarters. I must have headed east, walking fast. Did I stop at the crosswalks? Were there even cars on the street? The world parted like a sea, melting, bending, and unfolding. I'd gotten used to the ground shifting below my feet. I wanted my balance back.

I'm not sure if I wrote down the address, or if it stuck in my brain—with so many other names and numbers, indelible and carefully organized. Eighty Center Street. I passed through Foley Square, the Civic Center of New York City, and spotted my destination on the corner.

Up a few stairs and inside the doors, I approached a security desk. "We have a Rachel Williams here," the guard said into a phone, looking intently from me to the driver's license I'd provided upon his request. He passed back my ID and gave me a "Visitor" sticker, smiling and pointing in the direction of the elevators.

I followed directions to the Financial Frauds Bureau of the DA's office and sat at a table with three other women—two assistant district attorneys (ADAs) and a paralegal. They wanted to hear everything.

At last, I had found a space where my story was welcome, and even useful. It fell on ears that believed and understood. Anna had performed a long con, all right, and I wasn't the only victim. In many ways, this was the worst-case scenario for me—"we don't think she has a pot to piss in," as someone put it—but the truth also made things simpler.

ADA Catherine McCaw, the primary prosecutor on the case, suggested I try contacting American Express to dispute the relevant charges. And another thing, creepy but important: my coloring was not unlike Anna's—maybe a coincidence, but maybe not. I would need to consider changing my credit cards, bank account number, and even my passport. I took this directive as an opportunity to mention one of my theories: "Oh, and I think she's Russian," I said.

"What makes you say that?" asked McCaw. I told her about the Frying Pan, about Beth's suspicions and Anna's hardened demeanor during our questioning.

She couldn't tell me yes or no, but went as far as to say, "You have good instincts."

At last I could see new ways to be proactive. There was a whirring in my head as scenes and phrases replayed, fragments clicking into a pattern. I'd had a front-row seat to Anna's operations. My memories were relevant, and I wanted to be helpful. I told them what I knew.

"Did you ever consider a career as an investigator?" one of the ADAs asked me. As it happened, why yes, I had. As a third-grader in Knoxville, Tennessee (looking up to my grandfather, who'd been an assistant director in the FBI), becoming an agent had been my earnest *when-I-grow-up* plan. This was not how I had imagined it, but my time had come and I would rise to the occasion.

The meeting lasted around two hours. Finally, I stood up to leave. "Would you like this back?" asked Assistant DA Catherine McCaw, pointing to the black binder on the desk between us. I glanced down.

"No," I said. "I think I was making it for you."

––––––

I sat on a park bench between the Louis J. Lefkowitz State Office Building, where the DAs were located, and the New York County Supreme Court. I called my aunt Jennie. I called Janine. I called Nick, who had left the day before for a few months of travel—a separation that would prove to be hard. I then realized I had almost forgotten an appointment that Kathryn and I had made for that evening. The two of us were expected at the Lowell hotel for a tour of the penthouse suite (to consider as a future photo-shoot location) and drinks with the hotel's P.R. team. "Are you up for it?" Kathryn asked. I said I was, wanting to be in her company.

As we walked through the lobby of the five-star hotel, I barely noticed my surroundings. I was too busy ruminating, trapped in my own head. I vaguely remember the smell of flowers. The penthouse was nice. I bet Anna would have loved it—or maybe it was too classically luxurious—too authentic. Back on the ground level, Kathryn and I followed the publicists into the hotel's bar. I was the last one to enter. My pace slowed as I looked around—was it my imagination? Majorelle blue, geometric patterns, embossed leather, and low seating—it was Moroccan inspired. The irony was amusing, but I found it mildly triggering, having packed so many emotions into my memory of Marrakech, particularly when it came to hotels.

Light-headed, I slipped into the bathroom, took a few deep breaths, and splashed cold water on my face. After a few minutes, I found my group at a table in the back room. A waitress came by for our drink orders.

"What'll you have?" she asked, looking at Kathryn first.

"Oh, I don't know . . . What's good? What's your signature cocktail?"

"The Marrakech Express."

A knowing look, a nervous smile, an obvious choice. "We'll take two," Kathryn said.

Chapter 15

Flip Side

After that meeting at the District Attorney's Office, I became trapped within my memories. I moved through the city—from my apartment to work and back again—but saw very little of my physical surroundings. I was busy sifting through every remembered detail and scene from my time with Anna. For months, I'd been fixating on a timeline that began with Marrakech and ended with the Frying Pan. Now I ricocheted back to the start. *I met Anna at Happy Ending, a restaurant-lounge on Broome Street.* Where were the warning signs? How did this happen?

Words and gestures, once seemingly trivial, suddenly took on new meaning. "Things, like money, could all be lost in an instant," she'd told me—is this what she meant? How much didn't I know? What happened behind the scenes?

One and a half years' worth of archival footage spun back and forth on a reel. There were hidden layers in every scene. I combed through the memories when I should have been sleeping as a way of coping with my shock. The mystery had caused such mental anguish, but now that I knew that Anna Delvey was not real, I could chart a whole new course of action.

First, keep Anna in the dark. Enlightened as I was, I couldn't see any advantage to making her aware of what I now knew. Better for her to assume that I was still in my cave, watching her shadow on the wall. So I considered: What would I have done if I hadn't found the DA? Assuming that

Anna was still without a cell phone, I sent her a message through Facebook on August 4: *Anna, I really need to be reimbursed. I'm in huge trouble. My job is on the line. Please please please. I can't believe I'm in this situation. I really trusted you.* She didn't respond.

The next morning, I called American Express. Unpacking the story for a stranger—on whom I needed to rely—triggered a range of emotions. My tone, to start, was firm, matter-of-fact. Describing the breakdown at La Mamounia, it shifted to angry. And at last, explaining my attempts at reimbursement, it lost all semblance of composure. I contested the charges from La Mamounia: $16,770.45 on my American Express corporate card and $36,010.09 on my personal card. Disputes filed, it was back to waiting, an activity I now knew so well.

Next, it was time to tell my parents. Alone in my apartment that evening, I picked up the phone but found I couldn't make the call. I thought it might be easier to talk about the situation while I was outside, in the open air, rather than indoors. The emotional weight was too big for a contained space, and walking helped me think. I paced the streets of Lower Manhattan and summoned the courage to call. My mom answered the phone.

"Do you have a few minutes to talk? Is Dad around, too?" My dad was out for a campaign event, but now that I was ready, I couldn't bear to wait. "I need to tell you about something and it's not good. Before I start, I want you to know that I am okay."

I began with the trip to Morocco. My mom hung on my every word. Even though she knew the trip had happened, these details were brand-new. She interrupted. I didn't blame her. How could she know where the story would end? Was that it?

"Just wait," I said, an impossible request. "Anything you can think of, I've already asked, and anything you suggest, I've already tried." Overconfident maybe, but I'd come so far. "Answers will come as I go," I assured her. Out it came, from start to finish: the back room after Villa Oasis, Jennie and Janine, loans from Nick, lawyers, police, the confrontation, and the truth.

There was a long pause.

"Oh, sweetie." Her voice broke. "I am heartbroken that you went through that on your own, but I am *so* proud of you." Not having the energy to tell it twice, I asked her to let my dad know. A few hours later, he sent me a note: "Your daddy loves you oh so much."

I broke down and cried.

I spent the first weekend in August at Kathryn's house, in Bridgehampton, and that's when I began to write everything down. The amount of information was overwhelming—I hadn't known that it was possible to remember so much. It felt necessary to exorcise every detail. If I didn't write each of them thoroughly, whatever stayed behind might fester, or become lost inside forever. To move forward, I needed the story to live elsewhere—outside of me—intact. I found the process incredibly cathartic.

The prosecutors would not disclose the contents of their investigation: they'd taken my information on board without giving much back. Although this made sense as an operational necessity, it made it hard to know what parts of my story might be relevant. So, just in case, I gave them everything I could think of that could possibly be of interest, from obvious facts to far-fetched theories (labeled accordingly). After all, if Anna Delvey was just a character, a front for covert operations, anything was possible.

With little hope of recouping any money from Anna, why did I bother? At the time, I barely paused to ask. My scope was limited, and in my quest to make sense of the chaos, it was gratifying to join forces with a broader operation committed to the same task. It was also motivating for my negative experience to be repurposed and put to good use. And deep in my stomach, I wrestled with one other thing: If Anna had chosen to do this to me, her friend, what else was she capable of? What else had she already done? I needed to know.

As I went through my memories and records of our exchanges, I organized the data in emails to the DA's office. By cross-referencing messages and iPhone photos, I created a timeline of Anna's activities. I listed the names of people she had mentioned: her favorite lawyer, hedge-fund acquaintances, businessmen, and potential collaborators. For each of them, I included a link to background information and a summary of their relationship to Anna.

Along with the timeline and list of names, I submitted the audio recordings from the Frying Pan. I also shared my full text-messaging history with Anna, going back to February of 2017, when she'd given me her new number. The PDF began with my first message, *Hello new Anna,* along with her first response, *Hello stranger.*

I logged new information as it came to mind. My emails to the DA's office went out in bursts, a flux of miscellaneous data. I thought the prosecutors might follow the money, so I told them where she spent it. She got her hair done here, her eyelash extensions there. She used this app for car services, that app for fitness bookings, and another app for spa reservations. She had an interest in cryptocurrency. *I think she was running a Ponzi scheme,* I said.

I planned to block Anna from all of my social media accounts, but first I went through them and took screenshots of her posts. I documented as much information as I could find (names of people Anna was pictured with and locations when available). I made a list of her social media handles in case the DA's office hadn't seen them. It seemed important for them to know where she'd been: New York, Berlin, Paris, Venice, Miami, Dubrovnik, Los Angeles, San Francisco—so many cities around the world. I scrolled all the way back to the beginning, to see Anna's first post on Instagram. There it was, February 27, 2013—three years before I met her—a picture of a chessboard, black-and-white marble with gold and silver pieces. The game had just begun.

When I wasn't archiving, I spent my time alone or with Kathryn. I had drinks with Ashley once during this time and confided in her. I relayed the broad strokes, but never mentioned the DA's confidential investigation. Without batting an eye, she asked whether I wanted to move in with her, into her studio apartment, so that I could sublet my apartment to save money. I was deeply touched by her offer—an act of extreme kindness during a time I felt broken and jagged.

My Friend Anna

Fundamentally shaken, I retreated inward, lacking the energy to keep anyone fully abreast of my progress and theories. Even as the narrative continued to unfold, I knew that something about it was so absurdly transfixing that, once it was told, it would be hard to contain. It was the type of gossip you needed to bounce off another person to properly absorb. *Can you believe it?* And although there were plenty of people I trusted to keep my secrets, this one was liable to burn a hole into any place it sat for too long. The smaller my circle, the less I had to worry. And with so much else causing me stress, the decision to keep quiet was easy to make.

Work was a good distraction—I had my day job to maintain. That following Monday, I was in the *Vanity Fair* office, as usual. I was busy organizing a small photo shoot of Jeff Goldblum, finding someone to photograph the desk of Cecile Richards for a front-of-book page, and finalizing a menu for the photo department's annual "Summer Fling," an upcoming dinner at Cecconi's in Brooklyn.

It occurred to me, not having heard from Anna, that it would be natural to reach out again. It felt wisest to keep the chain of communication open—what did I have to lose? I sent her another Facebook message, as if it were a matter of routine procedure: *Am I meant to give up? Can you please contact your family? Hello?*

I'm not sure what I thought was going to happen, but thirty minutes later, her response came as a shock: *did you go through all my contacts or not yet.*

My heart fell on the floor. What did she mean—*contacts*? Was she asking if I'd spoken to her friends and acquaintances? Maybe she was referring to Tommy, since I'd brought him up to her at the Frying Pan. But if not him, who? Was someone playing both sides, talking to me and to Anna? It was the day after I'd sent that list of names—*contacts*?—to the prosecutors, but how could she know that? Had she tapped my phone? My computer? I disconnected my laptop from the Internet and looked nervously over my shoulder for the rest of the day. Her message shook me. I didn't respond.

But on Tuesday, Anna surfaced again. I was at my desk when my cell phone buzzed: the name "Anna Delvey" popped up on its screen.

Back at this [number], she texted. Did she have her phone back or was she using a computer? Either way, I didn't engage. An hour later my cell phone rang. It was her again. I watched the phone vibrate as if it were possessed.

In my mind, Anna had become a disembodied force, more of a specter than a human. If we were in a horror movie, she was the evil spirit who kept knocking on the door.

When I didn't answer the phone, she sent another text: *Call me back or provide a time for us to call you back asap regarding the outstanding issue,* it said.

Us? Who's *us?* "Outstanding issue" meaning reimbursement? Why was she being so cryptic? My view of Anna had changed entirely. All trace of my friend was gone; she was a stranger, and I was afraid. Even so, I found ways to be proactive. I alerted the DA's office that Anna was back on the grid. Thinking ahead, just in case, I downloaded an app on my cell phone that would allow me to record calls. Then I considered my words carefully and waited until I was calmer to respond.

That evening, I went for it: *You have all my info. You've had it for almost three months. My life has turned upside down because of you. When will I see something in my account?*

She responded a minute later: *It seems like you are misrepresenting the situation and the way I'm handling it to a lot of people.*

My heart raced so quickly that I felt sick. Anna's power play was aggressive. By taking the offensive, she made me question my own strength. By implying that I was outnumbered—was she really talking to *a lot of people?*—she made me feel like I was alone. Her attempt was perfectly twisted. Despite the physicality of my panic, I could see these manipulation tactics clearly and understood their objective.

This time, I took the upper hand: *The situation is clear. There is nothing to misrepresent. You owe me a lot of money. This debt has ruined my life over the last three months. If you think I'm not upset you are wrong. And you have not answered my question. I have nothing else to discuss.*

My Friend Anna

For a while, Anna and I left it at that. Neither of us had anything to add. I trusted the assistant district attorneys to do their job, and, as a way to feel constructive, I continued to write. Now and then, I would get phone calls from an unknown number. I never answered, but I assumed they were from Anna. Since she seemed alone and desperate, I expected her to spiral. The thought of her lashing out scared me. To feel safe, I watched her from a distance, keeping an eye on her social media.

During the time that I'd known her, Anna had always fixated on knowing about places that were new and considered cool, but I'd noticed that if she visited those places, she rarely posted about them online, at least not right away. This made it difficult for me to know where she was. And yet, while it didn't reveal her geographic location, her online activity in mid-August did unmask a certain state of mind.

drain you, read the caption of her Instagram post on August 10, an underwater picture of a woman. You couldn't see Anna's face, but in a black dress with her legs bent, it was definitely her. Although she hadn't geotagged the location, I remembered the scene from Marrakech. It was an image Jesse had taken in our private pool at La Mamounia. Was Anna's caption directed at me? I took a screenshot of the post and shared it with the DA's office, if only to give them an indicator of Anna's insensitivity.

That same day, she also posted one other photo: a close-up of her own face, lips pouting with pseudo-vulnerability. She mimicked a baby doll, puffy-faced with feminine features and a markedly vacant look in her eyes. She also updated her Instagram bio. "Let em eat cake," it said. Just like her tattoo, an homage to her idol, Marie Antoinette.

I followed Anna's activity on Spotify, so I could see the names of songs as she played them. Knowing that she was online and listening to music was agitating (what was she doing?), but I was convinced that the information might somehow be useful.

Again and again, she listened to one in particular: "Drain You," by Nirvana—a song about a parasitic relationship, written by Kurt Cobain, which must have been the inspiration for her Instagram caption. It was all a little too on the nose. How much was she doing on purpose? Her actions struck me as predatory and increasingly deranged. Though I was deeply unsettled, I couldn't look away.

Craving more insight, I consulted Anna's Instagram account to see the photos in which she had been tagged. This led me to Hunter, Anna's ex-boyfriend, so I scrolled through his account, too. Anna appeared in only a few of Hunter's photos, but in my state of mind, there was more that seemed relevant. For instance, his post from New Year's Day 2014, from the Soho House in Berlin, a photo of typed words on strips of paper:

```
               enjoy
        the little things
             in life . . .
           for one day
        you'll look back
                and
             realize
            they were
        the big things
```

Platitude or warning?

Judging by his posts, Hunter had also been to La Mamounia; he shared photos of the hotel in June 2015 and April 2016. Evidently, he and Anna had similar taste in travel, as well as in art, architecture, and design. I scrolled all the way back to his earliest posts. This time it wasn't a chessboard that caught my eye (although there were a few of those). It was René Magritte's *Le modèle rouge*—posted on March 21, 2011, without any caption—a Surrealist painting of hollowed out feet-shoes, complete with ten toes and untied laces, like boots made of flesh. It was a fitting reflection of how I'd come to see Anna. Her human form was just a vessel: sealed in its confines, her Machiavellian life force wore its skin like a costume.

Rapt and repulsed as I was by Anna and her nightmarish world, there was another issue I needed to confront. The situation with American Express was ongoing. Filing the disputes had been only the first step. Because the phone number was unfamiliar, I ignored a call from Amex one afternoon. I learned from a voice mail that they required some additional information regarding the claim on my personal card. (Because two cards were used, there were also two case numbers and the claims had to be processed separately.) After a round of phone tag, I spoke with a representative who had a few questions. Was my credit card stolen? No, I answered. Was it lost? No, again. Was I there at La Mamounia in person? Of course the answer was yes.

But how could my story fit into one-word answers? The nuance of the drama required a long-winded explanation, and I gave it. Just like before, when I first filed my claim, I started out calm and by the end of the phone call I was in the midst of a full-blown panic attack.

As a person, the representative sounded sincerely sympathetic and wishing to help. As a corporate cog, however, the representative seemed obliged to focus on ticks in a box. For Amex's purposes, the term "fraudulent" applied only when charges were made to a lost or stolen credit card. It was as black-and-white as that, and mine was a tale doused in gray. While this did not mean that my claim was rejected, it did mean that it had reached the wrong team. The Fraud Squad would redirect my case to the Customer Service Team. The Customer Service Team would then contact La Mamounia before circling back to me. Which meant more waiting. The looming threat of the unpaid balance filled me with a constant undercurrent of dread. I carried on trailing Anna.

Chapter 16

Eclipse

On the following Sunday, August 20, I drove a rental car with Grandma Marilyn and Noah to my aunt and uncle's house in Cape Cod for a brief vacation. My sister, Jennie, and her boyfriend would take a ferry out to join us on Monday. None of them knew anything about my situation with Anna, and I had no immediate plan to tell them. This was primarily because I wanted to avoid my predicament becoming the dominant topic of conversation during our visit. If I told them, they would have so many questions, and I didn't have it in me to patiently respond—the stress made me way too fragile, prone to anger, defensiveness, and fits of crying. Conversely, were they *not* to ask questions, I would feel self-conscious and annoyed by everyone tiptoeing around. No, I couldn't do it. I was too tired and too grumpy. I just wanted things to be normal. I needed a break.

Our first night on the Cape, Noah decided to sleep in a hammock on the back porch. My grandmother slept upstairs, so I was alone on the first floor. Lying awake in my bed, I logged into my Amex account on my cell phone. I checked my personal account first and then my corporate account, and that's when I saw a line that made my heart drop: "VALID CHARGE— PREVIOUS CREDIT REVERSED $16,770.45."

It was a quarter past midnight, but I was suddenly wide-awake. I pulled back my covers to stand up. Pacing in the darkness, I called American Express. It was too stressful to wait until morning. I spoke to a representative

215

and, through tears, told my story yet again. The representative reopened my case. When I hung up the phone, I looked out at the porch to see if Noah was sleeping. His eyes were closed, but I noticed that a window was open. I wondered if he had been able to hear.

The following morning, my sister and her boyfriend arrived, and at half past two that afternoon we assembled to witness the eclipse. From an aerial view, Cape Cod is shaped like an arm curling to flex its bicep. Midway between its "fist" (Provincetown) and "elbow" (Chatham) is Wellfleet, where my family gathered on the wooden roof deck of my aunt and uncle's house, perched on a bluff overlooking salt marshes and the bay.

It was a welcome distraction for me. We didn't have the special glasses you needed to look directly at the sun, so instead Grandma Marilyn showed us a trick using two sheets of paper. She punched a pinhole into one and held it above the other, so that light passed through the puncture to form a bright spot on the surface below. As the moon crossed in front of the sun, its shadow eclipsed the circle of light on the paper. Visually, the effect of her tool wasn't that impressive, but it was a joy to see how much pleasure Grandma Marilyn got from making and using it. The solar experience was unifying, like flying a kite. For a few minutes, dusk fell in the middle of the day and we humans were reminded of our tiny place in the universe.

On Tuesday, I received an email from the DA's office. Without revealing any details, it let me know that the investigation into Anna was moving forward. I was introduced to Officer Michael McCaffrey, who was working with Assistant District Attorney McCaw and had been copied on the email. Officer McCaffrey replied a few minutes later. "Hello Ma'am," his email began. He gave me his phone number and said I should feel free to contact him whenever I had a moment. The footer of his email identified him as a police officer in the NYPD's Financial Crimes Task Force. Although it was after six o'clock, I called him right away. Looking for privacy, I first sat on the roof deck, but then I came down and, barefoot, walked in circles around the yard. I told Officer McCaffrey as much as I knew. Now and then, he chimed in with a question.

After the call, I emailed him a zip file of my Operation Clarity folder, along with my notes on how I met Anna and the beginning of our "friendship." Then I forwarded a couple of relevant videos via text message. It was reassuring to open such an instant and accessible line of communication with someone whom I associated with safety. I told Officer McCaffrey that I was available and glad to remain involved in whatever capacity would be most useful. I imagined it would be just a matter of time before Anna was apprehended.

Returning to New York was unexpectedly destabilizing. Out of necessity, I had built up an emotional callus that allowed me to function in the midst of extreme stress. I hadn't noticed my callus before the trip to Cape Cod, but when I got home, rested but raw, I was abruptly struck by its absence.

We came back on a Sunday night. The next morning, as usual, I began my day by checking Anna's social media for anything new, which there hadn't been for weeks. My heart leapt. There were two new posts on her InstaStory. The first had been posted eleven hours prior: a close-up of thirsty-looking banana palm leaves in front of a red tiled roof. Anna wasn't in New York. The picture was too tropical, too green, too sunny.

The next post was from ten hours prior: thick red and white stripes filled the frame. Was it a pool chair? A painted wall? At the right edge of the image, I recognized Anna's foot and a sliver of her calf. Her toenails were painted blood red, and she was wearing sandals I hadn't seen before: rattan with a strip of circles, maybe seashells, that ran from her toes to her ankle. It was the week before Anna was scheduled to appear in a Manhattan court to face three counts of misdemeanor theft of services, and I felt certain that she was on the West Coast. I took screenshots of both images and texted them to Officer McCaffrey. And just to be sure everyone was aware, I also emailed them to the District Attorney's Office.

Seeing the posts from Anna was enough to shake my foundation, but what really knocked me down was the news from American Express just an hour later. I saw the email in my in-box: "An important message is ready for you to view in the American Express Secure Message Center." I logged in immediately. The message pertained to my personal card: "During our investigation, we contacted the merchant on your behalf and requested them to either provide an explanation or issue a credit for the charge in question. In response to our inquiry, the merchant has provided copy of signed charge receipts along with itemization which we have included for your reference . . . Therefore, the amount under review [$36,010.09] has been reapplied to your account, and will reflect on an upcoming statement."

White-hot terror. The attached receipt was the "preauthorization" slip I had signed when the La Mamounia staffers told me it was for a temporary hold. I called Amex while I walked down the West Side Highway toward my office. Again, I spoke to a series of representatives, and again I unraveled. By the time I got to Battery Park City, I was hyperventilating. I watched goldfish in the Lily Pond of Rockefeller Park as I struggled to slow down my breathing. After hearing my story (yet again), Amex agreed to refile my dispute. They were sympathetic and attentive; it was just that their boxes were square and my story was round.

That evening, at home in bed, I ended the day just as I had begun it, with a look at Anna's social media. On Instagram, she was at it again. In only the hour before I checked, she had posted a suggestive photograph of her bare legs, extended and crossed as she lay on a couch, with black fabric draped around her thighs. I scanned for any details that could be used to identify her location: the pattern on the couch, the style of the lamp, olive-green shapes on the white curtains.

While I was looking at my phone, Anna posted again. This time it was a self-portrait of her reflection in a full-length mirror. She was leaning against a doorway, wearing a black leotard with long sleeves and no pants. The photo was cropped so that it appeared off-center. The camera flash obscured most of her face. Only her right eye was visible.

Knowing that Anna and I were online at the same time made me feel strangely exposed, as though we were connected and she might somehow feel my presence. Likewise, it felt as though I should be granted special insight into her—what she was doing, who she was with, and where she was.

I sent screenshots to the District Attorney's Office, as usual. Any new piece of information that reached me—an Instagram post, for instance—

carried with it a certain energy. When it got to me, I held on to it long enough to interpret what I could, then by passing it along, I did my part to keep the current moving.

Tuesday, August 29, was a rainy day in Manhattan. It was the week before Labor Day, one of the last days of summer. Thankfully, it was quiet in the *Vanity Fair* office, so no one noticed when I slipped out for a two p.m. meeting at the District Attorney's Office.

Anna was the target of a grand jury investigation. In preparation for the hearing, ADA McCaw, who was prosecuting the case, wanted to ask me some questions in person. She asked that I bring a few items to the appointment, in particular an itemization of charges relevant to Marrakech. I was prepared.

The meeting was brief. I answered the queries and left my documents behind for review. The prosecutor was still deciding whether or not I would testify—if I did, it would take place the very next afternoon. She would let me know by tomorrow morning at the latest. With that, I walked home to await news.

Later that afternoon, when I was going through my miscellaneous papers from Morocco, I rediscovered the zippy pouch in which I'd kept every receipt. Nestled among them, I found an unrelated boarding pass. It was from Anna's flight to New York on February 18, when she dropped back into my life. "Anna Sorokin" flew business class on Air Berlin from Düsseldorf to JFK. Düsseldorf is a forty-five-minute drive from Cologne. I wasn't sure what to make of it, but seeing the ticket on this day of all days felt like the closing of a circle.

As usual, I passed the new bit of information along to the District Attorney's Office. In a separate email, four minutes later, I received word that they would like me to testify.

That evening, a compulsory scan of Anna's social media revealed a posting spree. A bevy of new photos had appeared on her Instagram page. The first three were all the same: nondescript palm trees against a blue sky.

Then there was the banana palm tree, again, against a red tiled roof. But one new photo caught my eye: *Nature morte*, read the caption. It was an image of Anna's foot resting in a small bowl with decorative leaves and a plum, among a collection of items on a wooden coffee table. Just beyond Anna's toes, an amber-hued candle was lit. And resting at the base of the candle was a chorded, forest-green tassel set in brass. I recognized it.

I did a quick Google Images search, just to be sure: "Chateau Marmont room key."

That was it. I knew it from past visits to the hotel for photo shoots. And the candle was the hotel's signature Alessandra candle, honey-amber with frosted glass. The rest fell quickly into place as I re-examined Anna's other recent posts: the lamp and curtains matched an image of the hotel's garden cottage; the thick red and white stripes were on a wall next to the pool. I had no way to know whether she was still there, but Anna's photos had been taken in Los Angeles. I arrived at the District Attorney's Office the next day at noon to be prepped before my testimony. When I got to the sixth floor, I sat down on a wooden bench to wait for McCaw. There were others waiting, too. Each of us was wearing a guest pass provided by the security guard downstairs. I glanced at the sticker on the man sitting next to me—and I recognized his name. Although we'd never met before, he was someone I'd heard Anna talk about. I had given his name to the ADA.

It was possible the prosecutor had found him independently, but I couldn't be sure. I had hoped that providing information to the investigative team would be useful, of course, but without their feedback I couldn't really tell if it was. Now, seeing this man here, I experienced a private feeling of affirmation. I was on target and my efforts were coming to fruition.

After a short lunch break, the other witnesses and I followed the prosecutor from the DA's office to another municipal building nearby. Inside, we were shown to a fluorescent-lit waiting room. It was *Office Space* meets Sunday school with a side of *Law & Order*. The room was lined with rows of battered and repurposed church pews facing a partial wall, on which hung two photographs: one of the Manhattan skyline at night with two vertical columns of light representing the Twin Towers, in remembrance of the September 11, 2001, attacks, and the other of the 9/11 Memorial fountains. Two houseplants poked up over the top of the wall: one was upright but slanting funny, and the other hung down between the two photos. There was nothing else to look at in the dull, utilitarian space.

Grand jury proceedings are held in private—no judge, no Anna, no opposing council—just a jury, the prosecutor (ADA McCaw), a court reporter, and one witness at a time. We had no indication of the timing or order in which we would testify. Periodically, McCaw would appear to call a name. A small group of us sat waiting for hours without speaking. At last, I broke the silence. Without divulging the specific nature of our testimony, we spoke lightly about the one thing we had in common: Anna.

I was one of the the last witnesses to testify. When it was my turn, I awkwardly lowered my tote bag to the floor, resting it against the wall, before turning to face the roomful of Manhattan grand jurors, nearly two dozen faces dotting curved tiers of seating that reminded me of a college classroom. There was a small table at the front of the room, and I sat behind it. The court reporter sat to my left, and ADA McCaw stood at a podium to my right, next to a projector. The foreperson, a young woman about my age, sat in the center of the back row and asked something along the lines of, "Do you swear to tell the truth, the whole truth, and nothing but the truth?" I did.

ADA McCaw began her questioning. "Good afternoon . . . Can you please state your name and county of residence for the record?"

"Rachel DeLoache Williams, New York County."

"Are you acquainted with someone by the name of Anna Delvey?"

"I am."

"How do you know Anna Delvey?"

"She was my friend."

I returned to the church pews after my testimony, which had taken longer than anyone else's. A couple of other witnesses were still there, waiting to be formally adjourned. I cast them a sympathetic glance, mindful that I had kept them waiting. McCaw let us know that it was the last day of the hearing, so we sat outside while the jurors cast their votes. They filed out in front of us when they were done. The experience was anticlimactic because we didn't get to hear the verdict. If they voted to indict, an arrest warrant would be issued. And then, only after Anna was arraigned, would the indictment be unsealed—that's when I'd get to hear the full scope of the charges. And if the jury chose not to indict—well, I wasn't really sure what would happen then.

On the last day of August, the day after I testified, I booked a flight to Tennessee for that same evening. I chose a return flight for the morning of Wednesday, September 6, the day after Anna was due to appear in criminal court to face misdemeanor charges. I was depleted, and felt that the trip would not only be relaxing but would also help put my parents' minds at ease. Though they were careful not to be overbearing, they had each been in touch with me separately to express their ongoing support and concern.

Before leaving for my flight, I received another secure message from American Express. They requested "a detailed letter describing the events surrounding [my] claim." I planned to write it while I was in Knoxville.

After work, I stopped by my apartment to quickly pack a bag. Nick had been traveling since the first week of August, and with no one else around to watch my cat on such short notice, I decided to bring her with me. Boo and I landed in Knoxville just before midnight.

The weekend passed without incident. I caught up on sleep, watched movies, and lounged around. Although I was glad to see my parents, I behaved like a total thin-skinned grump—overly sensitive and terribly cranky. Luckily, my family understood. Aside from the time I spent debriefing my parents, the days were largely Anna-free. Until Monday morning, on Labor Day, when I received a message from Officer McCaffrey. He needed a few details for his report and asked if I knew whether Anna was back in New York. She hadn't posted anything since the photos from Los Angeles, so I wasn't sure.

My Friend Anna

The following day was Tuesday, September 5, Anna's court date. During my morning check of her social media, I saw that she'd shared three new photos on Facebook. There was no location tagged: just three close-ups of her head—lips pouty and eyes blank, as usual. In the background of one, I could see a white umbrella, like those next to the Chateau Marmont pool. There was no way to know when the picture was taken, but I alerted Officer McCaffrey, just the same.

He texted back with a question: *You said she was really intent on not missing court, right?*

Yes, I told him, because that's what Anna had said at the Frying Pan. If she missed her court date to face the misdemeanor charges, she was afraid that when she left the United States she would never be allowed to return. That word stuck in my head: *misdemeanor. Mis-demeanor. Mis*, meaning wrongly or opposite; *demeanor*, meaning appearance. That was Anna. *But I've heard so many lies from this person it's hard to know what to believe,* I added.

Would she still respond to your calls/texts if you were, in theory, to reach out to her?

An ominous question, but I told him that the likely answer was yes.

Chapter 17

Turning

When my cell phone rang, I stepped onto the back porch of my parents' house to take the call. ADA McCaw and Officer McCaffrey were both on the line.

"She didn't show up," said ADA McCaw.

I should have known. When given a choice between two paths, Anna always took the one that was more dramatic. Through the fine mesh of my parents' screened-in back porch, I studied the trees, watching their leaves catch the wind and sway. September was a time for turning.

"If you were to text Anna, do you think she'd respond?" asked McCaw.

My heart snagged on a beat as I paused to reconsider the likelihood.

"Yes," I told her, just as I'd told McCaffrey.

It wouldn't be hard, I reassured myself as I hung up the phone. Just another shot in the dark. What was the worst that could happen? Silence?

It was the first text I had sent to Anna in almost a month. The tone was like that of so many texts that had come before, but now the purpose narrowed, as did the feeling of who was in control. My goal was to re-establish contact, and uncover her location. I sent the message at half past two: *Hey Anna. I've been thinking about you today, as I know you had that court date. I wondered how it's gone for you. In thinking back through everything, I can tell you must have gotten into some sort of situation that I don't understand. I can't imagine you intended for things to turn out the way they have. It seems like you must have gotten into trouble somehow. I'm sorry that you didn't feel like you could tell me the full story—and I'm sorry you're in this mess, however it happened.*

I meant what I said.

In case Officer McCaffrey had feedback, I took a screenshot of the overture and shared it with him. He approved. When Anna didn't respond, I followed up over the course of the day with gentle inquiries that ran little risk of betraying my motives. I knew better than to rush it.

Anna said nothing. News of her skipped court date appeared in the *New York Post*: "Wannabe socialite skips court, now faces arrest," which meant it was now public knowledge that she was wanted by the police. She must have known that, too.

When I touched down in New York the next morning, I pinged Anna with a question mark. Her silence lasted until almost five that afternoon.

I'm in a hospital since Monday, her text said. *Bad reception.*

I responded immediately with a barrage of questions: *What??! Are you ok? Are you in NYC? Should I come by? I remember you hadn't been feeling well. What happened?*

But she was done with answers for the day. A hospital? I remembered her heavy drinking, I thought of her suicidal impulses, and I wondered.

I sent everything to Officer McCaffrey, as usual. He was receptive but wanted to be sure I wasn't overextending myself emotionally, given that I was a victim in the case. I assured him that this type of contact was not outside the realm of what I'd be doing if I still didn't know the truth about Anna. Yes, I was nervous, but I was within my comfort zone. And, besides, if I didn't do this, who else could?

Officer McCaffrey and I made plans to meet later in the week, to re-examine my information and to see if there was anything he might have missed.

When I woke up the next morning, I saw Anna's next text.

In CA, it read.

Broad. California is a large state. Then again, progress was progress. I sent a screenshot to Officer McCaffrey. He suggested I ask for an address to send flowers, but I was afraid that Anna would see through any line of questioning that was too direct. Instead, remembering how badly she had wanted to see that *Mirage* installation near Palm Springs, I took a roundabout approach: *Are you out of the hospital now, and ok? Did you finally go to see Doug Aitken's glass house?*

After that, I waited.

At noon, the staff at *Vanity Fair* received an unusual email asking us to gather immediately outside of the planning room. The space was too small for our head count, and we overflowed into the hallway. After a few minutes, our editor in chief, Graydon Carter, appeared and announced that after editing the magazine for twenty-five years, he would be stepping down at the end of the year. Everybody was shocked and upset. It was as though someone had died—not Graydon, but *Vanity Fair* as we had known it. We had always known it would happen one day, but that did little to lessen the impact.

Then again, my world was already so out of whack that more change felt inevitable. Clichés are clichés for a reason: When it rains, it pours.

When I got back to my desk, I sent another text to Anna: *Do you need help? Where are you and what happened? Still in the hospital? Now I'm worried!!!* While I waited for her to respond, I confirmed a meeting with Officer McCaffrey for the following day.

Anna got back to me that evening as I was leaving the office.

Still here, she said.

I had just finished sending a screenshot to Officer McCaffrey when a second text came in: *Why dont you stay away from my toxicity like you suggest others do.*

Who had she been talking to? *Toxicity*—I had used that word in reference to Anna many times. Where had she heard it? We began a game of psychological jujitsu.

Five minutes later, I wrote back: *Anna, I have been TOTALLY freaked out. You can't blame me for trying to figure out what is going on. The amount of money outstanding is HUGE to me. I've been extremely upset. And then you went totally silent.*

Why should I be on the defensive? I sent another text two minutes later:

I can't believe that you think it's acceptable to be mad at ME in this situation. I'm the one checking on you even though you owe me almost 70k.

Nearly fifteen minutes passed. I sensed an open channel and instinctively knew that it was time to push, to lean in while I had the chance. I continued: *I've spent so much time with you since February and it seems like everything has just spiraled. When you stopped communicating I just kept thinking about everything. I thought maybe since it's Sept, you could actually access your trust and things would get better. I'm truly sorry that your family or whatever support you have hasn't come through for you sooner. It just seems like it's all unraveled. And as mad and desperate as I've been, I also feel sorry for you and worried. Why are you in a hospital?*

She didn't respond, but I had faith the message would land.

———

The Starbucks on the corner of Johnson and Gold Streets was busy at eleven o'clock the next morning. Three steps inside, I spotted Officer McCaffrey, seated but obviously tall, square jaw, slick hair, and with a gun on his waist. He stood to shake my hand. It was the first time we'd met in person. I ordered a coffee and took a seat. We went through the story again, from start to finish, and I answered his questions. He didn't divulge any new information, but the meeting in itself felt productive. At the very least, I was glad to put a face to the name.

After leaving the Starbucks, I sent another text: *Anna? I've restructured so much of my life to support this huge debt. I'm having constant panic attacks. The least you could do is communicate. I'm truly sorry to hear that you're in a hospital. What is happening to you?*

Three minutes later, I got a text from a random server who used to work at Le Coucou. Anna and I had gone to visit him once in his new job at some other bar, where he wore Hawaiian T-shirts every day. His message seemed benign, but its timing was suspicious.

Hey how have you been? he asked. If he was in touch with Anna, she could have been using him as bait, so that I might divulge my true opinions and motives. Act natural, I told myself.

Hey, I'm okay—how are you? I wrote.

I'm good! It's been a while!! he replied.

Yes!! Things ok for you at work? Still wearing the 🌼 🌻 🌸 *shirts?*

Of course I am. I miss seeing that pretty face of yours!

It has been a while, I noted.

Too long!! What's new with you?

Why was he asking? Was he just making small talk or was he digging for information?

Getting excited for the fall. Just hanging in there. Working hard. And you? I asked.

I love the fall!! Working hard as always but making sure to have fun. You need to come and visit me.

This conversation was going nowhere. It was entirely possible, even probable, that he was merely hitting on me, but at this stage of the game, wherever Anna was concerned, it behooved me to assume the worst—that he was her spy. I answered with a superficial *Oh do I?* and went quiet.

That afternoon, Officer McCaffrey asked me whether Anna had a Snapchat. She did, I told him, though she rarely used it. It was only by spelling out her Snapchat username in a text that I saw it with fresh eyes: *delveyed.* It read like a verb, and it described what had happened to me. Had Anna known that when she chose it?

The rest of the day went by, and Anna still hadn't responded to my texts.

I sent one message on Saturday: *does your family know that you're in the hospital?*

And another on Sunday: *I hope you are ok.*

Finally, on Sunday night, I received a response: *My family's accountant will arrange for your payment hopefully this week.*

Back to that old game again! Just when I thought it was over. It was a language of engagement we both knew so well. Well, if that was her chosen tongue, so be it. I would play along. Was I to believe that reimbursement was coming? Was she hoping I would silently wait?

Not wanting to scare her away, I let the message sit unanswered. We were busy in the office that week, anyway, prepping for the New Establishment Summit, which was quickly approaching. I would travel to Los Angeles in less than a month to help with production for Annie Leibovitz's group portrait of the conference speakers. Maybe Anna would still be in California. The Instagram posts from the Chateau Marmont made me think there was a good chance she could even be in LA.

On Monday afternoon, I attended a meeting to review plans for the photo shoot. Afterward, when I had a moment, I went back to Anna and gently pushed for more insight. *That would be an enormous relief,* I told her. *Are you back in NY yet? How are you feeling?*

Another day went by. Part of me wished that my investigation hadn't been quite so thorough before I found my way to the District Attorney's Office. Clearly I had touched on something (or contacted someone) that rocked Anna's trust. Then again, I had done only what any rational person would have: I had tried my best to solve the puzzle. She was just being paranoid, though perhaps rightly so.

On Instagram that evening, Anna hid all of the photographs in which she'd been tagged. Her account stayed up, but an entire section disappeared, the one that showed posts by other people in which she'd been identified. I had already taken screenshots of the photos she removed, so I sifted through them for clues. What was she trying to hide? Or was she merely pruning her personal "brand," knowing that people would be looking?

I walked to work on Wednesday, and not long after I arrived a text message appeared from Anna: *Im still in California, they will reach out in coming days.*

I assumed "they" referred to the family accountant. It was the third time she'd told me she was in California, but her answer wasn't getting more specific. *Ok. When are you coming back?* I replied. *I haven't seen you in over a month.*

I was hoping to hurry things along, but once again Anna was slow. In the interim, out of the blue, I heard from Kate. When she asked how I was doing, I gave an honest answer, and like a good friend, she gently pried. I expanded: *It's a bit complicated but I'm ok. Just went through a really hard time with that person who owed me money . . . haven't been paid back and don't think I will be. Plus Graydon announced he's leaving V.F. at the end of the year so everything is about to change in a huge way at work. and Nick and I aren't doing well. He's been abroad for over a month and [is] not communicating much. It's been a hard few months.* Seeing my own recap, put so succinctly, I suddenly understood why I was bone-tired.

Kate had the perfect series of reactions, beginning with *Oh my god Rach!!!!!!!!! You gotta tell me these things!!!!!* and closing with *I am here for you and love you.* It was a relief to have another ally in the know.

On Thursday, I was in Pier 59 Studios for a photo shoot of actress Hong Chau. The photographer was Erik Madigan Heck. In between set-ups, and after another day of silence from Anna and a conference call with Officer McCaffrey and ADA McCaw, I gathered the nerve to call Anna's phone. Since I dreaded the thought of hearing her voice, it was a relief when she didn't answer. I followed up with a text for good measure: *Tried calling you. Are you still in the hospital? What're you doing in CA?* Still no response. I sent parallel messages on Facebook Messenger and could see that she was reading them. What would it take for her to respond?

Worrying that she was really gone this time, at midday on Friday I decided to get creative. When I opened Snapchat to see whether she'd posted, I noticed a filter that I knew she would like. I used it to take a black-and-white picture of myself. A large satin bow appeared in my hair, centered like a baby doll's headband. The effect also enlarged my eyes and gave them exaggeratedly long lashes that looked a lot like Anna's extensions. I held my mouth in a pout and kept my long hair in front of my shoulders. My resemblance to Anna was exceptionally creepy—I had a hunch that it might work. On top of the image, I wrote a short message: "This Snapchat filter is very you." I hit Send.

That afternoon, five minutes after I sent another wave of text messages, Anna finally replied: *Bettina or someone else will reach out to you regarding the payment.*

And then another: *Im also aware of the messages you are/have been sending to other people and other comments from your side.*

She knew exactly what to say to mess with my head. Again, I wondered if my phone had been tapped. What did Anna know, and how? Or was this intimidation tactic just part of her skill set? If so, bring it on.

Not sure what you're referring to, I replied. *It's insane that I haven't been paid back after this long. You have no place to question my behavior in this situation. You haven't given me a straight answer to my questions in months.*

I was daring her to tell me the truth, which was hardly likely to happen, but at least I was on offense. I went on: *When are you coming back/can we just meet to go to the bank? What are you even doing in CA?*

I followed up the next day: *still no straight answers? I was such a good friend to you. I cannot understand how you think this behavior is excusable. At the very least you could be direct with me.*

———

The Florida Gators beat the University of Tennessee Volunteers with a sixty-three-yard Hail Mary touchdown in the final seconds of the football game on Saturday, September 16. My brother, Noah, and I watched from my apartment, and afterward we decided to go for a walk before grabbing some dinner. Without a specific destination in mind, we took a tour of SoHo. Noah pointed out the office where he'd just begun a new job as a video producer for a company called Group Nine Media. Meandering from there, we playfully bickered about who knew the neighborhood's streets better: me, who'd lived nearby for six years, or Noah, who'd worked there for less than two months.

My Friend Anna

Just before we settled on a spot for dinner, I got a message from Anna saying she would call me by Monday. The thought of her deflated my mood. By the time Noah and I entered Café Gitane, at the corner of Mott and Prince Streets, I was quiet and a little depressed. We sat at a table by the window, and I anxiously sipped water to calm my nerves. When the waitress brought over menus, I scanned mine briefly, recognized its French-Moroccan influence, and knew that it was time. Once my glass of wine arrived, I began to tell Noah the story. I started with the trip to Marrakech and brought him all the way up to the present. You could see on his face that it was a lot of information to digest. He listened with complete attention, such that when his dinner course arrived, he reached down to move it aside without thinking and promptly burned both of his hands. He spent the second half of our meal holding a glass of ice in each palm in an effort to soothe the burns. We would have laughed about it if the mood hadn't been so low. I could feel that he was sad for me, and that in turn made me sad, too. But somehow that sadness worked to bring us closer.

It was that same weekend that I focused on compiling supporting documents for American Express. I wrote a detailed letter describing the events surrounding my claim—"Anna Delvey (aka Anna Sorokin) was a friend," it began.

I also included copies of relevant email correspondence, an itemization of charges (along with receipts), and press clippings from the *Daily News* and the *New York Post*. I added mention of the grand jury hearing, hoping it might lend credence to my case.

Unsurprisingly, Monday came and went without any word from Anna.

The prolonged back-and-forth kept playing out in the background, while I made a simultaneous effort to put my energy toward the people in my life whom I really cared about. For me and many of my best friends, the time from our late twenties to our early thirties was a period of major transition. Kate was newly married. My other best friend, Taylor, had just gotten engaged. My friend Holly was to be wed within the month. Liz had just bought a condo. And Kayla was the first in my friend group to become pregnant. Something in my experience with Anna deepened my understanding of relationships, and reminded me how important it is to show up for the people you love. Financially, I was so deep in the hole that buying a flight to San Francisco for later in the month—to celebrate Taylor's engagement and to attend Kayla's baby shower—felt like a small drop in a big bucket. These people, these friendships, and these milestones were my priority, and I wanted to honor them through my actions.

By the end of the following week, I had recovered enough strength to resume communication with Anna. *Still haven't heard anything,* I nudged.

She responded at half past three that afternoon to say that she was *sorry for the delay.*

It's been four months, I replied. "Sorry for the delay" hardly seemed sufficient.

Are you back yet? I asked.

No, she replied.

I wish we could just go to a bank and get this over with. I'll be in CA soon—will you be in LA?

I'll let you know, she answered.

When? What are you doing now?

I'll be here for another week or [a] bit longer, she said.

In LA you mean? I'll be out the first week in Oct.

Yes, she confirmed.

Officer McCaffrey was impressed with my progress, but even so, it began to weigh on me. Unlike Anna, I saw trust in a relationship as a value to honor, not to exploit, and as terrible as she had been to me, to break that trust from my side felt unnatural. Nevertheless, I went on.

I haven't seen you in ages. Are you ok? I asked.

I was in ny the whole time until end of august, dont recall hearing from you then, she replied.

Anna, I was so intensely frustrated and mad at you. I had to distance myself. This has been so dark for me. I was tired of running in circles so I told you to contact me when we could talk about me actually receiving reimbursement . . . and then I didn't hear from you. I've found ways to cope but the past four months have been hell. Please understand how awful this has been. I understand there may be circumstances beyond your control but this debt has never been something I was able to sustain.

Thirty minutes later, she replied: *I wasn't having the best time either as you might have noticed. Nothing worked out the way I planned and for you to assume any of this was my intention is insulting and disappointing. Considering the time we spent together, I thought you'd be able to see through the situation without sourcing outside input from people who barely know me. In any case, I'm looking [forward to] settling this with you as soon as possible.*

There was an element to her approach that felt familiar. I scrolled through our recent exchanges—had she borrowed that "I've spent so much time with you" tactic from me?

I was desperate. I'm sorry for that, I told her. *This whole situation makes me intensely sad.*

She responded: *Obv im not using this as an excuse for the delay with your repayment, it's a separate thing.*

Officer McCaffrey was shocked that Anna was so talkative. To me, her loquaciousness confirmed what I'd always suspected: that she was inherently lonely. This tugged at my sympathy just as it always had, but still I moved forward. Now that she and I had worked through our trust issues, it was time for a lighter approach. I made a comment about the weather in Los Angeles versus the weather in New York.

The weather is the least of my concerns honestly, she replied. *Just trying to work things out back to normal.*

Back to normal? *Ha. You and me both,* I answered. *I've been struggling to get out of bed.*

How is everything else? she asked. *Hope you didn't get in much trouble with your job.* How could she not realize? There was nothing in my life that was untouched by the immensity of my ongoing stress. Obviously she didn't understand the weight of the damage she'd caused. Her desire for connection, to some degree, felt real, but she seemed to lack the internal chip that would allow her to comprehend another person's feelings. Officer McCaffrey encouraged me to downplay the damage, to avoid scaring her away. I told her about Graydon's departure and spared her my incredulity.

Then I shifted the focus back to her: *Are you feeling better? Why were you in the hospital? If you don't mind my asking.*

I will tell [you] later in person eventually, Anna replied.

I'd ask if you're doing ok but I guess it sounds like you're working on it. Do you have a nice place to stay for now at least?

Her answer dodged my question: *Yes a little break from ny helped.*

You have friends to hang out with in LA at least? I probed. *I feel like you're such a New Yorker. With all your black clothes.*

A couple, she conceded. *Also not drinking for couple weeks now.*

That week, I'd received a random invitation to rapper/TV personality Action Bronson's book-launch event. Remembering how much Anna had liked him, I shared a screenshot of the email with her and said it was too bad she wasn't around. We were back in familiar territory, texting like old pals. We ignored the world closing in around us, but it was only a matter of time. Each of us had our secrets. I was no longer the naïf, but I kept up the guise in order to trick the trickster.

What day are you coming to LA? Anna asked me. *For the New Establishment thing right?*

A perfect opening. *Yeah, either Sept 30 or Oct 1. Probably the 1st. I think I'll be at the Four Seasons, maybe [the] Chateau. Where are you staying?*

I'm in Malibu for now, she said.

Chapter 18

Passages

Malibu. Where would Anna stay in Malibu? I was driven to finish the puzzle, and its final pieces were coming together faster than I even realized. On Monday morning, the week before my trip to Los Angeles, Anna and I continued our conversation.

Where are you staying? Are you going to be there for the next week? Or are you coming back to NY sooner? I asked, letting her know that I would arrive on Sunday.

I think I will still be in Malibu, she answered.

I wish my Soho House membership included the one in Malibu, I said, to keep the conversation light. The more we chatted, the more comfortable we became with each other.

Apparently it's for residents only, Anna replied.

Yeah, exactly. Blah. Last time I was in Malibu I stayed at Malibu Beach Inn, right next to Nobu 🍣 🍱 📧 👻 It's nice to be so close to the beach. I thought maybe this time she'd take the bait, respond to something in my commentary that would hint at her location. But after almost four hours of silence, I was afraid I'd overstepped, so my next message served as a chaser: *Had sushi on the brain so I just had it for lunch.* 👍

She replied within the hour: *Let's try to get together in LA next week.*

What did I think was going to happen? Hadn't this been the goal? Momentum was building, and yet, as the investigation moved toward its conclusion, I was uneasy. Why did I have to be the one to betray her? And would she know that it was me? Anna had flipped a switch and become the character I knew before Morocco. Her reversal messed with my head.

Once again, I felt like a person whom she had chosen to trust—like I had in the beginning, when she picked me as her friend. But I had trusted Anna, and look where that got me? Was my hesitation an indicator that I was still susceptible to her influence? Knowing as much as I did and still feeling pity, I imagined what might happen to others who knew far less. Still, I didn't want to do it. I wanted out of the situation entirely, but I was stuck—damned if I did, damned if I didn't. For the time being, I could only keep moving forward.

When Anna called that afternoon, I was coming from the office, on my way to take the ferry from Wall Street to Brooklyn for dinner. I answered spontaneously, emboldened by her opportune timing as I walked, ahead of schedule, along the East River toward the pier. Her voice was exactly as I remembered it, distinct and high-pitched. Her tone was casual, un-affected by the dramatic tension of our recent past. It was astonishing how quickly we slid into our old dynamic: two friends catching up on the phone.

"I'm in rehab," she confided. She was supposed to be there for thirty days, she explained, and she had been there for two weeks already.

"I'm glad you're getting help," I replied. For some reason, I didn't ask what for. Maybe I assumed it was alcohol, or maybe I believed she was really just there to hide from the authorities, and meet other people who she could potentially con. "Do you get to go to the beach much?" I asked, homing in on her location.

"Yeah," she confirmed, "they offer beach walks." The center was just across the Pacific Coast Highway.

How else did she pass the time, I asked—were there tennis courts on the property?

There were, she answered, but lately she'd taken up golf. The facility had a relationship with a country club in Calabasas.

And whom did she play with, I pressed.

She had made a few friends, she told me.

Anna had entered an enclosed center that catered to the wealthiest people in their most vulnerable state—of course she had made a few friends.

After less than ten minutes, the call dropped, and Anna texted to say that she was off to her next activity. I studied my notes from the conversation and began to do my research.

A fair number of luxury rehab centers dotted the stretch of the Pacific Coast Highway near Malibu, but Officer McCaffrey and I focused on two, Promises and Passages, both of which closely resembled Anna's descriptions. Costing upward of $60,000 per month, the latter billed itself as the world's most luxurious addiction rehab center—and as such, for Anna, it seemed the likeliest choice.

Even though it felt like we were getting close, due to health care privacy regulations it wasn't so easy to check. Clinics were not required to admit law enforcement officials, nor to confirm whether a certain person was in residence. Assuming Anna knew as much, you had to give her credit.

The final week of planning for the New Establishment Summit was the most intense. Kathryn's assistant, Emily, and I stayed in the office until eleven p.m. almost every night. We wrapped up travel bookings and compiled scheduling documents. Once we were in Los Angeles, Monday would involve a full day of prepping, and the portrait itself would be broken up over the course of the two-day conference, on Tuesday and Wednesday. For each of the people to be photographed by Annie—Ava DuVernay, Maja Hoffmann, Anjelica Huston, Bob Iger, John Kerry, Richard Plepler, Shonda

Rhimes, and more than fifty others—Emily wrote out a short bio and gathered recent news for quick reference. Using headshots, I created a visual timeline for the shoot and then spent hours cobbling together supplemental research. By the time we landed in Los Angeles on Sunday afternoon, October 1, we were bleary-eyed but ready.

We switched on our phones after the flight to discover a company-wide email announcing that S. I. Newhouse, Jr., the chairman emeritus of Condé Nast, had died. I found a photograph of "Si," as he was known, taken by Jonathan Becker at the *Vanity Fair* Oscar party in 2000 and posted it to the *V.F.* photo department's Instagram account, choosing a quote from Graydon for the caption: *With [Si's] passing, at the age of 89, so goes the last of the great visionaries of the magazine business.* I was witness to an empire in transition.

Emily and I went directly from LAX to the Wallis Annenberg Center to help with the "load-in" and begin to set up. Two hours later, I was doing laps between our equipment holding room and the portrait site—firing off messages concerning a rental car, parking, raw almonds, wire baskets, a cooler with ice, water for the crew, and thumbtacks—when I received a message from Anna asking if I'd arrived. *Yes,* I told her.

Nice, where are you staying?

The Four Seasons, I answered, *but haven't been to the hotel yet. You still in your place?* I asked. *It's not Passages is it?*

Yes I am, she replied. *Pls don't tell anyone though.*

That place is supposed to be the best, I volunteered.

You can come visit, she deigned.

Anna seemed genuinely to miss our friendship. I was back in her favor.

Come visit today, she said again, offering to send a car.

There was just so much that she did not care to understand. Evidently, to her, my needs were an inconvenience.

I don't think I will have time to come to Malibu, I answered. *Are you free to come to Beverly Hills anytime in the next few days?*

Let me know your times, she said.

Could we do lunch on [October] 3rd?

Sure, she replied.

Nothing about this was easy. It seemed like Anna was sincerely happy that we were making plans again, and no matter how shallow she was, that weighed on my heart. Surely, there were elements to our friendship that contained some degree of authenticity. But what were they and what were they worth? For all I knew, everything was counterfeit—it's not as though Anna ever trusted me enough to reveal the core untruths that propped her up.

————————

Annie Leibovitz landed in Los Angeles on Monday morning, October 2. She came directly to the conference site and commenced with a full day of prep. Her large group portrait would be taken on an exterior set of wide steps adjacent to North Crescent Drive. Based on timing, and the research we'd compiled, she worked with Kathryn to map out a plan—deciding where each of the subjects would sit or stand within the composition.

I was working when I received another text from Anna: *Do you have time to come over to Malibu today by any chance? I need something from the outside.* Again, she offered to arrange for my car.

I'm on site all day, I replied. *What do you need?*

She asked me to give her a call. I said that I would in just a few minutes.

Around the corner, and out of the way, I first phoned Officer McCaffrey. It was the eleventh hour and I had doubts, not about whether Anna would show up to our lunch date—I was sure that she would—but about my willingness to proceed. What did I care if Anna got arrested? Whether she did or she didn't, the damage was already done. It wasn't going to reverse time, eliminate my stress, or restore my finances. Vengeance had never been my motive. For a long time Anna had scared me, but closer up she seemed less threatening. I harbored some lasting ill will, but how deep did it go? Was I really willing to instigate her incarceration?

Wasn't the surest way to clear Anna from my life simply to cut ties altogether? Was it possible to forgive her, to step back, and to move on? I'd come so far, but now I was hesitating, second-guessing.

The hardest obstacles to overcome were deep within myself: irrational loyalty, compassion, and passivity—collectively these were forms of self-sacrifice. Where did they come from? And how did they mark me? As naive? Damaged? Oh, how I hated the sensitive part of me that continued to make excuses for Anna, this person who had willfully dragged me through hell. Except it was this same sensitivity that set me and Anna apart. Even if empathy was partially to blame for my predicament, I had no wish to be without it. It was a weakness, but it was also a strength. I saw fellow people where Anna saw only pawns.

"Is this the only way she makes her money?" I asked Officer McCaffrey.

As far as he knew, deceit was her sole source of income.

Next, I called Anna. She asked if I would be willing to buy a large bottle of vodka and some bottles of Voss water, then pour out the water, transfer the vodka into the empty Voss containers, and finally bring the disguised vodka into her rehab in Malibu.

No, I told her. For starters, I was too busy with my job to leave, grocery shop, and spend hours in traffic driving from Beverly Hills to Malibu and back. So she came up with another plan. What if she had a courier do the grocery shopping? He could bring the items to me, I would repackage them at the Annenberg Center, give them back to the courier, and he would bring them to her.

"Is it even for you?" I asked.

"No, I don't do vodka," she said.

I wanted no part of it. I told her that the Annenberg Center was swarming with security. It would be much too difficult for a random courier to gain entrance, and I didn't have time to loiter around awaiting his arrival. It just couldn't happen. Catching myself, in an effort not to sound overly judgmental given the circumstances, I suggested that maybe we could figure it out tomorrow. She got off the phone quickly once she accepted that I wasn't going to help.

242

Back at the group-portrait site, I was seated on a lower step, leaning forward, elbows on my knees, holding very still. One at a time, other makeshift stand-ins moved into place around me. We relaxed in position as Annie studied our arrangement and her photo assistants checked the lighting. My cell phone buzzed at random, tucked within my back pocket. I ignored it until a break in the blocking session, and then pulled it out to check my messages.

How much time do you have for lunch tomorrow? Anna asked.

One and a half hours, I told her. (It wasn't true, but it didn't matter.)

Ok noon it is, she wrote back. *You choose the spot.*

I suggested a restaurant called Joan's on Third.

Ok, she said. *Do we need a reservation?*

I sent a screenshot to Officer McCaffrey. *Awesome,* he replied, *she can make one if she wants.*

Maybe make one? I'm not sure, I said to Anna.

They don't take any, she replied.

I think it's pretty casual, I answered. *They have delicious salads.*

I took another screenshot. *Perfect,* said McCaffrey.

God, it made me sad, lying like this. I could feel myself splinter—words on one side, actions on the other. How on earth had Anna done this for so long and with such apparent ease?

To help the Los Angeles Police Department identify her, Officer McCaffrey asked me to send him a few recent photos of Anna. Scrolling through my phone, a travelogue flashed before my eyes. Anna smiling in her sunglasses on the grounds of La Mamounia; walking through the souk, looking back at me with a grin; pouting in the self-portrait from her Instagram account; beaming, self-satisfied, at a table in Le Coucou. I guessed her height at five foot seven. *And she normally wears all black,* I added.

See ya tomorrow lady! I said to Anna, as I arrived at the hotel restaurant for a quick dinner.

Yes! she replied. *Will you be able to pick up the bottles for me before? I'm being driven by rehab people. Can't wait to see you. Been forever.*

It felt like forever, but in reality it had been almost two months to the day since I last saw Anna, when she had turned around to wave goodbye on the walk home from the Frying Pan. Had she forgotten that evening? It had been a condensed drama unlike anything I had ever experienced. The futility of hurled accusations bouncing off lies and shattering on the ground—it left me broken, injured in a way that may never fully heal. And what about her? It would take a mental-health professional to say for sure, but by this point it was my firm opinion that Anna was a sociopath. As far as I could tell, she ticked every diagnostic checkbox.

Had Anna experienced confrontations like the one at the Frying Pan before? How deep and how lasting were her bruises? She must have built up a tolerance. Conflict is inevitable if your every action is founded on self-obsession.

But then, I'm not sure that Anna could control her self-aggrandizing impulses—they seemed intrinsic to her nature. In Morocco, when I became collateral damage, she had made zero effort to protect me. Quite the opposite, she used me as her shield. Her selfishness was hard-wired, and because of it she made that choice. Was she sorry? Yes, but sorry like a child who had broken her favorite toy. She used me up and was sorry when I was gone—not sorry for my anguish but sorry for her loss. Now Anna was staying in a facility that cost more than she owed me, and not only was she unapologetic, she was asking me for favors. It was as if Marrakech had never happened.

Once upon a time, not long ago, I had been living my life and doing just fine. Anna's presence in my world had occurred suddenly and quickly expanded. Her influence spread undetected. While she bought me dinners and invited me on vacation, I deluded myself into thinking that, as reciprocity, my understanding, time, and attention would be enough. Meanwhile, under the guise of friendship, she tethered herself to my core. With every hour we spent together, her power grew. Where I felt connection, she felt control. Before I knew it, I was coming to rely on her. After Morocco, all that remained was a void—my life, hollow; her promises, empty; our friendship, without meaning.

I felt the loss of Anna, not as she was but as I had once perceived her to be. When I lost that, I lost a part of myself. When I became disillusioned with my friend, I became disillusioned with my faith in the innate goodness of all people.

Our final text exchange took place on October 3, 2017, starting at 8:39 a.m.

———————

Anna: Can you talk now?

Me: Sorry. Not right this second. Call you ASAP.

Anna: I'm leaving here now, not sure i'll have reception until our date, see you there.

Anna: prob be there bit early.

Anna: If you get a chance to get like 3 vodka bottles and big water bottle 1 or 2 to fill that in.

Me: Ok see you soon!! Sorry it's crunch time here.

Anna: And maybe 1 bottle of white wine with screw top and ice tea to pour that into.

Anna: Thank you.

Anna: See you at noon.

———————

The goal of the shoot was to achieve one group portrait containing more than sixty subjects, not all of whom were available to be photographed at the same time. Adding to the riddle, time with every subject was limited—a few minutes before or after speaking engagements—while town cars sat waiting and handlers stood by. For maximum efficiency, each subject's position was predetermined. The stairs outside of the Annenberg Center were dotted with little neon strips of tape: a left foot here, a right foot there. On Tuesday morning, a group of us divvied up small squares of paper, each one containing a headshot of a subject along with his or her name. We scurried

245

up and down the steps neatly taping our squares to the ground. It was my job to know where each person would go.

The text from Officer McCaffrey arrived at 9:18 a.m. *Call me,* it read.

I ducked around the corner, cell phone to my ear, bracing myself.

"They got her," he said.

Anna was arrested by the Los Angeles Police Department as she left Passages that morning. She was in custody, on her way to wherever it is that criminals who are arrested in Malibu are taken for booking. At noon, the very minute I was scheduled to arrive at Joan's on Third, I was of course still on location for the photo shoot. I sent a series of messages to Anna:

> Me: Hey, I'm running like 10mins late—almost there
> Me: Are you close?
> Me: I don't see you.
> Me: Anna?
> Me: I'm sorry I had to leave. Maybe you're at the wrong location???
> Me: Text me later when you get back on WiFi and we can find another time to meet.

I never went to Joan's on Third for lunch, so why bother pretending that I had? Was I afraid that she would discover my involvement in her arrest? Most definitely. But that wasn't the only reason. As Anna had done with me, I wanted her to believe my lie.

On Wednesday, Larry David wore photochromic glasses that darkened in the sunlight. As Annie was taking his picture outside the Annenberg Center, his glasses kept dimming into a shade that obstructed too much of his face. Eager to please, he would take them off and stash them temporarily inside his blazer until they regained their clear transparency. Then he would pull them out in a flash, like a cowboy drawing a pistol, place them on his face, and pose while Annie fired her shots. When the glasses darkened again, the process would repeat.

No one on set could keep from laughing, but I was distracted by my phone. Every few minutes, I received an incoming call from Houston, Texas. No matter how many times I ignored it, my phone would ring again. Eventually, I answered and I heard a robot make an announcement: "This is Global Tel. You have a collect call from—" I hung up.

And yet, in the same way that Anna kept reaching out to me, I found myself compelled to continue reaching out to her. Even though I knew she had been apprehended, I would send her text messages for days to come. Nothing profound, just pebbles dropped into an abyss. Each of us reached out wondering if the other one might be there.

A week later, I sent my last text to Anna: *Find it strange I haven't heard anything from you,* I wrote. And as sad as it was, I meant what I said.

Chapter 19

Rebalance

After her arrest outside Passages in Malibu on October 3, 2017, Anna spent twenty-two days in Los Angeles County's Century Regional Detention Facility. Officer McCaffrey picked her up from there on October 25. He would later tell me the story. It was the first time he'd seen her in person. He introduced himself and explained that he had come to take her back to New York County.

"Why am I going back to New York?" she asked.

"Because there's a warrant for your arrest," he said, unable to discuss the specific allegations without her counsel present—which was just as well, since she didn't even ask what the charges were.

On the five-hour flight, Anna sat calmly with Officer McCaffrey in economy class, read a magazine, and ate a vegetarian meal.

From JFK, he brought her directly to Manhattan Central Booking, where she would spend the night. As he was preparing to leave, Anna spoke up.

"Hey, can I ask you something?" she said.

Finally, he thought, she was going to ask him about the charges.

"Can you get me some contact solvent?"

Meanwhile, that same evening, I was texting back and forth with Kathryn. The *New York Post* had just published an article with the headline: WANNABE SOCIALITE BUSTED FOR RIPPING OFF LUXURY HOTEL, JET COMPANY. It described Anna as "a grifter socialite armed with an

249

alias and a taste for the high life" who had been "busted for ripping off a string of upscale businesses—including a luxury Moroccan hotel and a private jet company."

I wasn't mentioned, thankfully, though neither was La Mamounia. Instead, the article reported that Anna had "allegedly stiffed Sir Richard Branson's five-star resort Kasbah Tamadot out of a $20,000 bill after a months-long Moroccan jaunt."

The facts seemed a bit muddled (Anna had stayed in Morocco for less than a month) but the piece included the first public mention of the trip, which made me nervous that the paper would soon find out about and start reporting on my disastrous friendship with Anna. I was aware of my position as a *Vanity Fair* employee, as well as the daughter of a man running for Congress, and I really didn't want that to happen. I could see the headlines coming, dragging me, my employer, and loved ones through the mud.

I sent the article to Kathryn. *No mention of my situation thank god,* I texted.

If it comes out, it comes out, she replied. *It will not reflect poorly on you. Only on her.*

It suddenly occurred to me: regardless of whether my name was mentioned in the press, it would likely be revealed during the judicial process. I'd been so focused on the investigation, Anna's arrest, and, after that, my ongoing debt and emotional recovery that it just hadn't dawned on me that I could become part of the story. I sent a text to Officer McCaffrey. Yes, he told me, if press attended the arraignment, they might learn my name.

I relayed the news to Kathryn. *I'm going to deactivate my Facebook. Insta is private. Deleted my full name and workplace, although it can easily be googled. I'm dreading this. Just called my parents to give them a heads up,* I went on. *Turning off my website with contact info, too.*

It will be fine, she wrote back. *Might be a storm of interest but will pass . . . just ride it out like a good wave in Montauk* 🏄.

The arraignment is at 9:30 a.m. tomorrow, I told her. I was not going to be there. I had no desire to be in the same room as Anna. At the same time, the fallout of my relationship with her had consumed my life for so long now that I couldn't help but be curious to know what would happen.

Kathryn picked up on that. *I assume it is open to the public,* she replied. *I'll be there.*

The next morning, in a nearly empty courtroom at 100 Centre Street, within the criminal division of the New York State Supreme Court, Anna appeared wearing a disposable black jumpsuit. I saw photographs later that afternoon, after the press posted them online. Her hair was down and looked either oily or wet at the roots. A criminal-defense lawyer named Todd Spodek accompanied her. I wondered if he was the same lawyer Beth had spoken with. I wasn't sure. During the arraignment, Anna was formally charged with six felonies and one misdemeanor. Kathryn called me immediately afterward with three key updates: Yes, there was press. No, Anna was not offered bail. And yes, she entered a plea of not guilty.

The scale of the deception set out in the indictment came as a shock. I'd had no real understanding of the scope of her alleged crimes. She was being accused of stealing approximately $275,000 through a variety of scams, and of attempting to steal millions more. One of her most successful tactics was "check kiting," a fraudulent practice that takes advantage of the several days banks need for deposited checks to officially clear. First, Anna opened checking accounts with Citibank and Signature Bank. Then, she wrote checks from one account to the other. She didn't actually have the funds to cover the checks, but the money would show up in her account, and she would immediately withdraw it before the banks figured this out.

According to the indictment, between April 7 and April 11—around the same time she'd confirmed our reservation at La Mamounia—Anna deposited $160,000 in bad checks into her Citibank account and then transferred $70,000 out of that account before the checks bounced. In August, post-Marrakech, she opened an account with Signature Bank and deposited $15,000 in bad checks. She was able to withdraw approximately $8,200 in cash before those checks bounced. When Citibank and Signature detected the fraudulent activity, they shut down her accounts and contacted the New York Police Department.

Anna was also accused of falsifying documents from international banks—UBS in Switzerland and Deutsche Bank in Germany—showing overseas accounts with a total balance of approximately €60 million. The indictment detailed how she had taken these documents in late 2016 to City National Bank in an attempt to secure a $22 million loan for the creation of her art foundation and private club. When City National Bank denied the loan, she showed the same documents to Fortress Investment Group in Midtown. Fortress agreed to consider a $25 million loan if Anna provided $100,000 to cover legal and due-diligence expenses.

On January 12, 2017, Anna secured a line of credit on her account with City National Bank for $100,000 by assuring banking executive Ryan Salem that she would wire money from a European account to repay the loan within days. ("We always believed that she had money," Salem would later testify. "She seemed to speak the language. She understood the financial jargon that you need to know to interact and transact in this environment. . . . I went to bat for somebody who at the end of the day was not somebody to go to bat for.")

Anna gave the $100,000 to Fortress to cover the expenses associated with her loan application. The wire with City National Bank's reimbursement never materialized.

One month later, in February, Anna re-entered New York City—and my life. Fortress had already spent approximately $45,000 of Anna's City National Bank money on their due diligence. According to the *New York Times*, Spencer Garfield, a managing director at Fortress, later testified that Anna soon "ran into problems providing details about the origin of her wealth. For starters, she claimed to be born in Germany, but her passport showed she was from a Russian town." (I took this to mean that Anna had more than one passport, since the one she'd sent me a picture of to book her flight to Marrakech listed Düren, Germany, as her birthplace.) "When Mr. Garfield volunteered to go to Switzerland to meet her banker there [in order to verify her assets], [Anna] abruptly withdrew from the deal, telling him her father would just give her the money."

I remembered Anna telling me that her father had gotten wind of the deal and didn't like the terms. After Anna backed out, Fortress returned the remaining $55,000. According to the District Attorney's Office, Anna used this money to fund her lifestyle: personal training with Kacy Duke, her stay at the 11 Howard hotel, and shopping at Forward by Elyse Walker, Apple, and Net-a-Porter. Anna squandered tens of thousands of dollars within the span of one month. By March, her bank balance was negative $9,000, according to ADA McCaw. She never paid the private jet company Blade for the $35,000 plane she had chartered to Omaha in early May, on the weekend before our Morocco trip.

In the DA's press release announcing the indictment, my story also came out. "SOROKIN invited a friend on an all-expenses paid trip to Morocco," it read. "During the trip, SOROKIN offered her debit card for payment knowing it would be declined due to insufficient funds. . . . SOROKIN never reimbursed her [friend], and made excuses when asked about the status of the re-payment." Court documents included my first and last name, but miraculously the press didn't discover my job or associations. As Kathryn put it via text: *There must be a lot of Rachel Williamses in NYC.*

Nevertheless, I was on high alert. When I received a LinkedIn "connect" request from a features photo editor at the *New York Post*, I deleted my profile picture and set my account to private. I would continue to stay off the radar for months to come.

At the same time, I still owed American Express tens of thousands of dollars on both my corporate and personal credit cards. (I asked the colleague responsible for reviewing my corporate expense reports to ignore the charges from La Mamounia, which he did without question because there was a credit for that amount while Amex was reviewing my claim.) I finally accepted the loan offer from Janine to cover part of the balance on my personal account. This included the charges for the Morocco flights, the Villa Oasis trip, all of our lunches and dinners outside of the hotel, and the dresses Anna had picked out in the medina. Janine sent funds directly to American Express on my behalf. She and I drafted and signed a loan agreement, and I began making monthly payments toward her reimbursement.

This did not cover the La Mamounia bill, however, which I was still disputing separately. These charges were split across my personal and corporate cards, and the claims I'd filed with American Express were still pending. While waiting for the credit card company to reach a decision, I was not responsible for paying any of the charges in question.

Until they suddenly began reappearing on my monthly statements. American Express had investigated my case, contacted La Mamounia, and turned down my claims. I received the news while I was at work and immediately searched for a space where I could make a phone call in private. I found an empty cement stairwell that smelled of building materials and dust, sat down on the steps, and stared at the blue industrial pipe across from me.

"Representative," I said, the sound echoing off the walls. I heard the phrase "This call may be recorded for quality-assurance purposes." *Good,* I thought, *I hope everyone is listening.* I was tired of repeatedly describing what had happened. I was transferred from person to person until they found the right department. I told my story, my voice tripping midway over the lump in my throat. Then I overflowed with broken emotion.

I called, called, and called again, reopening the case, only to have the disputes closed once more and the charges reposted to my account. Every time it happened, I called to refile the disputes.

And then there was a breakthrough.

Two weeks after Anna's arraignment, I received a letter in the mail pertaining to my corporate card. "While pursuing your claim on the above referenced account from HOTEL LA MAMOUNIA MARRAKECH MOROCCO, we have maintained credit(s) of [$16,770.45] and advised you we would contact the merchant on your behalf." I skipped ahead frantically, overeager for the verdict: "our previously issued credit(s) will remain on your account."

I read the message five times before cautiously accepting that it *might* be good news. Then I took a photo of the letter and sent it to Kathryn and Nick to make sure they read it the same way.

I THINK this means that Amex has protected me from the charges on my corporate card!!!!!!!! I wrote.

Looks like it 🙏 *!!!!!!!!* Kathryn responded.

I think it might . . . . . !!!! 👆 Nick agreed.

At first I read it as the other way around, I replied, *but CREDIT was money issued back into my account. A charge would have been money taken out. Plus it's not showing up in my account so that seems to be a good sign. Good grief.*

I was scared to believe it but also too afraid to call American Express for clarification. (Could they change their mind?) But as time went on, my pessimism gave way to joyful acceptance, dampened only by the uncertain fate of the La Mamounia charge remaining on my personal card for $36,010.09, more than twice the amount forgiven on the corporate account. Considering Anna's indictment and the decision on my corporate account, surely more good news would follow, right? I dared to think positive.

Given all of my progress, I had hoped that I would feel better during the ensuing winter months, but the truth is that I didn't. I remained depressed and struggled with constant anxiety. The monochrome gray of Manhattan in winter only made it worse. I also lost my grandfather right before Christmas, the one who lived in Spartanburg, South Carolina. He was ninety-six, surrounded by loved ones, and by his own account "ready to go" when he died. But there will never come a day when I don't miss him. I felt like I was always on the verge of tears and as if my breathing wasn't doing what it was supposed to, my lungs never seeming to get full. Writing everything down helped, so I focused on that as much as I could.

On January 30, 2018, the day after my thirtieth birthday and two months after the good news about my corporate card, I was walking from the subway to work when I received a message regarding my personal card. "We are crediting your account for $36,010.09," it read. "This credit will appear on an upcoming statement. We always aggressively pursue the arrest and prosecution of any individual(s) that have made unauthorized charges. If we need additional information from you we will contact you before 03/15/2018 or you may consider this case closed. . . . We regret any inconvenience you have experienced. Thank you for the opportunity to assist in this matter. Sincerely, Global Fraud Protection Services."

I stood stock-still in the Condé Nast lobby and broke down crying with joy and relief. I took a screenshot of the message and immediately sent it to my parents, as well as to Kathryn and Nick.

I can't believe it—I said to Nick—*I feel like I can breathe properly again.*

I texted the news to my closest friends. *I don't even have words for how relieved I am* 😭 🙏, I wrote. *I'm scared to even believe it but it's real. I fought hard. My claim was denied so many times. Cosmic that it happened today, my first full day of 30.*

It was the end of the nightmare—or so I thought.

Without explanation, in early March, the charge reposted to my account. I hadn't received a message of any kind. I had only logged in to the American Express website, and there it was. When I saw the balance, I started to shake. "I think there's been a mistake," I said on the phone. "I contested those charges, and the dispute was already resolved."

The representative said there was nothing in the system to suggest the decision had been reversed. She saw only the same message I'd received back in January, saying I would be protected from the $36,010.09 hotel charge. Of course, I wanted so badly to trust that she was right, but it seemed too good to be true. So, at the end of the day, I called again, to see if anything had changed.

This time I received the news I'd been dreading. American Express had, indeed, backtracked—after contacting La Mamounia regarding my claim and once again receiving the signed preauthorization slip as evidence.

"But you've known about that slip the entire time," I argued, insisting it had been signed under pressure and false pretenses. I had included clear mention of it in the written summary Amex had requested, describing the sequence of events surrounding my claim. "You knew about it when the decision was made in my favor, so why is it being brought up again now?"

The representative was sympathetic, but because there wasn't any further explanation in the system, he had nothing else to tell me. My best course of action, he said, would be to contest the charge again. So that's what I did. I reopened the dispute, and we started back at square one.

My Friend Anna

Unfortunately, the Amex reversal wasn't the only significant event of March 2018. As I was boarding a flight to Los Angeles for the *Vanity Fair* Oscar party, I received a LinkedIn message from a reporter named Jessica Pressler, who was working on a piece about Anna Delvey for *New York* magazine and was interested in speaking with me.

I kicked myself for not realizing that my LinkedIn account could still receive incoming messages. I panicked, didn't respond, and spent the next twenty-four hours wondering what to do. I had been writing about my Anna ordeal since the day after the Frying Pan intervention. To me, the narrative felt too long and complex to be shared in an article. But if it was going to happen, I decided, I wanted to tell my story myself, in my own words.

Vanity Fair published my article—a personal narrative, describing the making and breaking of my friendship with Anna—in April 2018, on the *Hive* section of its website. (The article subsequently appeared in the magazine's summer print issue.) *New York* magazine published Jessica Pressler's article, a comprehensive piece of investigative journalism, in late May.

I knew there was something about Anna that was *catching*, but I could not have anticipated just how big a media sensation she would become. My article was published on a Thursday, and almost immediately I was bombarded with a flood of messages asking about book, film, and television rights. On the following Tuesday, I received a message from an agent at CAA who had read my article and obtained my email address through a shared connection. At the time, I was feeling vulnerable, in over my head, and in need of wise counsel, so I gratefully accepted the agency's offer to help me navigate territory that was dauntingly unfamiliar to me.

Not long after that, HBO optioned my article for a potential film or television adaptation, and Netflix optioned Pressler's article for the same. Over the summer, people from around the world who had gone through similar experiences reached out to me. This reassured me that I had done the right thing by telling my story. And there was mutual comfort in knowing we were not alone. The support and encouragement I received from friends and strangers inspired me to keep on writing—especially since I knew there was a lot more to tell. So I spent most of the summer doing just that, writing down my story, while continuing my day job at *Vanity Fair*, which I still needed and very much loved.

Yet, there were bizarre consequences to the story's success, too. Walking through Manhattan's Greenwich Village in the fall of 2018, I saw a trendy-looking man in his mid-thirties, wearing a white T-shirt with the words "Fake German Heiress" on the front in black letters. I stopped dead in my tracks, staring in disbelief as I processed this strange twist in reality. It was as if I'd fallen into a dystopian TV thriller and might turn the next corner to discover a flash mob of strangers wearing Anna Delvey masks.

A quick Google search revealed a range of Anna Delvey–inspired T-shirts for sale, one of which read, "My Other Shirt Will Wire You $30,000." It bothered me to know that other people were laughing at something that had caused me such distress.

Still more people were clinging to Anna as an anti-Establishment hero. I understood the impulse to applaud someone who was taking advantage of the stereotypically self-important New York art scene, banks, and investment groups. But as a hardworking young woman from Knoxville, Tennessee, who had moved to the city with nothing but an entry-level job, it didn't feel like this interpretation of Anna and her crimes was quite accurate. Rather, it seemed like people were seeing only what they *wanted* to see in Anna, instead of who she actually was: a fraudster whose narcissism was despicable and whose scheming was indiscriminate.

And yet, faceless social media users cried out, "Free Anna." If Anna was the hero, where did that leave me?

I kept writing all through the winter. Even when it was hard, it felt cathartic and productive. Slowly but surely, everything that had come off the rails was getting back on track.

But then, in early January, I read in the *New York Post* that Anna had rejected an offer of three to nine years behind bars in exchange for a guilty plea. This was bizarre to me, considering that all of the evidence stacked up so heavily against her. (Swindling banks leaves a paper trail.) So I thought she would reconsider before her case actually went to trial.

Two weeks later, on a Thursday afternoon in January 2019, I was sitting with my headphones on in the *Vanity Fair* office listening to Nina Simone while organizing the files on my computer's desktop when an email arrived in my in-box with the subject line "People v. Anna Sorokin." It was from Assistant District Attorney McCaw. Anna's trial had been scheduled, and I was likely to be called as a witness. I wasn't braced for the news.

I immediately thought of having to see Anna in person, after so long, and the idea made me sick. When I walked through crowded places, I sometimes had the irrational fear that I would run into her, which always made me break into a cold sweat. I had no wish to ever see her again.

I tried to absorb what this meant, being asked to recount my experience in front of a roomful of strangers. Would there be press? Would I be able to find the right words? How would I keep from crying? No, there would be no chance of that. What if I passed out? Had that ever happened before?

And how would Anna look at me? Would she still think of me as a friend? I know the idea seems outlandish, but Anna had done exactly that, well past the point that most people in her position would have known our friendship was over. *Why hadn't she just accepted a plea deal?* I imagined she was ten steps ahead. There must have been a reason. Did she want a trial for the notoriety? I'd learned that in addition to optioning Jessica Pressler's article, Netflix had optioned Anna's life rights. Was she going to trial simply for the drama? For the publicity? Had this been her plan all along?

On February 5, I was sitting at my desk at work when I received a phone call from an internal number and a name I didn't recognize. I walked down the hallway to an office, as requested, and that's when I learned that I was being laid off due to corporate restructuring. The news came as a blow, but I had been in publishing long enough to know that these things were often unpredictable. In recent years, there had been a lot of turnover at Condé Nast. Kathryn had left the magazine before me, almost one year to the day, along with fourteen other top staffers, who were laid off after Graydon Carter's exit. In fact, I was one of the only ones left who had worked under Mr. Carter at *Vanity Fair*. I calmly packed up my belongings, without crying, until *V.F.*'s deputy editor called and graciously offered to connect me with some former colleagues of hers at other publications. Suddenly things felt very real. So when my desk was empty, Kathryn met me downstairs in her car to scoop me up—along with the office junk I'd accumulated over the previous eight and a half years—and we went out for a drink, toasting the bittersweet closing of a chapter.

Much of the next two months I spent dealing with everyday chores like switching my health insurance and cell phone plans and filing for an extension on my taxes. Nevertheless, the bulk of my time I devoted to writing. And I did a lot of writing. So much in my life had changed, and putting it into words helped me find meaning in the chaos and eased my anxieties.

Jury selection began on March 20, 2019. Initially, I tried to avoid reading about the trial in the news, but my friends and family sent me links to articles, and I couldn't resist. In his opening statement, Anna's lawyer, Todd Spodek, offered the jury a line from the song "New York, New York," made famous by Frank Sinatra: *If I can make it there, I'll make it anywhere.* "Because the opportunities in New York are endless," Spodek suggested. "Sinatra made a great new start here in New York, as did Ms. Sorokin," he said. "They both created a golden opportunity."

A great new start? I thought. *Assuming a false identity in order to cheat and steal?*

"Anna had to kick down the door to get her chance at life," Spodek continued. "Just like Sinatra had to do it his way, Anna had to do it her way."

It felt to me like Spodek was sugarcoating Anna's criminality—making it more palatable, not only to jurors but to the court of public opinion, and to the possible movie and TV-show audiences down the line. The crux of the defense was that "Anna had to fake it until she could make it," which, to me, sounded like a clear admission of guilt. As in, Anna had to fake it (commit the crime) until she could make it (get away with it). Even Spodek had to admit that my former friend's methods were "unorthodox" and "possibly unethical."

"Through her sheer ingenuity, she created the life that she wanted for herself," he argued. "Anna didn't wait for opportunities, Anna created opportunities. Now, we can all relate to that. There's a little bit of Anna in all of us."

Speak for yourself, I thought. But then again, if you were a criminal defense lawyer and your client had committed crimes leaving evidence so damning that it couldn't be denied—check fraud, for example—you would have to get creative, too. So I guess he was only doing his job.

The majority of the media coverage was focused on what Anna was wearing. This fascination had taken hold after she appeared in court wearing a black choker and a low-cut black Miu Miu dress. Photos of her courtroom outfits spread like wildfire across the Internet (under headlines such as *W*'s ANNA DELVEY'S COURTROOM CHOKER LOOK IS SO ON-BRAND). *GQ* then published a story reporting that "Soho Grifter" Anna Sorokin had a fashion stylist, Anastasia Walker, dressing her for the trial. This sent social media users into a tizzy.

I felt like I was watching some kind of a dark social experiment through a one-sided mirror. According to the *New York Post*, Netflix had staffers attending the trial. I also understood that, in addition to being Anna's criminal defense lawyer, Todd Spodek was representing his client in her entertainment dealings as well. So from the outside looking in—with press coverage and social media as intermediaries—it seemed to me that Anna was treating her own criminal proceedings as a business opportunity.

The press covered her every outfit and move. I scrutinized the photos of her, looking for any sign of guilt or remorse. It's true that there were pictures of her crying, but only beneath headlines referring to "FASHION MELTDOWNS." It was the same thing I'd witnessed at the Frying Pan, when she had said that she was crying because the *New York Post* had described her as a "wannabe socialite." As far as I could tell, Anna's emotions were more or less dependent on the way she appeared to the outside world.

When she seemed to like what she was wearing—according to *Elle* magazine, a plunging Michael Kors shift dress on one day, a sheer black Saint Laurent top with Victoria Beckham trousers on the next—she would walk brazenly into court, coyly smiling for the cameras, and turn around from the defendant's table to take stock of the crowd and bask in the attention. But when Anna *didn't* like what she was wearing, she put on a different show. According to the *New York Post*: "The haute ordeal began Friday morning when Sorokin, 28, arrived from Rikers Island in a tan prison-issue sweatsuit and refused to don the civilian outfit provided by authorities. An irritated [Judge] Kiesel sent her lawyer, Todd Spodek, into the holding cell to talk Sorokin into appearing. When the attorney came back, he said she was weeping and complaining of nausea. Sorokin told him that vindictive jail staffers were sabotaging her designer ensembles 'to interfere with her being able to wear the clothes.'"

"Again, with all due respect to your client, she seems a bit inordinately concerned about her clothing," New York State Supreme Court justice Diane Kiesel told Spodek, as reported in the *Post*. "This is a trial. She is a defendant in a criminal case. I am sorry if her clothing is not up to her standards, but she's got to be here."

To me, however, the press missed the bigger question: Where was Anna getting the money to fund her criminal defense, wardrobe included? Who was paying for her stylist (who, according to *Elle*, was "hesitant to reveal the exact details of her arrangement with Sorokin" but did disclose that she was "getting paid for the gig" and that she and Anna would "continue working together in the future")? Was Netflix funding any of this? Legally, Anna is not allowed to profit from her crimes. But Netflix can. I wondered what loopholes there might be in the law that would allow Netflix to act in their interest, and Anna's, by spending money to amplify and elevate Anna's case, as an investment in Anna Delvey, the phenomenon.

Or did Anna have some unknown benefactor who stepped in to finance her lawyer and stylist? Leading up to my testimony, these are the questions that occupied a certain space in my brain.

A few days before I was scheduled to testify, I discovered an article about Anna on the website of *Komsomolskaya Pravda*, a daily newspaper published in Russia. Anna's birth name was Anna Vadimovna Sorokina, it said. She was born in Domodedovo, a town twenty-one miles south of

Moscow. Her father had worked as a truck driver, and more recently selling air conditioners. Her mother had once owned a store, but after the birth of Anna's younger brother, she had become a housewife. (*So Anna does have a younger brother,* I thought to myself, wondering if he really played chess.) Anna's family left Russia for Germany in 2007, when she was sixteen, and moved to a small town called Eschweiler, thirty miles west of Cologne.

The article included quotes from several of Anna's former classmates in Russia. "[Anna] and I . . . were best friends," said one named Anastasia. "True, people were afraid of her. Anna is very strong in character, not everyone could stand it. Her mockery could easily hurt. But she always did it very subtly." This quote reminded me of a story that Anna once told me from her childhood. A girl in her class kept going home at the end of the school day with bruises, something that mystified the teachers, and Anna told me that she had been the one pinching her. At the time, I was unnerved to hear this and didn't know what to make of it.

I continued reading. Another classmate, Nastya, remembered that Anna's favorite movie was *Mean Girls*. Nastya said that she and Anna identified with the film's cruel but "popular" lead characters and liked that they were "negative heroines." To me, this explained a lot about the type of character Anna Sorokin was trying to emulate.

Toward the end of the article, I read a few quotes from a man named Vadim Sorokin, Anna's father—who was clearly *not* named Daniel Decker Delvey, as Anna had said. "There is nothing so special about this story. . . . Many people want to find out something about my daughter from me, but by and large I have nothing to do with it."

"She studied in Russia up to the 8th grade," he told the reporter. "In school . . . she was on the honor roll. Before the arrest, we did not know anything about her life in the United States. My daughter never sent us money. On the contrary, she took from us! Naturally, we are very worried about her. She has such a selfish character; we can't do anything about it. We gave her a normal upbringing. I do not know, by nature it is with her."

The words "by nature" jumped out at me. The term was awkwardly formal, I assumed, because of the translation, but it felt so true to my under-standing of Anna. Her self-centeredness and greed were *by nature*.

"To a certain extent, yes," said Anna's father, "naturally, she is guilty,"

On the morning of Wednesday, April 17—one year, eleven months, and two days after my departure from Morocco—I arrived at Foley Square, across from the District Attorney's Office. Stepping out of the cab, I clumsily slammed the door into my knee. I froze, clenching my eyes shut, momen-tarily paralyzed by the throbbing pain. I had spent the previous four days mentally preparing for my testimony, agonizing over every detail. Now that it was finally time, all I needed to do was listen carefully, move at my own speed, answer the questions, and tell the truth. The aching in my knee would serve as a helpful reminder to slow down and be present.

I entered the New York State Supreme Court with Assistant District Attorney Kaegan Mays-Williams, a prosecutor who had been assigned to the case alongside ADA Catherine McCaw.

Mays-Williams had prepped me for my testimony and would be the one conducting my direct examination (asking me questions in front of the jury). The courtroom was on the seventh floor. I was silent as we rode up in the crowded elevator, aware that a juror or reporter might be listening to anything I said. I was so nervous. *Feeling strong, feeling ready*, I kept repeating in my head.

Mays-Williams and I exited the elevator into a short hallway that dead-ended in the center of a long corridor lined with wooden benches. I spotted Nick and Kathryn right away. They stood to hug me, and I briefly introduced them to the assistant district attorney before she left us to wait for me to be called. The three of us sat on a bench, watching jurors and reporters file by toward the courtroom. A couple of men with long-lensed cameras snapped my picture from down the hall. I felt exposed, self-conscious of my every move, and hypersensitive to my surroundings.

We waited about an hour before a court officer came up to me and said it was time. I nodded, looked at my friends for reassurance, and walked ahead of them to enter the courtroom alone. The officer leading the way was a stocky, fifty-something blonde woman with a kindly disposition. She was unexpectedly chatty.

"Are you a photographer?" she asked as we walked.

"Only for fun," I answered, "I worked in the photo department of a magazine." I didn't tell her that I'd been laid off. She told me about her son who was a photographer—or at least I think that's what she said. I was distracted. Near the end of the hallway, she stopped and turned to me.

"Ready?" she said.

"Ready as I'll ever be," I responded.

Then she opened the door and yelled, "Witness entering!"

Escorted by the court officer, I somberly walked down the aisle, dressed in a nondescript, navy silk button-down, black slacks, and black pointed-toe shoes. Imagine, if you will, the opposite of a wedding ceremony. To my left and right, church-like pews were filled with people who turned to look at me. Some of them even took my picture. But none of them actually knew me, nor did I know them. They were not my friends or loved ones, whom, aside from Kathryn and Nick, I had asked not to come, wanting to limit their exposure to the press and, most importantly, to Anna. She was already there, of course, sitting next to her lawyer, but I wouldn't look at her until I had to.

"Watch your step," said the court officer, as I made my way up a few stairs to the witness stand, between the empty jury box and the judge. I remained standing, as instructed, lifted my right hand, and swore to tell the truth. Next, twelve jurors—six men and six women, varied in age and ethnicity—walked past me to take their seats. I prepared to formalize the nullification of my friendship with Anna Delvey. ADA Mays-Williams asked me whether I saw the person who had committed the crime against me anywhere in the room.

"She's there," I said, pointing to Anna, looking in her direction for the first time and meeting her stare. She was smirking, with the corners of her mouth turned slightly upward and a mocking look in her eye. Was she trying to unnerve me? Her attitude now struck me as juvenile. It strengthened my resolve. I was asked to describe something she was wearing, so I said that she had on dark-rimmed glasses.

"Let the record reflect the witness has identified the defendant," said Mays-Williams. After that, I barely looked at Anna, ignoring her presence almost entirely. It was surprising to me how little she affected my composure. I think it was partially because she no longer seemed mystifying. I knew who she really was now. In addition, back in the summer of 2017, I had already confronted her with *everything*, so I wasn't accusing her of anything new.

I was more concerned with the jury, feeling a vital need for them to listen, understand, and know I was telling the truth. I tried to answer the questions calmly, but when I was asked to describe what had happened on May 18, 2017—the day that Anna had convinced me to put down my credit card at La Mamounia—I started to cry. I quickly collected myself and continued answering the questions with as much composure as I could summon.

There were more tears when I had to read text messages and emails out loud and describe the way Anna's deceit had affected me. I couldn't prevent the feelings of powerlessness, anxiety, and betrayal from resurfacing—they were embedded in my memories.

I had been told beforehand that my testimony would likely take one full day, but my direct examination by the ADA took longer than expected, which left Todd Spodek with only fifteen minutes to begin his cross-examination of me. So I was asked to come back the next day.

The next morning I sent a group text to my family. *Gearing up for day two. Cross examination,* the message said. *Climbing back into my armor. Feeling strong. Feeling ready! Going to breathe. Take my time. Tell the truth. And that's all there is to it.*

Go get 'em sweetie!! replied Uncle Bill.

You got it. Now go give it, said Aunt Jennie.

The amen chorus is warming up and by your side. Love you, wrote my dad.

Yes! And don't let anyone put words in your mouth! Uncle Jim added.

Yes, [Uncle Jim] is right, Aunt Becky agreed. *A pause before answering will allow you to breathe and gather your thoughts. Your integrity will come shining through! We love you.*

Cross-examination was the part of the trial I had dreaded the most, and for good reason. I understood its importance, but from ten in the morning to one in the afternoon, I sat in the witness stand and tried to defend myself—without *sounding defensive*—against a character assassination. Spodek attempted to portray me as opportunistic for letting Anna buy me dinners, training sessions, and a decadent vacation, which of course she never paid for.

He paced around while he spoke, gesturing animatedly with his arms. He was not dissimilar from the lawyers I had seen on television and in the movies. Each time he asked me a question, I took a breath, repeated his words in my head, and did my best to answer as accurately as possible. It was a test of my patience, and mental acuity, to have someone question my every move and motive. Snapping back at him would have reflected poorly on me, so instead I concentrated on telling the truth as calmly and succinctly as possible.

I stayed collected and straight-faced for a long time, but eventually he struck a nerve. Aware that I had a book deal and that my story had been optioned by HBO, he accused me of using the trial as content for entertainment. I felt all of my pent-up defensiveness and anger begin to erupt. I spoke more firmly, no longer able to contain my irritation. "I didn't want the trial, or my testimony, to be misconstrued as a ploy for my own benefit, *because it is not*," I snapped.

I was the victim of a con. I didn't choose this. His accusation sent my head spinning—particularly because I felt so sure that he and Anna were the ones doing just that, putting on a show. I looked out at Todd and Anna and, in the audience, saw Jessica Pressler, who I already knew was working with Netflix. It was surreal.

But then again, Nick and Kacy Duke were also there, having come in a touching gesture of support. There were no HBO staffers or book agents, no publicists or stylists in attendance. I hadn't treated the courtroom like a publicity opportunity. I wore the exact same outfit two days in a row. After day one of my testimony, there were photos of me ugly-crying on the Internet. This was *not* splashy or fun, *not* entertainment—this was me pushing a damn boulder up a hill because my friend Anna had turned out to be a con artist and had taken advantage of me, as well as of so many others.

I looked out at the room, afraid I might find it was only a movie set. I imagined everything shifting—the way it happens in dreams—into a nightmarish unreality. I felt an urgent need to call everyone back to real life. Spodek kept pushing. My memory of his exact wording is fuzzy—my ears were filled with the thrum of my own anger—but what I heard was "You *want this*—this is good for you, isn't it?"

"This is *not* about entertainment," I said staunchly. "It is about law and order and a crime. . . . This is about something I went through."

I looked at Anna and the crowd of people and I wanted to scream, *Don't you see?*

I heard Spodek say, "But this *is* entertainment. It worked out pretty well for you, didn't it?"

What does that have to do with the crime that was committed? I wanted to yell. Yes, I had found a way out of the wreckage. Would my case have been stronger if I hadn't? Should I have stayed lost and broke? Would that have made me a better victim?

"This is the most traumatic experience I've ever been through," I said, my voice breaking. "I wish I had never met Anna. If I could go back in time, I would. I wouldn't wish this on anybody."

The cross-examination concluded minutes later. As soon as the judge turned to excuse me, I stood up from my chair in the witness stand and, without pausing, walked angrily down the courtroom aisle and out the door. While I waited for Nick in the empty hallway, I closed my eyes, clenched my jaw, and breathed deeply through my nose. Nick emerged seconds later.

"I don't want to be here," I said urgently. "I need out—need to go. I'm done."

Without lingering, we strode to the elevator. I had lasted as long as I could in that place, with Anna there, and all of the press. I had withstood the relentless questioning of my character. It had been miserable. I'd had enough.

My Friend Anna

The moment we were safely outside and half a block away, I crumbled, sobbing in the middle of the sidewalk. It needed to happen. I had to release all of the pressure and emotion I'd been suppressing. So for a minute, I let it all go while Nick gave me a hug and said I had done great. Once I calmed down, we walked a few blocks to the Odeon for lunch. While we waited for our food, I stepped outside to call my parents, who were anxiously waiting to hear from me. I did my best, I told them, but it had been hard. They were so proud of me, they said.

The next day, I flew to Knoxville to spend Easter weekend with my family. When I arrived to McGhee Tyson Airport, my mom, dad, and brother greeted me with a giant hug and a bouquet of flowers. It was good to be home. My sister arrived the next day, and the five of us hung around the house. Outside, the dogwood trees were blooming and the springtime air was warm. I wanted to stay longer, but I knew that Anna's trial was almost over, and I felt like I needed to be in New York when it ended. My time in Knoxville was just long enough for me to catch my breath before the jury made up their mind.

I traveled back to Manhattan on Tuesday afternoon. All day, I'd been keeping an eye on Twitter, thinking that's where news about Anna would be shared first. When I got home from the airport, I collapsed onto the sofa. That's when I saw a tweet saying the trial's closing arguments had ended. *Now I can only hope,* I thought. It was all that was left to do. The rest was up to the jurors, who were beginning their deliberations.

Even though I tried to distract myself, by watching a movie and talking to friends, I couldn't resist hitting the Refresh button on my Internet search for Anna Sorokin–related news every fifteen to thirty minutes.

That evening, I saw articles online summarizing the closing arguments made by McCaw, for the prosecution, and Spodek, in Anna's defense. According to *Rolling Stone,* Spodek referred to my testimony as a "performance" worthy of an "Oscar." This made my blood boil; he had been the one performing—not me.

The jury deliberated for longer than anyone expected. Wednesday came and went without news. When I first returned from Knoxville, I had been feeling calm about the impending verdict, relatively at peace with whatever might happen. But the longer it took, the more anxious I became.

On Thursday evening, after another full day of jury deliberations, I saw a tweet from a *New York Times* reporter: *A note from the Anna Sorokin jury at 4:55: "We the jury would like to inform the judge that we feel unable to reach a unanimous verdict because we fundamentally disagree. How would you recommend we proceed?" The judge sent them back to continue deliberations.*

My heart sank. I did some online research to understand what this could mean. In criminal-court cases, New York State requires a unanimous vote by the jury to find the defendant guilty.

So, if one single juror was holding out, insisting that Anna was innocent (or at least not guilty beyond all reasonable doubt), the other jurors would need to agree to declare her "not guilty," or they would have to convince the holdout to change his or her mind. They also needed to reach a separate verdict for every individual crime of which Anna was accused.

If the jurors were really deadlocked, the judge would declare a hung jury, resulting in a mistrial. Then the government would have a choice: it could either abandon the prosecution entirely or set a date for another criminal trial, starting from scratch with a new jury. *Surely, the prosecution would proceed with a second trial,* I thought. *But if it came to that, would I have to testify all over again?*

And then, less than two hours later, I saw another tweet: *The jury has reached a verdict in the #FakeHeiress trial. #AnnaSorokin #AnnaDelvey.*

That's all it said. I sat cross-legged on my bed, refreshing Twitter and my Internet browser, begging the computer for more information. I frantically called Nick and began to hyperventilate.

"Either way, Rachel," he said, "you're going to be *fine*."

On April 25, 2019, the New York State Supreme Court jury found Anna Sorokin guilty of eight of the charges against her (five of the charges from the indictment plus three from the earlier stiffed hotels and dine-and-dash incident), including attempted grand larceny in the first degree, grand larceny in the second degree, grand larceny in the third degree, and theft of services.

Anna had used phone and computer applications to create voice mails from fictional bankers and to falsify bank documents. She created emails for fake personas—such as "Bettina Wagner"—after searching Google to learn how to "send untraceable fake emails."

The jury did not, however, find her criminally guilty in her actions toward me or toward Fortress Investment Group. When I first heard the news, I was crushed. How did they get it so *wrong?* But then, I adjusted my perspective. ADA McCaw, ADA Mays-Williams, and Officer McCaffrey (who by this point had been promoted to detective) each called me, independently, after the verdict was announced. Sometimes when jurors are stuck in deliberations for longer than expected—if there are a few stubborn holdouts on either side—they "split the baby." In this case, that might have meant giving Anna a "not guilty" verdict on certain counts.

During their deliberations, the jurors had asked the judge questions about the role of intent in determining criminality. When Anna proposed our vacation in early May, she had just deposited a heap of bad checks into her bank account and withdrawn $70,000—what for? She used some of it to pay her bill at 11 Howard, but what was her intention with the rest? Did Anna *intend* for me to pay for the vacation? How could she have known that my credit cards would even cover that much money? I certainly didn't. And did Anna *intend* to pay me back? Is that why she had wired me $5,000? If she had gotten a multi-million-dollar loan from someplace, do I think she would have repaid me? Maybe. Probably. I do think Anna honestly wanted me as a friend.

But everything changed when she gave me a nonfunctioning debit card to pay for our flights, betting I'd volunteer mine instead. She could have played it differently. When she was without a way to pay, she could have made up some excuse and canceled the entire trip. Except that Anna's visa really was expiring and she needed to leave the country. Going to Canada, Mexico, or a nearby Caribbean island wouldn't work. For her visa to reset, she had to go farther. So she picked Morocco. Someone else had to foot the bill while she figured out the next move in her shell game.

The verdict doesn't change what really happened. My story is just the same as it ever was. Anna is going to prison for four to twelve years—she began her sentence at Bedford Hills Correctional Facility for Women in Westchester County, New York, on Wednesday, May 15, 2019. And my involvement in her arrest and the judicial process was never solely about my case. It was also about preventing her from doing this to other people. And in that regard, I think I succeeded.

A few weeks after the trial, on the same day that Anna entered prison and exactly two years after the Marrakech trip, I found myself on the corner of Howard and Lafayette Streets. I looked up at 11 Howard, thinking of all that had transpired and trying to let go of the unpleasant memories that caused me to avoid this little section of Manhattan for so long. Strangers casually walked by Le Coucou; others came and went through the hotel's front doors. The characters I had once spent so much time with were long since gone. I made my peace and moved on.

Minutes later, I was walking east on the sunny side of Grand Street, between Mulberry and Baxter, when my phone rang. It was a woman from American Express. She told me that I would be protected from the charges— the remainder of the La Mamounia bill. Standing on the side of the street, I cried, overcome by relief and gratitude.

The nightmare had finally come to an end.

Epilogue

The thing is, I'm not sorry. I'd be lying to you and to everyone else and to myself if I said I was sorry for anything. . . . My motive was never money. I was power hungry. I'm not a good person.

—Anna Sorokin, *The New York Times*, May 10, 2019, the day after being sentenced to four to twelve years in prison

Almost everyone I have spoken to knows someone who has been scammed, if it hasn't happened to him or her directly. Trust is a healthy and normal part of human nature. And yet it's hard to talk about this sort of experience because too often people are quick to be judgmental, to blame the person who was tricked rather than the trickster. Many often assume that individuals who are susceptible to cons—ideal marks—are characteristically naive, greedy, or foolish, explains author Maria Konnikova in her book about con artists, *The Confidence Game*. But when it comes to actually predicting who will fall for a scam, she writes, "personality generalities tend to go out the window. Instead, one of the factors that emerges is circumstance: it's not who you are, but where you happen to be at this particular moment of your life. If you're feeling isolated or lonely, it turns out you're particularly vulnerable. . . . Given the right fraud, it seems anyone can be a victim." I believe that applies to what happened to me, as well as to most of the other victims of scammers with whom I've now spoken.

Many run-ins with con artists and sociopaths are far worse than mine was. Every day, people lose more than I did—and they do so to schemes that don't involve fine dining, saunas, or five-star hotels. Some people get scammed out of things that can never be recovered, or experience damage that can never be repaired. It could have been much worse.

I have tremendous respect for people who have suffered through long-term toxic relationships and found the strength to recover from the psychological damage inflicted on them. I do not equate my experience with theirs. My time with Anna was relatively short. She was not in my most intimate circle, and I was surrounded by supportive friends and family.

And for the most part, I have it together now. Anna is in prison. I've made my money back and repaid my debts to Janine and Nick. I have my health. My loved ones are safe. And look at all that I've accomplished—this book, for example.

I'm aware of my good fortune—to be loved, supported, and to have the resources I have—but that doesn't mean this experience hasn't taken its toll. My struggle continued long after Anna's arrest. The stress of navigating the financial burden lasted for more than a year, as did the emotional impact of Anna's deceit. I slipped into depression and stayed there so long it became my new normal. I carried my anxiety everywhere. I hyperventilated, cried, lost hair, barely slept. I lashed out at loved ones and fought with myself. To this day, I sometimes feel too vulnerable to leave my apartment. Some nights I lie awake spiraling into negativity, looking for proof, wherever I can find it, that all of my most irrational insecurities are true. I am lucky to be surrounded by patient friends who convince me that they are not.

I've come out on the other side, and I've changed as a person. I see the importance of listening to my own voice and giving myself permission to speak up. I understand that, no matter what they say, people show you who they are through their actions. I believed that my friend Anna was a wealthy German heiress. I didn't pay close enough attention to the things I saw in her that didn't fit this pattern, the eccentricities I rationalized and the complexities I dismissed. Those were the details that revealed who Anna really was. I spent so much time begging her for the truth when, in fact, the lie was all there was.

I'm not always successful at it, but I try to put what I've learned into practice: I have to remember—time and again—to stop worrying about what other people think of me. I remind myself that sometimes it's okay not to be okay and that healing takes time. And I'm more open with my loved ones—sharing the good things and the hard things—because that's what real friendships are for. It wasn't an experience I'd wish upon anybody, but I did gain something valuable. Instead of losing trust in others, I found the strength to trust in myself.

Afterword

Fake News, True Crime, What Next?

On February 11, 2021, Anna Sorokin was released on parole from the Albion Correctional Facility in upstate New York, after serving three years of her four-to-twelve-year sentence.

Someone from Fortress Investment Group—I need $720m by the end of next week, DM me, she tweeted that same afternoon, from a freshly restored Twitter account with a bio that read, *I'm back.*

I believe everyone contains hidden depth, but from a distance Anna looked static, like she had emerged unchanged from prison, with new schemes and old priorities. Wasting no time, she checked into the swanky NoMad hotel in midtown Manhattan—paid for, according to the *Sunday Times*, with money she had received from Netflix—and hired a film crew to follow her around.

"I'm just kind of filming everything I'm doing right now and I'm going to see what to do with it later," she explained in an interview with *Insider*. "I just got out of prison, like two days ago. So it's me like getting all this stuff from Sephora, me opening a bank account as soon as I get permission from my parole officer . . ."

Makeup, money, and a vanity project.

"I'm nothing but consistent," she wrote in response to a comment on one of her Instagram posts.

And it would seem this is true. After being exposed as a criminal, what choice did she have, given her soaring aspirations, but to double down on the persona that made her notorious?

But the two years that have passed since the publication of *My Friend Anna* have affected me differently. It's hard to understand something until you're beyond it. Only then, if you have the wherewithal and interest, can you look back and see the real shape of a thing. As I reflect on my friendship and fallout with Anna, I see how much it taught me—the importance of channeling my energy toward positive people and healthy relationships, how to set limits, and when to walk away. And I see how it made me stronger. I'm asked on occasion whether I'm grateful for the experience, and my answer is of course not. But I'm proud to have overcome it well enough for such a question to seem reasonable. I am not grateful to Anna—if it were solely up to her, I'd be broke and broken, which ironically might have made me a more sympathetic victim—nor am I glad to have endured her betrayal. Rather, I am grateful to have had the privilege and opportunity to speak and be heard, to have met countless kindhearted people along the way, and to have discovered my inner resilience—though I wish I'd never had cause.

Today I have found a sense of peace, which I owe in large part to the catharsis of writing this book and to the support I received in response to its release. After years of feeling like a shell of myself, moving forward while facing back, and spending days and months tucked away as I stitched artifacts and memories into a narrative sequence, sending it off into the world made me feel as though I had finally caught up with the present and could begin to look ahead. I spent the evening of the book's publication date at a launch party surrounded by my family and friends, celebrating the end of one life chapter and the start of the next. When someone—I think it was my former boss Kathryn—clinked her glass and nudged me to speak, I felt a wave of gratitude rock my composure, rising from my chest to my throat before filling my eyes, a feeling too big for words.

If you had told me years earlier that one day I would write a book and embark on a book tour, I wouldn't have believed you. And if you had told me that one day I—who was so shy as a kid that my little sister had to order

278

for me in restaurants—would also lose my fear of public speaking, I'd have called you insane. But compared to the pressure I'd felt stepping into the witness stand when my emotions were still so raw, press interviews seemed like a breeze. That's not to say I wasn't daunted by the level of interest and nervous to reemerge in the public eye. I most certainly was, but as I spoke with reporters from across the globe—from *Good Morning America* and *Nightline* in New York, to Sky News and the BBC in London, on to podcasts in Ireland, and morning shows in Australia—I was buoyed by the notes of encouragement I had begun to receive and made braver by the knowledge that my story might serve as a cautionary tale or help those who have had similar experiences to feel less alone.

On a Sunday that August, I drove along the familiar streets of my hometown to Union Ave Books, a locally owned shop in downtown Knoxville. The space was filled past capacity with people perching in the doorways, overflowing into an adjacent room. My family was there, along with childhood friends and many faces I recognized. I was nervous—maybe the most nervous I had been before any of the other book events I had done—but it was a different sort of nervousness. Preparing to speak to a roomful of strangers, I'd think, *Will they like me? Will they understand me? Will they get where I'm coming from?* But preparing to speak in front of a roomful of people who had watched me grow up, who knew my family, and who lived in the place I came from, I thought, *How will this change what they think of me? Will I still be the person they thought I was?* I was prepared for awkward consolations, to be partly understood and politely supported, but instead I saw tears and smiles, nods of recognition, and was hugged and applauded. I stayed for over an hour signing books and heard one phrase repeated often: *Your parents must be so proud.*

One of the trial's most lasting effects took time for me to recognize. The defense attorney, in his attempt to undermine my credibility, twisted fragments of truth into fiction, teaching me that my every move could be yanked out of context, relabeled, and picked apart. In response, I developed a reflexive self-consciousness and, afraid of what others might think, became my own biggest critic. But in the months that followed the book's release, this newfound anxiety was eased by emails, messages, comments, and phone calls from countless individuals.

From mental healthcare providers:

I'm a psychologist by training and appreciate your thoughtfulness about your former friend's pathology and the ways that any of us could have been vulnerable (who doesn't know the feeling of giving into someone's bad behavior because we were raised to be respectful of our impact on others?).

From those who work in the criminal justice system:

I'm a former correctional officer, and even knowing how sociopaths work, I was fooled by one on the job . . . Sociopaths are slick. I can understand how easy it is to be fooled by them.

From people sharing insight and reflections:

I wanted to reach out to you. Firstly, to tell you how much I loved [the book], so much I've actually read it twice. And secondly to say that on my second reading, I realized that your book isn't about Anna's con and the money you lost, but instead about the breakdown of a relationship . . . I felt your emotions, your heartbreak and betrayal, and I sincerely hope that you have recovered and regained your trust in people. Thank you for sharing your story with the world x

Hi Rachel, I think I wrote and erased this message a thousand times because I never ever write to strangers. However I felt the need to tell you that I really enjoyed your book. When I first read your *Vanity Fair* article I thought to myself, well, I guess she deserved it, because she tagged along on this trip etc etc. (mean, I know, sorry) but after reading this book I quite understand why you've been her friend and that you're a kind person who wanted to be there for someone. It helped me reflect on myself a bit, how I judge people based on hearsay and I'm going to work on that. So, thank you and please keep writing. I'm happy to see that you're turning a bad situation into something good. :)

From others offering encouragement:

Beyoncé would be proud that you took debt-ridden lemons and turned them into page-turning lemonade. 🍋🍋

And from many who had gone through similar experiences:

No doubt other people who have been fraud victims have contacted you; I am also such a person. . . . Thank you for having the courage to publish your experience. It makes those of us who have been victimized feel less foolish, perhaps, less naive, and certainly less alone.

These voices silenced my self-doubt, called me back to myself, made me feel as though I had done the right thing by sharing my experience, and restored my belief in the goodness of people.

My joyful calm lasted for several months, until October 2019. My aunt Becky had come to New York for work. I was walking her back to her hotel after we had dinner together at the Odeon, the same restaurant I'd gone to six months earlier after I had finished testifying in court. I looked at my phone and saw that a friend had sent me a link to an article about *Inventing Anna*, a Netflix miniseries created and produced by Shonda Rhimes, based on a *New York* magazine article titled "How Anna Delvey Tricked New York's Party People," by Jessica Pressler. Without saying a word, I immediately clicked the link and waited for the website to load, feeling vulnerable but bracing myself because I wanted my aunt to know that I was okay, to see that I was strong, happy, healthy, and equipped to roll with the punches.

Because I was not involved with the show, I learned at the same time as the rest of the world that it would feature Katie Lowes as a character named

"Rachel," described by Netflix in the following terms: "A natural-born follower whose blind worship of Anna almost destroys her job, her credit, and her life. But while her relationship with Anna is her greatest regret, the woman she becomes because of Anna may be Anna's greatest creation."

I absorbed the words as I reread them, this time out loud. *The woman she becomes because of Anna.* Seven little words in one fell swoop laying claim to a lifetime of becoming. *Anna's greatest creation.* Stripped of my agency, accomplishments, truth. I saw my pain reflected on my aunt's face, a woman who has loved me since I was born. I felt the sludge of dormant anger reawaken and I wanted to scream. *In what world is it acceptable to describe a real-life person as anyone else's creation?* Were we meant to believe that the woman I had become was not on account of the parents who raised me, the love I shared with family and friends, my own efforts or personal growth, but *because of Anna*, someone I had been friends with for less than one of my thirty-two years?

When I made the decision to sell the film and television rights to adapt my story (not to Netflix, but to HBO), I had expected there would be times the dramatization of my experience would make me uncomfortable. I had understood that stepping into a spotlight came with certain risks. But this Netflix description felt shocking. I said good night to Aunt Becky and decided to keep walking, needing to blow off steam. It felt fitting to me that this news had come on Halloween, an evening that had already dredged up old anxieties as I had prepared for the possibility that, as I walked around lower Manhattan, I might encounter the bad wigs and black chokers of more than one Anna Delvey. I sidestepped the crowds along Church Street, scanning the faces of strangers, feeling cut off from their jubilation—flat, deflated, stuck where I didn't belong. I remembered a speech I had recently read, given one year earlier by Shonda Rhimes as she accepted the Luminary Award at *ELLE*'s Women in Hollywood Celebration. She had been unapologetic and fierce, and it stuck with me. "I'm getting this award for inspiring other women," she had said, "and how can I inspire anyone if I am hiding? . . . We need to set an example . . . I am awesome and we are awesome, which is another way of saying we have power and we are powerful women. And when we say we have power, we are really saying we deserve to have power. We deserve whatever good thing it is we are getting."

Yes, I wanted to say, *I do have power*—not *because of* Anna, but *in spite of* her. Power that wasn't *hers* but *mine*. I had the power to choose whom to believe in, the power to make a mistake, the power to fall apart and the power to piece myself back together. I wasn't hiding. I had stepped squarely into the light, cracks still visible but with my head held high.

————————

Over one year later, on February 12, 2021, the day after Anna was released from prison, I was at my parents' house in Tennessee. I'd had no forewarning, and it was my dad who gently broke the news after he heard it from a friend. I was surprised and relieved by how little this update affected me, but interview requests soon came rolling in from journalists across the US and abroad. At first, I ignored them, not wanting to rehash the details of a victimization that was now in my rearview mirror, and feeling like it would be presumptuous to speculate about whether Anna had changed or what she might do next without giving her a chance to show us. She had done her time and that was that. I hoped for the best.

But while I turned down press requests, I watched media outlets give Anna a platform without holding her to account, with weirdly convivial interviews in which she tried to pass off criminal behavior as a form of high art. One US morning news show, as if to justify their programming, highlighted Anna's expressed interest in prison reform, an urgent and complex issue that demands serious attention and critical analysis but was reduced to a superficial soundbite. Anna knows what to say in order to open doors, but until she has actions to back up her words, she may as well be saying, "the check's in the mail."

Talk is cheap and con artists are good at it, I wanted to insist, *Why are we handing one a microphone?* Except then I realized that was precisely why—because Anna, a brazen female con artist with highbrow taste, lowbrow morals, and no apparent regard for the consequences of her actions, gives the media exactly what they want: clickbait.

I read the headlines—*Fake Heiress Anna Sorokin Says She Takes Being Branded a 'Sociopath' as a Compliment . . . Says Her Prison Sentence Was 'a Huge Waste of Time' . . . Sets Her Sights on Influencerdom with a New Vlog Series.* I understood the implications of this sort of coverage, the glamorization of criminality, and wondered who would speak up. I did not want it to be me. I felt that Anna, as a person, had proved herself to be deserving of our awareness, not our attention. And yet, as much as I wanted to shout this message from the rooftops, I recognized it would be easy to mistake my concerns as merely the words of a bitter ex-friend when in reality the issue was much larger than my past drama with Anna, larger than Anna, too, and larger than any one story—it was a big-picture problem.

Forty-two days after her release, Anna was taken into custody by US Immigration and Customs Enforcement and detained after a judge made note of her interviews and antics and declared her "a danger to society."

From Bergen County Jail in Hackensack, New Jersey, Anna spoke to a reporter from the *Telegraph.* She said that if she were to agree to leave the country, she would likely be released, but she preferred to be detained in the United States than free in Germany. "I have a whole life in New York," she said. "If I have to spend a week or two in jail to sort it out, I think that's reasonable. When you look at it like a mathematical equation it adds up."

When you look at it like a mathematical equation. This is what gets me. Should we as individuals make decisions based on the same risk-benefit metrics used by big companies? Take, for example, Netflix: If they were to decide that the *benefit* of the drama between Anna and me as they had written it exceeds the financial *risk* of a possible defamation suit brought forward by a single individual with limited funds, whose claims might only bolster the false narrative she aims to correct? What toll does that take on us as human beings? Does *strength of character* now refer to a person's entrepreneurship—to the marketability of their crafted persona—instead of their integrity? At what point does the price of entertainment exceed its value?

Afterword

I did the math. According to BBC News, who obtained a copy of the *Inventing Anna* contract through a Freedom of Information Act request, Netflix paid Anna an initial fee of $30,000 pre-trial. This money—just as I had suspected—"went directly to her lawyer, Todd Spodek, to cover a portion of his fees," reported the *NY Post*, citing court filings. They subsequently paid more for a consultancy fee and the rights to adapt her life story, bringing her payment up to $320,000. This money was frozen so that victims of her crimes could file lawsuits to make claims, which some of them did. But the remaining funds went to paying the balance of her attorney fees and then to Anna herself. "Using the prison phone just before she got out, Sorokin enjoyed a Net-a-porter shopping spree, buying among other things, Celine sunglasses, a $720 Balenciaga hoodie and Alexander McQueen and Nike trainers," reported the *Sunday Times*. When asked where she got the cash, Anna replied "I still have some money from Netflix," before vaguely referring to other unnamed projects.

In response to a serial killer who received widespread press attention after he committed a murder spree in the mid-1970s, the "Son of Sam" law was created to keep criminals from profiting off their stories. In its modern form, the law gives the New York Crime Victims Board the power to decide whether any profits earned by criminals should be rerouted to their victims. But how do we define profit? And what about that window of time before a verdict is reached?

When asked if crime pays, Anna told BBC *Newsnight*: "In a way, it did."

Do we care more that she made this statement than we do that it seems to be *true*?

If your crimes are splashy enough, a media company could snatch up the rights to your story pre-trial so that you're able to afford a top-tier lawyer who can then minimize your penalty. You could be paid so much money that even after your funds are frozen and victims are repaid, you have cash left over. And not only that, if fame is what you're after, you'll have built yourself a "brand," created a platform, and found an audience. It's a gamble but, thanks to Netflix, Anna Delvey shows us it's possible to win.

"Netflix declined to talk to the BBC about whether their payments may have affected the justice process," I read in an article. "The OVS [Office of Victim Services, responsible for enforcing the Son of Sam law] has clarified that Netflix came to them initially, it did not need to chase them, and all US rules were followed." Was this meant to put our minds at ease? Isn't it worse that these facts happened according to the rule book?

Just because something is legal doesn't mean it's right.

In his opening remarks during the trial, Anna's attorney tried to present her as someone who, like so many others, came to New York with sky-high dreams and a willingness to hustle. The idea of "making a brand-new start of it" here, he said, "resonates with people all over the world." What if he's right? Is this the example we want to *resonate with people all over the world*? "Any millennial will tell you, it is not uncommon to have delusions of grandeur," he argued. As a millennial myself, I reject this as false, but it's not the millennials I worry about. It's Gen Z and those who come after, those who look to "influencers" for behavior to imitate based on what our society rewards. "She's a role model to some people," her lawyer said later in an interview with *60 Minutes Australia*, "She's obviously famous. People like engaging with her. Her social media is blowing up. So, I hope that she can harness all of this into something really positive, productive, and monetize on it. I hope she can make a real business out of it."

Is the model set by Anna really our American Dream?

"My life is performance art," her current Twitter bio reads.

Ask yourself: What's happening behind the scenes?

"I always was Anna Delvey," she said to BBC *Newsnight*.

Is it possible for a charade to be all that there is?

"I think that's part of the trap," her own attorney said to the *Sunday Times*.

My final point is this: People, like ideas, only have as much power and influence as we give to them. Without even realizing it, I gave Anna enormous power and influence over me—power and influence I then spent years working to reclaim. Anna is clever. She can be funny. I, too, used to find her amusing. Like others do now, I once marveled at her audacity, at the way she plays by her own rules, at the grandiosity of her dreams, and at her ridiculous, outsized confidence. It's easy to be captivated by larger-than-life characters who defy our expectations, especially when we think we have nothing at stake.

But what I learned through this experience is that your attention is an investment. Giving someone your attention is the act of being influenced, whether or not you're aware of it in the moment. And especially in this age of constant stimulation, with endless people and stories competing for your clicks, likes, follows, and time, your attention has value. It has power. It's worth something. Be careful where you spend it, and understand the cost.

Acknowledgments

I could not have written this book without help, encouragement, and support from colleagues, friends, and family members—to whom I am deeply indebted.

I'm grateful to Aimée Bell, my editor at Gallery, who helped me find my voice and, as a former *V.F.* colleague, provided early reassurance. My appreciation extends to Katy Follain at Quercus for her constructive insight. Thanks to Max Meltzer for his patience and sharp editorial skills and to eagle-eyed Adam Nadler. It has also been a pleasure to work with Jennifer Bergstrom, Elisa Rivlin, Jennifer Weidman, Jennifer Robinson, and the entire team at Gallery.

My sincerest gratitude goes to Mollie Glick and Michelle Weiner at CAA for their advocacy and wise counsel. I am also indebted to John Homans and Radhika Jones for their support in publishing a portion of this tale within the hallowed pages of my favorite magazine, as well as to Graydon Carter, Chris Garrett, and Susan White for all that I learned under their leadership.

I would like to express my admiration for Assistant District Attorneys Catherine McCaw and Kaegan Mays-Williams and Detective Michael McCaffrey for their sensitivity, dedication, and utmost professionalism from beginning to end.

I'm profoundly thankful to Kate for reminding me that *sometimes it's okay not to be okay*; to Liz for her fierce love and loyalty; to Taylor for

Acknowledgments

her tireless generosity; to Alicia, Holly, Ashley, Olivia, Natalie, Sarah, and Lacey for their love and kindness during this difficult time; to Mary Alice, Lindsay, and Emily for their solidarity. A special thank-you to Ariel Levy for listening at a pivotal juncture and pointing me in the right direction, and to Kacy Duke for her positivity and compassion.

My deepest thanks to Janine for believing in me when I felt scared and alone, and to Dave for his advice and steadfast friendship.

Words are inadequate to convey my gratitude to Kathryn MacLeod, who has taught me so much during the decade I have known her. Kathryn, thank you for your mentorship, friendship, and unflinching support—through thick and thin. Many thanks also to Mark Schäfer and Ilene Landress.

Nick Rogers kept me sane and alive while I wrote this book and reminded me in hard times to *change my thinking*. Nick, I am forever indebted to you for the love, patience, and support you have given me over the course of many years.

I would like to express my endless appreciation for my wonderful and loving extended family—thank you, Aunt Jennie, for your graceful candor and inspiring influence; Uncle Bob, Aunt Becky, Uncle Bill, Uncle Jim, Aunt Mia, Uncle David, Uncle Marty, and Aunt Amy for sharing your wisdom and encouragement; and Grandma Marilyn, for opening your home to me and making my dream to live in New York City possible.

Mom, Dad, Jennie, and Noah, thank you. I love you beyond all measure.